Advance Praise for *Celibate*

Maria Giura's *Celibate* is an impassioned portrait of a self in utter struggle over, and ambivalence about God, family, sex, and love. Giura exquisitely draws the reader into the turbulence that was her life but also compels the reader to believe that now, finally, she is on the right path, that now she has reached her truth and peace. An exhilarating page turner.

— Kathleen McCormick, author of *Dodging Satan*

Deeply human and finely wrought, *Celibate* is Giura's strikingly honest examination of her battle to hang onto her faith in the midst of trying to understand—and free herself from—her complex relationship with a Catholic priest.

— Michael Steinberg, author of *Still Pitching: A Memoir*

A beautifully rendered and heartfelt look at the place that contemporary women have in the Roman Catholic Church and one brave woman's struggle to reconcile her faith in this context.

— Leslie Heywood, author of *Pretty Good for a Girl*

Celibate tells a different kind of vocation story. Vivid and passionate, it speaks to both the afflictions and the victory that can come from discerning and following God's voice. A gripping memoir from first to last page.

— Jana M. Bennett, author of *Singleness and the Church: A New Theology of the Single Life*

In *Celibate,* priest, woman, and Church are tangled together in a romantic, forbidden web, and the boundaries between Church and society-at-large blur to the point of clear transparency. A poignant must read.

— Anthony Julian Tamburri, Dean, John D. Calandra Italian American Institute

celibate

a memoir

celibate

a memoir

Maria Giura

Apprentice
House Press
Loyola University Maryland

First Edition

Paperback ISBN: 978-1-62720-214-5
Ebook ISBN: 978-1-62720-215-2

Printed in the United States of America

Designed and edited by Christina Damon
Promotion by Meghan DeGeorge
Author photo by Danny Sanchez

Published by Apprentice House Press

Apprentice House Press
Loyola University Maryland
4501 N. Charles Street
Baltimore, MD 21210
410.617.5265 • 410.617.2198 (fax)
www.ApprenticeHouse.com
info@ApprenticeHouse.com

Also by the Author

What My Father Taught Me

Peace and
Blessings!
Maria Ginsa

*For JC
and for JM*

My truths are all foreknown,
This anguish self-revealed.
I'm naked to the bone,
With nakedness my shield…

—*Theodore Roethke*

Contents

Note to the Reader xv

Chapter One: The Long Loneliness 1

Chapter Two: After Mass 31

Chapter Three: Telling Father 53

Chapter Four: Courting 73

Chapter Five: Confessions 97

Chapter Six: Mystic 117

Chapter Seven: Nellie 139

Chapter Eight: Candidacy 153

Chapter Nine: Novitiate 183

Chapter Ten: Exit Interviews 217

Chapter Eleven: Dream 259

Epilogue 275

Acknowledgments 283

About the Author 289

Note to the Reader

No one in this memoir asked to be in it. Yet here they are.

I've written only those parts of their lives that directly intersect with my story. I've prayed for the wisdom to write them as real as I can and have done my best to acknowledge when I've done them wrong. I've changed all their names and, where possible, without compromising the emotional truth of the story, some details. I thank each of them in advance, especially my family, for understanding that I *had* to write this story.

Vivian Gornick says about memoir that, "It's not what happened; it's what you made of what happened." I think it's both, but I understand what she means. If I had chosen a different life—or it had chosen me—my interpretation of the past, especially my childhood, might be different. I present to you this account, the only one I can.

Chapter One

The Long Loneliness

I first noticed Father Infanzi in the way that matters during his second year at Saint Stephen's. It's not that I hadn't noticed him before. It was impossible not to. He was thirty—four years older than me— tall and lean with black hair parted to the side, and he said beautiful things like *God loved us into existence.* But it wasn't until my sister Janine introduced him to my family after Easter Sunday Mass that he really got my attention. It was a cool, sunny day with the fragrance of daffodils in the air as we waited on a long line to greet Father outside the front doors. When it was our turn, we all smiled and said hello, and my step-dad Tom complimented his homily. Father said, "Thank you," and then, shaking our hands and blushing, said to my sisters and me, "Wow, *four girls.* You all have the same blue eyes," but when he got to me he held my eyes a beat longer than he did theirs, and I felt a sharp pulse of attraction. After we walked away, my sister Julie said, without a hint of irony, "He'd be perfect for Maria." Nellie, the youngest, rolled her eyes, and my mother shot back, "*Julie!*" but with a smirk. I nearly gasped. He *was* perfect—smart and handsome and personable but also a touch shy to make him sweet. He made me feel more special in that moment than the men I dated, sometimes slept with, so I wouldn't have to be alone. After that, whenever he said Mass I thought *good* but walked out the side door and didn't greet him. He was a *priest*. Besides, the last thing I wanted to be reminded of was celibacy. I'd been running from it ever since I was eight and, sitting in St. Bernadette's one night, I felt God calling me to become a nun.

It was after five o'clock Mass on a Saturday, and I was headed out the door when something made me pick up *The Tablet's Special Vocations Issue* and stay a while. Nestled into hewn rock high above the altar was the Blessed Mother in a beautiful white dress and powder blue sash with fourteen-year-old Bernadette kneeling beside her and gazing into her face. It looked like a giant circle of love surrounded them, but not one that made me feel left out like I had ever since Nellie was born. I walked a few feet down the long aisle, sat down in a pew, and opened *The Tablet*. There in the center-fold in big bold letters was GIVE *YOUR* LIFE TO GOD. I stared at it for a while unsure why God would want jealous eight year old me to give my life to Him or what that even meant until I turned the page and saw picture after picture of smiling nuns and priests. God was telling me to become a nun. I was sure of it. Why else had I picked up the paper that week and not another? Why weren't there any pictures of regular people? Why did it say *Give* and not you *Can* give? I knew nuns and priests marry God, and I felt a tug on my heart, but I was embarrassed and afraid. When I got older I wanted a husband I could see and feel, who would talk to me with a real voice. I wanted to feel special and beautiful, the way I did when James Gardini touched my hair in school, not plain and invisible the way I did during Princess Hour when my mother and teenaged sisters transformed the kitchen table into a pink baby spa and took turns bathing Nellie's cherubic, glistening body. It felt like there wasn't enough love even though Baby Jesus had promised me there was the previous Christmas Eve when He whispered it to my heart during Communion. It felt like his Father was giving me an order like Papa always tried to give Mommy. Sometimes he'd pound his thick fist against the dinner table, and I'd jump.

I brought *The Tablet* home that night but didn't say a word. I was afraid if I talked about it, I'd make it real and God wouldn't leave me alone. I filled out some of the return cards for more information, but I never mailed them, and then one day *The Tablet* got thrown away with *The Daily News*. I still went to Mass every week even when my mother couldn't take me, but I wouldn't stay afterward anymore, and as the months went by, the calling dimmed, though not my hunger. One day when my mother was kissing Nellie all over and calling her *Gioia*, joy, what she used to call me, I cried out, "*What about me?*" Janine and Julie looked at me with open mouths, but my mother narrowed her eyes like I was mean, which devastated me. From the moment Nellie was born, my mother saw her blond, fair-skinned self; she didn't want Nellie, who was the baby like her, to feel as insecure as she had growing up in the shadow of older sisters. For the first time in my mother's life, she wasn't working and could enjoy being a mother. She had also almost lost Nellie. The doctor had told her that because she was thirty-five and had had tuberculosis, the pregnancy could kill her. The appointment for the abortion was scheduled, but the night before, twisting and turning in bed, my mother knew she'd never be able to answer to God or live with herself. Nellie was a miracle.

If my father had been there for us, I don't think I would've been as needy or jealous. The only time I had with him was a few minutes on his lap, but he'd either jump up nearly dropping me, or he'd fall asleep with his arm across me like a bar. Even though my mother worked the same grueling hours in the pastry shoppe as he did, he believed it was her job to raise us and wouldn't help with anything not even to run to the pharmacy to get us medicine. She didn't mind the hard work or the serving; they fulfilled her. But she couldn't stand that he was never home for us, that he was mean. When I came down with recurrent bronchitis at three—probably from his chain smoking—and she had to stay home with me for weeks, he blew up. I imagine my father yelling, "*Non puoi!*" the huge vein in his forehead throbbing as my mother shouted back, hands on hips, her face pulled in a little, "*Watch me!*" Sometimes he'd wear her down so much, she'd take us to Grandma Giulia's or one of our aunts for the night, or she'd lock him out. It got so bad once that she packed our bags and took us to Kennedy Airport to board a plane somewhere, but Aunt Anna and

4

Uncle Dom showed up at the gate just in time to change her mind. For a while my father would do better, take some time off to be with us, but it didn't last, and he'd be back to driving him and her into the ground. Then, after seventeen years of second chances, when I was nine and Nellie was one, she told us they were divorcing. I stormed out of the kitchen demanding, "*Who's going to be my father now?*" What I really wanted to say but didn't dare was, *Bad enough you dropped me for Nellie. Now you're sending away the man who kisses my hair and calls me Bella?*

My mother, Nellie, and I became a family within a family. We did everything together, including all my ball games where my mother was in the stands with Nellie in the stroller next to her fisting a sippy cup, the two of them rooting for me. I finally had someone who needed and looked up to me, but Nellie was so gorgeous with golden locks and such a *fungita*, pouty lips, that none of us could keep our hands off her. Her looks were only half of it. Once Julie had a friend over who had an enormous pimple on the tip of his nose, and two year old Nellie said, "What's that *ding* on your nose?" Even my mother hid a chuckle. There was no way I could compete with that. When Nellie misbehaved, my mother screamed and punished her and cancelled our plans, but then they'd snuggle and make up like I wasn't there. The fact that I was growing chubby and awkward made me more insecure. My mother did everything for me, but I felt I couldn't say what I really felt without upsetting her, so I kept it in and made believe I was perfect. In fourth grade, I passed a note to my friend Leslie that said I wanted to "do it" with some boy whose name I don't remember, but I used the nasty word Frankie LaVerde taught everyone in school. In sixth grade, when I was far enough from home I started rolling up my skirt. In seventh, I hid in the Brooklyn Public Library to read the dirty parts of Judy Blume's *Forever.* One summer, I even bullied two sweet, overweight kids in the neighborhood.

When my teachers took us to church, I looked forward to it, paid careful attention, loved the clean way my soul felt after receiving Penance and Holy Communion. But it wasn't until I was fourteen that I really started searching for Jesus. Initially I'd chosen a large communications high school, but I was intimidated by crowds, so it was hard for me to make friends. I wandered the loud hallways alone until I got to the quiet library carrel where I listened to "You've Got a Friend" and imagined Jesus singing to me. When I transferred to a Catholic girls' school the following semester, I still felt lost, because everyone had already made friends. I started wearing the cross I received at baptism and showing up to Prayer Group every Tuesday morning where a Sister of St. Joseph led a faith sharing. There'd be a candle burning and a song like "Here I Am Lord" or "Be Not Afraid" playing, and I'd cry. The following summer when I turned fifteen and James Gardini asked me out, I told Julie, "*If I don't marry James, I'm becoming a nun.*" I was trying to keep my hopes low, so I wouldn't get hurt, but I also had a feeling that I wasn't meant to get married, that it wasn't what God wanted, or what I was born to do. I don't know if I remembered that night in St. Bernadette's. I just knew that I felt more peace with Jesus than I did with James, and I sensed that would be the case with every boy. Still, when James kissed me, I started dreaming of taffeta wedding dresses. When he broke up with me two months later, I was crushed.

At the end of sophomore year, I threw out the poem my mother had written for me about how she hoped the world would never steal my innocence. After reading Ronald and Nancy Wilkins' *Man and Woman* in Sister St. Paul's religion class, the only book from high school that I saved, I wanted to remain pure, but the thought of it made me feel more invisible. A lot of the girls in my school teased their hair and wore diamond ankle bracelets their boyfriends bought them and hiked up their skirts higher than I did. Except for the occasional awkward boy I met at a dance, I felt that no one ever saw me, as if God had thrown a sheet over me to keep me for Himself. In spring of senior year, when my friend Leslie found The Nautical, a bar that let us use fake ID, I fell for Gary who I made out with even though he didn't buy me drinks and who cancelled on me a week before the prom. It only got worse in college where I fell for more Garys. I even fooled around with one who had a girlfriend. I told my mother I had sorority meetings that went late and that I'd be staying in one of my sister's rooms, but sometimes I'd wind up in a guy's room, and though I didn't lose my virginity, I came close.

A year after college graduation, there was Dave, six foot and athletic with a slight overbite that made him good-looking in a sweet way. He drove a hundred ten miles round trip every weekend to see me. I finally had a lover, someone who made me feel beautiful, who made me an even number. I knew he wasn't the one, but I was enjoying myself. As time went on, I was afraid that if I broke up with him, God would finally get me for Himself. There were also the voices of my southern Italian ancestors in my head: *All your cousins your age are married or engaged. What about you? Cos'e` questo soulmate? You're next in line on both sides of the family.* And my own voice. *What about me? Why can't I just want this? Why can't Dave be enough?* I held on for two and a half years. Five months before we broke up, when my mother found out that we'd been sleeping together, she was livid. "*What you've pulled is absolutely unacceptable under my roof,*" her light blue eyes piercing mine as I faced her, my bed in between us, my heart pounding. I was sorry but only because she had found out. Now that I knew how good sex could be, I didn't want to give it up. If I didn't get married, the only life my mother and the Church would deem worthy was a nun's. Three months later I moved into the apartment in Julie and her husband Nick's house. I wanted to have something to show for myself in place of marriage, so I wouldn't feel like a failure. I had to get away from my mother's and Nellie's fighting, which had become impossible since my mother and Tom married.

On the night I left, she and I were standing at the top of the landing while Tom brought the last of my things to the car. Her anger had cooled months earlier. Now I was the hurt, angry one. I didn't want to move out knowing that I'd be breaking up with Dave soon, that I'd be alone. I wanted her to march to the front door, spread her arms across it, and tell me not to go—that she and Nellie would go for therapy, I should wait another year or two when I wasn't so afraid to move out, it was okay if I never got married, she loved me no matter what. All I'd told her was that I didn't want to marry Dave, which she sensed I blamed her for and I denied, but it was true. I subconsciously blamed her for my calling: maybe if she hadn't named me after the Blessed Mother or nicknamed me *Baby Jesus* when I was small...I was jealous that all she'd ever wanted was to marry and have a family. It didn't matter that I saw how dearly she was paying for it again. I was certain I'd do better. I had no idea I was wounded. Except for Dave, I attracted emotionally unavailable men like my father who could never bring himself to say, "I love you," or "I'm proud of you" or "Tell me about your day." I told myself that Papa hadn't known any better, that he loved us, which was true but not enough. All I'd ever had were some fleeting moments when I'd feel a rush of his attention and affection. It was my mother's love that always carried me, but it was Papa I was excusing and protecting. I romanticized marriage, making it an eternal honeymoon, but deep down I distrusted men and commitment. I wanted a prince to find and save me, to fill the deepest desires of my heart. What I needed was a Savior.

Four months later when I got home from a New Year's cruise that I took with my family, I collapsed from the grief. I knew that moving out and breaking up with Dave was going to be hard, but I didn't know it would feel like someone had died. The singles scene on the cruise was awful. I felt like God had abandoned me. I was terrified He was going to use the silence of my apartment to trap me into the calling I didn't want. I felt a dark voice close in on me: *It would be so much easier if I weren't here tomorrow.* I cried out, "*Jesus, please take me.*" I didn't want to die; I wanted to be delivered, but I didn't want to give up my will, find out for sure what God's was. If He allowed His own glorious Son to be crucified, why would He ever love or take care of a nobody like me? I still went to Mass but I left as soon as it was over, afraid I'd hear God whisper, *Come Follow Me.* I told myself that just because I felt called to be a nun when I was a child didn't mean it was real; how did I know there wasn't someone else out there for me? If God wasn't going to give me a husband, I was going to find one myself.

I dated as often as possible. There was Mark, the blue-eyed paramedic my cousin Gino introduced me to (I don't remember why it didn't lead anywhere); Vincent, the strawberry-blonde architect who started cancelling our dates because his ex was back in the picture; and Tim, the thirty-year-old lawyer I went out with for three months who wanted to quit his job and move to the south of France to paint. After a few dates, he started shutting down, showing up late, stopping at his mother's for something to eat even when he and I were going to dinner. Maybe he smelled the *Bride* magazine I'd bought after three dates. He even asked me to drive. When he didn't read the anger in my pause, I gave in, because I didn't want him to break up with me. Sleeping with him only made me angrier, kept me from Holy Communion. When he got up at five to put on sneakers, I couldn't believe it. "*You're leaving me to go running?*" I asked, humiliated.

There were stretches when I enjoyed being single, like when my coworker Henry and I rented a house on the Jersey Shore, and he invited his friends, and I invited mine or when I threw parties, and my apartment was brimming. I was happy bringing people together, but when they left, or I had too much time on my hands, I felt helpless and panicked. Except for the gym and my job as an admissions counselor, I didn't have a lot going on. My close friends were either married or unavailable, like Silvia who was in med school or Kara who lived seventy miles away. I wasn't involved in anything—a charity, a team, not even a hobby—to pull me out of myself. I joined a couple of young adult groups, one for Catholics in Manhattan, but if I didn't see anyone in the audience who looked attractive and well-adjusted, I walked out when the guest speakers were on their last syllable. Three day weekends with no plans were the worst. I'd start out hopeful on Saturday mornings, do three miles on the treadmill with the stereo blasting and the blinds thrown open to let the sun pour in. Then I'd make a pot of cinnamon decaf and a batch of corn muffins and give myself some kind of project like cleaning out my drawers, but when I was done and had forty-eight hours to go, all the nothing made me feel so miserable that I curled up on my couch sobbing, convinced God had forgotten me, but also, in the back of my mind, terrified that He hadn't.

Things got especially bad the second winter in my apartment, one of the stormiest in history. Just as we dug out from one blizzard, another hit. Nick helped me with all the shoveling, but all I thought was, *I'm alone.* The one date I almost had with an investment banker from Julie's firm on Valentine's weekend got cancelled because of another storm and never got rescheduled, because Julie hadn't thought we were a good match to begin with. I should have trusted her, but I didn't. When I broke up with Dave, she was loving and sympathetic, but since then I felt she was avoiding me. In retrospect, I couldn't blame her. I was needy and holding a grudge from childhood that I wasn't fully aware of. While I was always trying to close the six year gap between us, she was usually looking for me to run her errands. It didn't help that until I was seventeen I felt homely around her like the summer I was twelve and wore knee-length sweat socks, because I wasn't allowed to shave, and she asked, "What's with the thick knee socks in 90 degree heat?" When I started going out with Dave, my insecurities disappeared, but now that I was alone, I felt twelve again. One day when she calmly corrected me for not bringing the garbage out in time, I snapped, *Sorry, I'm not obsessed with garbage removal like you,* taking a shot at her domestic life, which I secretly envied. I wouldn't even call her until one night when my fear and dread were so bad I didn't know what else to do.

It was the end of the first day back to work after another blizzard, and everyone was gone, even my intensely dedicated boss Doris. The office was silent except for the wind against the thin paned windows. I had finished calling a few student applicants and had settled in to write a couple of cover letters. Even though working in Admissions was a good fit, I fantasized about a job in publishing, certain it would be easier and more glamorous than schlepping to high schools two hours away where students walked passed my Westerly College table toward the far more popular Villanova. My first two sentences came quickly, but then I couldn't think of anything else, and the more I tried the more defeated I felt. I was resentful that instead of working on Madison Avenue, I was in a hundred-year-old house where I couldn't keep the space heater on without blowing a fuse. I started telling off one person after another in my head: Janine and Julie for double dating and not including me; Doris for getting upset with me for not inviting her to a counselor's birthday that someone else had planned; my mother for not intuiting how unhappy I was. I shook my head, saved the cover letter, and brought up my resume hoping for some kind of inspiration, but when I saw my name and objective, I felt empty, and that's when it happened. The image of a nun in full habit flashed on the screen before me, her face indistinct like in a dream. I gasped, pushed my chair back as she disappeared, reappeared, and then disappeared again. I stared at the computer until it rebooted itself. I started to cry; then I was sobbing.

Still shaking, I drove home convinced that it was God hunting me down. Why not? Throughout the Old Testament, He was jealously cruel to get what He wanted, but then I wondered if I'd hallucinated the nun, if this was connected to how depressed I felt. I finally broke down and called Julie but didn't say a word about what had happened. I knew how nuts I'd sound, and I didn't want to admit I felt a calling. The first time I dialed, I hung up, but I dialed again, and after apologizing for bothering her even though she didn't sound bothered, I tried to explain, tears welling in my eyes.

"Jule, I don't know what to do, what's wrong. I think it's starting to scare me that I'm going to wind up alone forever. Since Dave and I broke up, I haven't been with anyone for more than three months. And most times I don't even want to go out. I'm just going through the motions. I feel I have no control over making things better. I can't make the right guy find me."

"Not having someone must not be easy at times, but I don't think that's what this is about. You haven't been yourself in a while," she said kindly.

"But it's the only thing that makes sense, that seems concrete. What do you mean that I haven't been myself?"

"Maria's bubbly. *You're* bubbly. You like people and being out there doing things. But what I've seen you doing lately is withdrawing and then being angry about it and seeming so disappointed in us, in *me*."

"I'm *bubbly*?" I asked, embarrassed to own up to the other.

"Yes, you're the girl lovin' up the camera in our home videos," she said, referring to the one when I was about five. On one reel, it's New Year's Eve, the only holiday my father was home for, because he loved his lobsters. I have a party hat on and my doll in my arms and am doing a fast can-can next to Dick Clark on the TV, and Papa is sitting on the edge of the couch in chinos and white tee, looking at me as if I'm his only daughter, which makes me tilt my hat and ham it up more. In another reel, we've stopped for a picnic on our way to Niagara Falls, one of two family vacations we took, and Papa's chasing me around our big, brown boat of a Cadillac. I'm running as fast as I can, pretending I don't want him to catch me. When he does, I squeal as he scoops me up in his arms and holds me in the air like his prize.

"Do you think this has to do with the fact that I'm convinced Papa's absence hasn't affected me?"

"Him, yes. But also, things in our house were never talked about," Julie said. "And each one of us deals with it differently... " She also said I shouldn't be embarrassed about going to a therapist, so a month later I tried. When I told the therapist that I felt I wasn't meant to get married, she said that I just hadn't met the right one yet. Had she said, "Okay, so let's explore *why* you feel that way," I might have trusted her enough to show up again. I was convinced no one would understand; yet I wasn't sure I wanted anyone to, so I didn't try another therapist. I certainly wasn't going to talk to a nun or a priest. However, after Janine introduced us to Father Infanzi on Easter, I did officially register as a parishioner at St. Stephen's. I even went to a new parishioners' meeting, but I left right after Father finished speaking. I was too intimidated and attracted to talk to him. His homilies were smart, interesting mini-lessons from the time of Christ, and he opened them with adorable anecdotes like the time his older brothers lowered him by his ankles into a sewer to get a baseball. Maybe when I joined a dating service the following month, I was hoping there'd be someone like him out there. I told myself it'd be fun. If I didn't like the men, I'd have one drink and leave. But I was angry it had come to this. If it was meant to be—if God loved me enough—He would've already found me someone.

My first date was scheduled for when I got back from a short trip to South Beach with Nellie. Initially I was thrilled to be in such a beautiful, bustling place, but by five on Friday, the scene on Collins Avenue overwhelmed me. Roller-bladders in thongs wove through the crowd at dizzying speeds like Adams and Eves on wheels, and in the street, guys and girls dressed the same way sprouted from cars that blasted techno and hip hop so loudly the bass pounded my skull. The next day while Nellie was on a towel thumbing through the catalog of the college she was attending in the fall, I was in the blue-green water with my eyes closed trying to feel peace. As a child I loved how weightless I felt in the ocean, how if I rode the waves at the exact right moment, they'd raise me up and carry me safely back to shore, but now I felt alien and unmoored, pulled apart from the Source like the flute in Rumi's poetry. I didn't realize that at the heart of my unhappiness was my deep distrust of God. I opened my eyes and walked several steps farther into the ocean when I felt what I thought was seaweed. Looking down, I saw something stringy and purple coiled around my calf like a snake as a horrible burn shot up my leg. I started screaming and trying to run, but the ocean floor felt like it was sucking me in, though when I looked back down it was completely still except for where my effort was forcing up little volcanoes of sand. When I finally made it to shore, I collapsed, gripping my swelling, reddening leg. I looked up at people whose faces were wobbly and closing in on me. I heard Nellie ask,

"*Ri Ri, What happened? Are you okay?*" felt paramedics hovering, laying compresses, announcing, "This sure is early for man-of-wars."

A few Friday nights later when my TV blew, I was convinced God had broken it. I was also sure He was behind the man-of-war and the fact that I didn't feel a connection with any of the men from the dating service. I'd never been attacked by nature before, and it felt so personal. For the first time since that night after the cruise two years earlier, I tried reaching for Christ. I grabbed note paper and pen and began writing *Dear Christ*, feeling foolish like I was writing to a ghost, but then the words poured out. *I'm not happy. I'm embarrassed. I feel trapped. I don't know where else to turn. I don't know why Your Father is doing this to me. What have I ever done that's so wrong? Why are all these things happening? You're the one who is gentle and loving, you're the one who suffered. You're so perfect and good. Please help me, Jesus, please, please help me. I'm not even sure what my dreams are or ever were, Lord, just that this is not them, not what I thought my life would turn out to be. I'm crushed.* I don't know what else I wrote, just that my tears made the ink run down the paper. I took a deep breath and signed the letter, *Love always, Maria.* A few days later feeling no better, I tore it to pieces.

Around this time, my Aunt Anna told me about Luisa Piccaretta, who, in 1878 when she was thirteen, Jesus appeared to in a vision on the Via Doloroso crying out, "*Anima, aiuta mi, aiuta mi*"—Soul, help me, help me. After that, she offered herself to Christ as a victim-soul. In order for her to understand everything he told her about the Divine Will, he removed her spirit from her body, a separation so disturbing that even after he returned it, only certain Catholic priests could release her from her death-like rigidity. For sixty-five years she survived on nothing but the Holy Eucharist, and in 1898, she began writing the thirty-six volume Book of Heaven, which included all that Christ had told her. It took her forty years to complete. I nodded respectfully as my aunt spoke zealously, but I was horrified. Yes, Luisa miraculously never got a sore, but she was still confined to bed for thirty-nine years. Why would she say yes to such ghastly suffering? How could God ask for it in the first place? Why did a gentle, petite, unmarried soul from southern Italy deserve such a sacrificial calling?

I was nothing like Luisa. I railed. Why was God asking me to give up the powerful sex drive *He'd* given me? How was I supposed to have any intimacy without it? Was my life just supposed to be work, being a dutiful employee for the college? Why was I expected to walk into every family occasion without someone who belonged to me? I even felt left out and strange at church where all the petitions and announcements were for married couples and families, where the only other single people were seniors. This is why I felt increasingly drawn to Father Infanzi, especially one November Saturday when I saw him lovingly greet a little boy with Down Syndrome after Mass.

Father was shaking people's hands, his green chasuble swaying slightly as a breeze came in the door, when I saw the little boy step toward him. He was four or five with a round face and brown eyes with wide, heavy lids. Father extended his hand to him, and he shook it, looking up at him as if he was a superhero. Then Father knelt down to meet the boy's eyes, and they smiled deeply at each other. They looked so pure and happy that I lost sense of myself. The picture of Cardinal O'Connor holding his miter in both hands became an 11 x 14 blur of red on the wall, the last snatches of conversation slurred, and everyone but the two of them faded away. They didn't care that the other was strange; all they saw was each other's light. For the first time in years, I didn't feel odd or guilty or afraid. Father made being celibate look beautiful, painless. As he stood back up and the boy's mother put one hand on her son's shoulder and they said goodbye, he suddenly felt deeply familiar, like I'd known him forever.

A month later I was sitting in a training workshop to become a lector, the lay person who reads at Mass, hoping Father was in the building, that he'd stop by. As I heard the back door open, I kept my eyes on Charles, the coordinator, afraid someone might detect my attraction. Sure enough, the deep voice from the back of the room was Father's. My heart sped as I turned around. There he was, all 6'1" of him in black pants, white collar sitting below his Adam's apple, and black shirt rolled up to his elbows accentuating his biceps. He looked even more handsome without his robes, like a young Cary Grant. "Don't let me interrupt all of you. I just wanted to say hello," he said taking a deep breath, which I found endearing, until Charles continued speaking, and Father folded his arms tightly across his chest like he was offended. A couple of women kept their eyes on him, but I quickly looked back at Charles. Just because he walked into the room everything was supposed to stop? He didn't seem like the humble, holy priest I'd spotted a month earlier. He seemed a touch arrogant, childish. I struggled to keep his body out of my mind for the rest of the night.

The next time I saw him on the altar with his hands pointed in prayer, I thought him adorable again. Each time I was the lector at one of his masses—which happened every month or two—and he stood behind me in the processional, I worried that he might be looking at my rear end. Just the possibility that he could be attracted to me was unnerving and exciting. After Mass I walked out the side door not the front, trying to avoid him and the nagging question of my own vocation. But then one Saturday in April, he showed up on my doorstep at work. All the interviews were over, and I was waiting for the student tour guide to finish up with the last family when I heard creaking from the front steps and the screen door open. I assumed it was the family returning, so I continued the call I was on, but then he appeared in front of me. I moved my eyes upward to his collar and face and held his gaze until I hung up.

"Father Infanzi?" I asked, trying to hide my shock.

"You're a lector from St. Stephen's," he said. "Maria?" though he didn't remember I was Janine's sister.

"Yes. What are you doing here?"

"I was asked to come and hear confessions."

"Are you sure? We're not a Catholic college. We have Catholic students, but I don't think we'd have confessions available on just any Saturday."

"I'm pretty certain I'm supposed to be here," he said taking out a piece of paper, clearing his throat before saying the name on it.

"There's no such person here. Maybe you're supposed to be at St. Vincent's University up the road?" I asked as casually as possible, so he wouldn't feel silly.

"Oh, you know what?" he said, slapping his palm against his forehead, "That's right. I just turned into the first college I saw." A thin film of red spread across his face, and then he paused, looking as surprised as I felt. "*Thank you.*"

"You're welcome."

"You work here?"

"I'm an admissions counselor."

"Oh. Well it was nice bumping into you like this," he said, looking at me longer than he needed to. As he left, I watched him out the window and then looked away quickly in case he turned back. When I was done, I walked outside where the magnolia trees were starting to bloom and felt stunned. It was one thing that of all the hundreds of parishes Father Infanzi could have been assigned to, he was assigned to St. Stephen's but showing up on my doorstep on the one Saturday a month I work? It had to be about my calling, didn't it? It had to be God sending him, a priest, to finally make me face it. But could God be *that* cruel? Father seemed to be everything I was looking for in a man, the perfect catch. I wasn't wise or religious enough to consider that maybe *I* was unconsciously drawing Father to myself or that this might be the work of the devil preying on my weak and immature soul. After this, I sometimes went out the front door to greet him. We'd shake hands and smile; he'd compliment my reading, and I'd compliment his homily, and he'd stare as I pretended not to notice. I didn't tell anybody about my attraction to him, not even RF, the therapist I began seeing when my depression had gotten so bad I started running red lights to get to work on time.

She was in her forties, had shoulder-length brown hair, and listened intently. In the first few sessions, she asked me what I remembered about my mother and father when I was a child. All I could recall about my mother was that I was always afraid she was going to leave. Once when I was five and napping in the early evening, I woke up to the dark, the only sliver of light coming from the lit-up gondola in the enormous oil painting above the couch. I called, "Mommy, Mommy!" but no answer. Terrified, I went into the kitchen where she was supposed to be at the stove cooking dinner, her glasses fogging from the boiling water, but all I found was the glaring yellow light. I don't remember anything else after that. When I asked her about it years later, she said she'd never leave me in the house alone, that she was always afraid she'd lose *me*.

My father was gruff and always working, and in the evenings when I had a few minutes on his lap, he'd conk out with his arm across me. I'd feel trapped but afraid to wake him, because I knew how tired he was, and I didn't want him to think I didn't love him. After he and my mother separated, I only saw him a few hours a month when he'd take Nellie and me for a meal. I didn't remember that he'd sometimes cancel, leaving the two of us in our dresses and barrettes, holding hands. He'd come over for special occasions, but he never stayed long. After he remarried when I was sixteen and

I visited him and my step-family, he'd swallow down some steak and bread and then leave for the caffè, the business he bought after he sold the pastry shoppe. Or he'd go downstairs to watch soccer in the dark.

RF asked what I knew of my family's history of depression, which was scant even though three women on my mother's side suffered from it. I wondered if my mother was ever depressed because of her tendency to withdraw at times, but I never asked, because I was afraid she'd think I was trying to dig up something negative. RF also asked about my dreams. There was the kind I'd been having ever since I moved out. My mother, Janine, and Julie—Nellie was never in it—are doing something fun together and excluding me. When I ask if I can join them, they dismiss me, sometimes make fun, or act like they don't hear and walk away, which devastates me. In another dream, my five year old half-sister Daniella has asked our father for something, but he's ignoring her. I don't know if it's me or my step-mother who yells, "*She needs you, and you're ignoring her.*" In a third dream, my mother and I are in a big, dark house where she has misplaced a baby she is not trying to find, and I'm angry. I showed RF a blurry picture of me when I was about a year old standing in my crib after a nap, my hair bent with sleep, my diaper pulling away from my waist. The picture is proof that I *wasn't* alone, but, because I felt that way now, I told her that I looked as if I'd been holding myself up for a long time before anyone came for me.

I also told RF that my sisters rebelled as teenagers but that I didn't, that I fantasized about rebelling now, cutting my hair and dyeing it, or quitting my job and that when Janine and Julie went out together with their husbands, I felt left out the way I did when I was little. After a couple of sessions, she told me I should get Alice Miller's *Drama of the Gifted Child*. Sometimes if parents didn't get to be children themselves, their children learn to hide their needs and memories "in order to meet their parents' expectations and win their love." They pretend to be well-behaved, reliable, and empathetic and are mortified when they find out they're not. Grown up, they feel alienated from themselves and rely on their partner, their achievements, or their own children to make them feel good. The book explains that loneliness can be caused by the loss of self in childhood, that denying it can lead to depression, and that we cannot really love if we don't know the truth about our parents and ourselves. It sounded as if it could be describing me, especially the part about pretending, but just the thought of owning up to it made me feel as if I were betraying my family, especially my mother. Besides, how I could trust any of these statements if I didn't know much about my parents' childhoods and couldn't remember much of my own?

One day, certain that my religious calling was causing my depression, I finally blurted to RF, "I think I'm supposed to become a nun." She asked me why I thought that. "I just know. Because nothing ever works out with men." I still didn't say anything about Father Infanzi. I didn't want her to think badly of me or presume that he was the only reason I thought I had a vocation. After this, neither one of us brought it up again for a long time. She was rightly interested in helping me discover why I didn't give good, available men a chance like the kind, devout teacher I met at a Catholic young adult event who took long walks on the beach with his ill father. "He doesn't *wow* me," I said. I was comparing him to Father Infanzi who did, whose homilies I took home in my heart especially the Sunday he connected *Beauty and the Beast,* the French original that I'd never seen, to the love between a husband and wife. When he said that the first time he saw his father cry was during this movie, I started crying. Who was this man who got to watch tender movies with his father and who believed that a husband's love for his wife should mirror Christ's sacrificial love for his Bride, the Church? I had learned a little about Pope John Paul II's—now St. John Paul II's—Theology of the Body in high school, but I had forgotten most of it. Now Father had stirred my longing for this kind of love all over again. I started looking for it in him. That's why I was devastated a few weeks later on the day of Janine and Phil's wedding when he forgot me.

It was after the ceremony, and he had already taken off his chasuble and alb and was busy retuning hymnals to their slots and gathering stray papers. *What good care he takes,* I thought as I stood on the side in my sleeveless, navy blue gown looking at his bare forearms. One of Janine's girl-friends had just told me I looked like Audrey Hepburn with my hair up, but nervously waiting for him to notice me and compliment my reading of "Love is Patient" from Second Corinthians, I felt more strange than pretty. When he looked up, I extended my hand, "Father, the ceremony was beautiful, and your homily really good," but he merely shook my hand, said thank you, and slid out the pew as if he were headed to something better. Even if he didn't recognize me with my hair up or still hadn't remembered I was Janine's sister, didn't he remember my voice? Didn't he see how pretty I looked? How could he forget me? He was just like my father who was outside, antsy in a tux, who had barely given me his cheek for a kiss, never mind a word about how well I'd done. *I'm just another parishioner,* I thought, and walked out into the June sun where my sisters were posing for pictures without me.

I had no business feeling disappointed. Father didn't owe me anything. But he'd bumped into me at work only two months earlier. We'd had conversations. What was wrong with him? I had no idea how needy I was. On one hand, I was drawn to the purity and freedom I saw in him, what I wanted to be and to have but couldn't accept; on the other, I desperately needed him to pay attention to me the way my father never had. Not only was I attracted to another unavailable man, this time I'd found someone completely off limits, the perfect man with whom to rebel against God and my family. Six months later on the night of the Advent concert, I got Father to remember me for good.

I was one of five lectors reading Scripture passages that were interspersed between choir music. Four of us were there, but the fifth seat beside mine was still empty. As I looked in the program to see who it was, there was Father Infanzi's name. I couldn't believe it. He was going to be seated next to me for an hour. I looked at the crucifix, trying to focus on

God the way I always did before I lectored but never could. I worried I'd trip over the words or that I wouldn't be able to get my hair back if it fell in my face when I bowed. Now I was also thinking how glad I was that the pants I wore made my backside look good. That's when I heard from the side aisle the clack of a man's shoes against the tile. I crossed my legs and pretended to be interested in the program as Father slipped into the seat next to me wearing a black bomber jacket, the kind the boys in school used to wear.

"Hi Father."

"Hello," he said, cold air and the scent of mouthwash wafting off him. Too nervous to look in his eyes, I watched him tug the pleat of his pants, stretch his leg out, and reach in his pocket with his other hand, a movement I found as alluring as a man shaving. He took out his reading, leaned his elbows hard into his knees as he looked it over for a few seconds, and then put it back, unlike me who had practiced five times and still felt nervous. Then he removed his jacket, his left arm hovering just behind my head so that if he lowered it, it would've fallen right around my shoulders. Twisting around to put it on the back of his chair, he finally realized, "You're Janine's sister."

"Yes."

"How are she and Phil?"

"Good."

"She's a nice girl."

"I like her."

He paused, then laughed.

For the next thirty minutes songs were sung and readings

read, and then during the third reading, Father went completely still. I turned my head just enough to find him asleep. I thought about tapping him but felt too self-conscious. When the lector was done, and the flautist began to play, Father shuddered, his elbow nudging my rib, the contact waking him. "Did I just elbow you?" he whispered. "It's okay," I said. He didn't apologize, just looked at me as if he was seeing for the first time. The flute fell softer and softer, cue that I was next.

"Good luck."

"Thanks."

I bowed at the foot of the altar and with clammy palms lit the pink candle in the wreath, the one that symbolizes joy, as I tried not to think about Father. Once at the lectern, I saw the rows of people stretched out in front of me and Monsignor Brennan facing the altar in a seat that had been placed especially for him in the middle of the aisle like an island. He was wearing a straight, full-length black robe with a wide purple sash, the kind you didn't see monsignors wear anymore, the kind that Father de Bricassart wore in *The Thorn Birds*.

I adjusted the microphone even though it was fine, looked down at the paper even though I had practiced looking up. "During those days Mary set out and traveled to the hill country in haste to a town of Judah where she entered the house of Zechariah and greeted Elizabeth...," I recited, my voice even despite the rumbling in one leg that was so terrible I leaned heavily on the other for support. I gazed up a couple of times avoiding Father's face except toward the end when I finally looked in his eyes. I folded my reading and walked off the altar, thinking, *He's not going to forget me now,* as I looked at him one last time to see if he was still watching. He was. Then I quickly looked away again and sat down but not before I saw that his face had gone from white to pink, from unaware to roused.

Chapter Two

After Mass

After the concert, Father asked me if I'd light the candle on the Advent wreath at Mass. I said yes, hiding my delight. A couple of weeks later I sent him a Christmas card with Shirley Temple standing on tippy toes in her short skirt to hang an ornament on a tree. When he thanked me for it on Sunday, he looked at me like he didn't want me to go. Then after Christmas Eve Mass, I kissed him on the cheek. The following week he asked if I'd wait until he was done greeting parishioners, so we could talk a few minutes. As he finished, he slyly popped a mint, and then walked over and said hi, his fresh breath curling into the air. He was in his clerical clothing and jacket—had taken off his vestments as soon as he reached the back of the church—and I was in my long, beige coat and a pair of heels, which I always wore so I'd look taller. The church patio had cleared out except for a straggler or two, and the ushers had locked up the heavy maple doors. With almost a foot's difference between us, Father had his hands jammed in his pockets like he was trying to hide his excitement, and I was looking in his eyes trying to disguise mine. "You read the readings beautifully," he said, blushing, and I said, "Your homily was great as usual." Then he asked me about my job and family and, except for clearing his throat several times, he let me talk, which I loved. When we finally said goodbye, we hugged each other from the waist up as he nervously patted my back.

For the next three months, I walked out the side door. There was always such a long line of parishioners out the front waiting to shake his hand. I was afraid of what I'd started. I also knew Father would be disappointed when he got through the line, and there was no me. The fact that I could have this kind of effect on a man, on him, assuaged my unhappiness, made me feel in control at least for a little while. There were times when therapy made me feel more broken, like the day I remembered when my father had taken Nellie and me to Beefsteak Charlie's and afterwards to the hotel he was staying in on Shore Parkway until he found an apartment. The waitress told him how gorgeous Nellie was, as I cut her meat and went up to the buffet three times. Then when we walked into his room, the haze of stale cigarette smoke made us cough as Papa put on the Mets game, closed the thick, dark drapes, and snored in the chair. I thought, *How sad.* I sat Nellie on the bedspread dotted with burn holes and tried teaching her *Miss Mary Mack,* pretending I didn't feel lonely as the sun choked its way from beneath the hems. After a few minutes, her eyes got so heavy, I laid her golden head on the pillow. Alone in the dark with the glare of the TV and Papa's snores mixing with Ralph Kiner's voice,

I started to cry softly. After a half hour I couldn't take it any longer. I wiped my face and nudged Nellie awake so her crying would wake my father. When I got home, I pretended I was fine. I didn't want to bother my mother. She always had so much to do. I was afraid she wouldn't understand. Once I told RF, I cried for hours.

A few days before Palm Sunday, Father called me to ask if I'd fill in for a lector who had cancelled. He'd gotten my number from the parish files. Standing in my blue and white kitchen, I vaguely felt he'd crossed a line, but I was too excited to complain. When we spoke again after Mass, I looked in his hazel eyes and gushed, "Father, you listen. So many people don't; they're just thinking about what they're going to say next. It's *nice*."

Then Good Friday happened.

I was with Janine at the three o'clock service, the hour that Jesus died. The church was cloaked in purple and swelling with people but quiet except for a sporadic cough. I was saving a seat for my friend Silvia who had something to tell me but didn't want to wait until I got home from church. I tucked my hair behind my ear just in case Father Infanzi was one of the celebrants. Then he and two other priests including Monsignor Brennan were processing down the center aisle. Instead of heading for the presiders' chairs as they would during Mass, they prostrated themselves on the altar. Silvia slipped into the seat next to mine, we kissed hello, and she waved at Janine.

I looked at the altar and felt an odd sense of satisfaction—Silvia and Father Infanzi in the same place. She and I'd been friends since third grade except for the first semester of high school. Since I was going to a different school than she was, I was hoping I'd make a new best friend. She was always so perfect and pulled together: her straight dirty-blonde hair never out of place, her science scores always higher than mine, her sins hardly worthy of confession. The night of our eighth grade awards ceremony, I'd had enough, but not because she was valedictorian. I had won the English award. It was all I'd wanted, but back at her house after the ceremony, she asked me to take a picture of her and her father. My father had not been there. I'm not sure if my mother or I even bothered to ask him. When I looked through the lens, Silvia and Mr. Pelusi both 5'7" and holding her certificate in front of them, looked like a couple—heads cocked, Neapolitan pride flooding their faces, especially his. I felt invisible, but I wasn't sure why, which only made it worse. A few months later when we went off to high school, I tried to break it off with her. But when I transferred to Catholic school half way through the year, she stopped me in the hall one day and asked, "Ri, can we be friends again?"

I bowed my head thanking God for Father, when out of the corner of my eye I saw the emerald cut engagement ring on Silvia's hand that she'd splayed on the pew in front of us. I'd known this day was coming—she'd been going out with Greg for a year—but I'd pretended it wasn't. She was my only single friend left. Stung, I looked at the altar trying not to see the ring, but it pressed on me, springing up from the pew like a big, perfect bow, growing to the size of my envy. I wanted to drop my head on my sister's shoulder, but she wouldn't have understood. Even if she and the rest of my family knew that the only reason I was dating Rick—a friend of a friend who had called on Valentine's Day—was so I'd have something to do on Saturday nights, they'd never suspect I felt a calling. They'd tell me I was only twenty-seven, I'd meet the right one, there was plenty of time.

I steadied myself as I looked at Father Infanzi on the floor. There was no way he was celibate because he couldn't get a wife. He had a choice, which made his priesthood a beautiful sacrifice. It didn't matter that he had lifted my phone number or that whenever we spoke he looked like he was struggling *not* to say something. All I saw now was a perfectly sweet, good looking man who would've made a wonderful husband giving his life to Christ. How did he do it? When the men rose from the floor and continued the liturgy, I was certain Father helped me overcome my jealousy. I lifted Silvia's hand, looked directly at the gem, and mouthed as genuinely as I could, *C...o...n...g...r...a...t...u...l...a...t...i...o...n...s* and *W...o...w*. She smiled and mouthed in return, *I k...n...o...w*. After church, when Silvia showed off her ring to me, I proudly introduced Father Infanzi to her.

The next night at the Easter Vigil after Father had sung the Exsultet, and I approached the lectern to read, I looked in his eyes. It was a split second, but I could see how excited he got. After Mass I told him, "I didn't know you could sing *too*," and he laughed and said, "You look *nice.*" I walked away feeling lit up but unsettled, the same way I felt four days later when he called again. It was one thing for us to talk after Mass, another for him to call a second time for no reason. It felt wrong. I wanted his attention but on my terms. I'd told myself that this was just a budding friendship. His phone call had threatened that. For the next several weeks I walked out the side door again, but I was soon in line at the front door once more. His relief when he saw me was intoxicating. We started talking after Mass nearly every week. In June, when he was leaving to go on a cruise, I sent him a bon voyage card: *I wish you some lucky strolls in the casino.* I thought celibacy such an enormous sacrifice that he deserved a little fun. When he called to thank me, I felt the knot in my stomach again, but I said, "You'll be missed." Two weeks later, I asked him out to lunch.

I was standing near my car after Mass stalling, hoping that if I gave Father enough time to finish locking up the gates he'd come over before I drove away. I'd spent the previous weekend with Rick at our friends' pre-wedding festivities in upstate New York, but I thought about Father Infanzi. I'd sent him another postcard: *After driving beside Seneca Lake for a half hour, there's still more lake. As beautiful as it is, I'm truly a city girl. Hope you're doing well.* I got in my car, put the key in the ignition, and pretended to search for something in my pocketbook. A minute later, Father was a few inches from my window telling me how special the postcards were. Then he told me that he was going on a second vacation, this time to the Midwest to visit his family and to go to Vegas. "Wow," I said, feeling a little jealous, though I wasn't sure why. *Priests go to Vegas?* When he added that he'd be gone for a month, I looked away and back at him. Then, before I lost my nerve, "Maybe when you return, I could show you around the college, and we could go to lunch?" He blushed and laughed nervously. Putting his hand in his pocket to calm himself, he said, "That would be very nice."

Five weeks later on my 28th birthday, we were sitting in a quaint Italian restaurant, the salt tang of New York Harbor sweeping through the French doors. I was wearing a long flower-printed dress with short sleeves and had my hair pulled up softly on the sides. He was wearing khakis and a light pink button-down shirt with a beeper clipped to his belt in case the rectory needed him. Ordinarily I would have waited for him to call, but the day after he got home from vacation I called him. My birthday was the following week, and I wanted to spend it with him, not Rick who I'd slept with the night of our friends' wedding. Afterward, I felt just as numb and disconnected from myself as I always did, but I hadn't gone to confession, because I didn't want to promise I wouldn't do it again.

As we looked at the menu, I told Father how good the pastas and fried calamari were. "I like pasta puttanesca," he said. When he couldn't find it, I pointed to it, the sight of my hand near his making him blush more. After the waiter took our order, I complimented Father's pronunciation. "A lot of people say *calamary*. It's so wrong, it hurts the ear."

"*I know,*" he said laughing. "That's my half Italian side."

"Your father's father is from Puglia?"

"Right," he said, impressed that I'd remembered. "And both your mother and father were born in Italy. You're the real thing."

I shrugged my shoulders to be cute, which made him laugh harder. "You studied Chemistry at Fairfield, right?"

He looked impressed again. "Yes, and you graduated from Westerly."

I nodded. "Then the fall after graduation, I went to work in the Admissions office."

"Where I bumped into you like a clod last April," he said, rolling his eyes.

"It was an honest mistake. Soon after that is when I got the career placement director position, and that's what I've been doing for the last year." By the time the waiter arrived with our platter of calamari, we were talking a steady stream. Both our mothers went back to college in their forties to become health care professionals; we were third-born and mildly introverted, almost always falling into the role of listener; his mother's name is Maria. I asked him what he does in the parish even though I already knew, and he asked me about my job and the graduate course in autobiographical writing that I was taking, both of which I enjoyed so much it showed on my face. I told him I wanted to write a memoir one day, though I didn't tell him that I cried in my professor's office when he asked me what my very first memory was, and I couldn't remember a thing. Half-way through our main course when we came to a pause, he started to laugh. "I'm sorry," he said. "I've just never had lunch with a girl like you before."

It was the moment when I should have steered the conversation toward vocation, asked him when he first felt called to the priesthood, told him that I also felt a calling, so that he wasn't wondering for one more moment why the two of us were having a three hour lunch on my birthday. But I was making him laugh with a spontaneity I'd forgotten I had. He was hanging on my words. He seemed so different from the men I dated: innocent and child-like and easy to charm. I was looking for some answer to my life, something pure to save me and give me the courage to take the next step toward God. One of the reasons I was attracted to him was because I couldn't have him, *wouldn't have to* have him, or owe him anything, but now all I cared about was how I might be able to keep him. For the three hours that we talked and ate and paused while the sun danced its shadows on the hardwood floors, I was running as hard as I could from God. As we waited for Father to get his change, he said abruptly, "I'd be happy to be the priest at your wedding."

At first I felt an odd sense of relief. He didn't say *if* you get married. He said it as if it were certain, and hearing it from a priest, I allowed myself to think that maybe I had this whole calling thing wrong. Maybe I *had* misunderstood God all these years, but then I felt a sharp twist of irony. If I were to get married, I was pretty sure I'd want to marry *him*. He was everything I wanted in a man. Why did he have to say that? I couldn't not feel what I was feeling. We had so much in common. The more I got to know him the more I felt I'd known him before, that it was our fate to meet. Maybe he was a gift from God, so I wouldn't have to be completely alone; I'd be happy and fortunate just to have him as a friend. This couldn't be the end. All I managed to say was, "That would be nice, Father."

Later that night, when Janine, Julie, and I were gathered at my mother's for cake, someone asked me if I had done anything special. I said as casually as I could, "I went to lunch with Father Infanzi." The only one who seemed a little upset was Janine whose mouth tightened. "*You did?*" My mother asked intrigued, "What did you *talk* about?" imagining herself sitting with him. Then she added, "I always thought it'd be good for you girls to have a priest-friend." And from Julie, a completely innocent, "Where did you go? That sounds really nice." If Nellie were there, she probably would've been onto me, but she was twenty and never wanted to be with us. Right before my mother placed the cake in front of me with nine flickering candles, one for good luck, I boasted, "It was a *three*-hour lunch."

Less than a week later, Father asked me out for a second lunch. While we waited for our food, he told me that one day when a woman had come to the rectory to talk to him about her marital problems, all he could think was, *Go away, lady! Why can't you be Maria?* I bristled. I wanted him to prefer me, but I didn't want him to own up to it *that* way. Besides, why was he bringing up another woman? When he asked if something was wrong, I said, "No," but I was distant for the rest of lunch. Did all the unhappily married women call on him? Was he responding to them the way he was to me? When I walked out after Sunday Mass with a frown, he asked if he'd done anything wrong. I said, "Your comment made me nervous." Two days later I received an apology in the mail: As privileged as he felt to be a priest, he needed to remind himself that he could cause great harm when he betrayed one's trust in him. I had no reason to feel nervous in my own church, which I'd be attending long after he left. He was sorry. It's what I thought I wanted to hear until I got to the part where he said *he wasn't trying to start anything*, that he planned to be *a faithful priest until he died*. Now I felt jealous of the Church. When I called to accept his apology, he told me that he had just gotten home from helping a single mom whose house was in need of repair.

No priest had ever helped my mother or spent time with Nellie and me once our father was gone. It seemed like an odd form of charity. The next time I greeted him after Mass, I shook his hand as if he were any other priest and said, "Have a good week, Father." He said warmly, "You too, Maria" and then reached in to give me a peck on the cheek, but he didn't ask me to stay and chat. I walked away feeling slighted, more resolved to keep my distance. In the meantime, Rick and I broke up by Labor Day, and I met Sam, a physician's assistant who rescued me from a table of misfit singles at a wedding in October. Fifteen minutes into our first date, with the pain still palpable on his face, he told me that his ex-wife decided on their honeymoon that she didn't want to be married. I was hoping he'd like me enough to forget her, but I knew from the obligatory kiss he gave me on our third date that I was wrong. I still went home four nights in a row hoping for a blinking red light on my answering machine. By Thursday, I had to accept that I wasn't going to hear from him. It was the same week that Grandpa Nino died, my mother's father with his bald head and mischievous blue eyes who wanted all of us to run businesses from home so we didn't have to pay taxes, who always said, "Go the straight way," and "*Se Dio vuole,*" if God wants, and who prayed the Rosary for us every day. Grandpa whom I loved, with whom I couldn't walk or talk with because of his Sicilian dialect and missing leg, which he lost the year I was born when he was walking home one day and a drunk driver crashed into him.

I pulled out a pot from the set my mother had bought me for when I got married and put water up for pasta. While I waited, I obsessed. Maybe if I had said or done something just a little bit differently, Sam would have called. Here was more proof that I wasn't meant to get married. Something would have worked out by now. As for Father, if God had wanted us to be together, he would have allowed us to meet before he entered the seminary or at the very least before he was ordained. How could God send me such a wonderful man I couldn't have to corner me into a vocation I didn't want? I was leading on a priest I wasn't sure I trusted and blaming it on God. All these months I hadn't said a word to him about my calling: letting him believe that I was available, sending him mixed messages as I dated other men, trying to get back at him for something I couldn't put my finger on. Just because I was jealous, didn't mean Father was doing anything wrong. He was reverent and dutiful on the altar, spoke so admiringly and proudly of Christ. If God wasn't giving me a husband—if He expected me to lead a celibate life—then at the very least He owed me a special male friend. He *owed* me Father.

Once the pasta was done, I reached into the cabinet to get the colander, and that's when I saw the bulletin from St. Stephen's sticking out beneath it. I tried not to read the list of priests' names but saw *Father James Infanzi, Parochial*

Vicar. I shut the cabinet quickly and ate my dinner staring at the wall. *It's not a big deal if I call him. He's celibate and looks happy. Maybe he can help me. But it's going to look like I'm interested in him that way. No it won't. I haven't done anything wrong. But what would I start by calling him? He'll probably ask me to lunch again and then what?* I looked at the phone, then away, and then back again. *It's not unusual to call a priest when your grandfather has died.* Before I knew it, I was dialing the number and asking for Father Infanzi. He expressed his condolences, but I could hear a breathless excitement in his voice. We spoke for a half hour about my grandfather and how difficult Janine was taking it, and about how hard I found dating, though I implied that *I* had turned Sam down. Sounding relieved, Father said, "He must be crushed." I said, "I don't know about that" and he said, "That's hard to believe," which made me smile. When I asked him how his week was going, he said he got stuck late a couple of nights doing more repairs for the single mom.

"The same woman whose husband left and has three sons?" I asked, disappointed that she was still in the picture.

"I told you about her?"

"Yes, of course. Why? Is anything—" I stopped and waited until he was done clearing his throat, expecting his perfect attention. "Is anything wrong?"

"No, no, I just didn't remember telling you about her."

"Did you do contracting work before the seminary?"

"Yes, in fact my two good friends, Matt and Roger? I told you about them."

"Sure."

"The three of us were talking about going into contracting, but then I decided to become a priest. Matt was pretty upset."

"He probably felt abandoned."

"I think you're exactly right."

"Father, does this woman plan on paying you at all?" I asked, growing angry at her.

"No, nothing like that. I told her I wouldn't charge her."

Before I could think or say anything else, he was telling me how happy he was that I'd called, that it was Sam's loss, that he'd pray for my grandfather, and then, "Maria, is there any way we could go to lunch again? I promise not to make any more inappropriate comments."

I clutched the receiver, my doubts erased by the sound of my name in his voice. "Do you think that's the best idea?"

"I don't see why it has to be a problem."

And then as if it was any less dangerous, "What about coffee instead?"

I let him pick me up at my apartment on a Thursday night, though I waited outside for him. I ordered cappuccino, and he ordered tea before he brought the waitress back, "You know what, can you make that an Irish coffee?" Facing me from behind him was Audrey Hepburn from the scene in *Breakfast at Tiffany's* in which her character, a call girl named Holly Golightly who's still dressed in the black gown from the night before, is looking into the window of Tiffany's to soothe her fears. She's beautiful and polished and goes to a lot of great parties, but as the movie unfolds we learn she's running from the truth. Father asked me how I went about helping students get jobs, so I told him about the company visits, the on-campus recruitment, the job consortia, as I tried my best not to get foam on my lips. He remarked admiringly, "You're *so* together."

After that night, I called him to wish him a Happy Thanksgiving, and in December we saw each other four nights in a row at the parish mission and spoke twice for an hour. I still didn't say a word about my calling. A week before Christmas when we went for coffee a second time, I asked him in to bless my apartment. He shook holy water and made the sign of the cross in each of the rooms including my bedroom where the floor lamp cast a dim glow on the ceiling as I stood in the doorway, so he couldn't see me and my bed at the same time. Turning around, he looked in my eyes and said, "What a *cozy* place you keep."

A few days later I was at a rectory near work telling a priest I didn't know that I had a vocation. The sight of Father liking my bedroom had unnerved me that much. But sitting across from the trim, forty-something Father Relici who was donning an Augustinian black capuchin, I couldn't bring myself to say "nun." It wasn't just celibacy that troubled me. I didn't want to take a vow of poverty either. I didn't want to wear a habit or live in a convent. If I had to have a vocation, I wanted to be like a diocesan priest, like Father Infanzi who got to keep his paycheck and had his own car and bank account. The only way a Catholic woman could give her life to God and be independent was to remain single, but what was the use of that? Even if I were certain the single life could be a real vocation, people would never understand. They'd ask me, "Haven't you met anyone?" or think, *What a shame she never married.* I wanted a title, something that would explain me, a life that would make me feel worthy and visible. I blurted, "Father, I feel called to the clergy."

"Are you saying you want to convert, so you can become a female minister? Because in the Catholic Church, clergy means priests and deacons, men only."

"Oh no, I'm Catholic. I think I just got my words mixed up," I said feeling humiliated but determined. I told him how my relationships lasted three months tops and how I thought that was a sign from God that I wasn't meant to get married. I said nothing about Father Infanzi. What would I have said, *I'm falling for a priest, and I think this confirms I have a calling?* Then I added half-jokingly, "Not all the guys I dated were losers," but Father Relici didn't grin, not even a slight upturn of his lips. I tried to recover with, "Some were very *nice* guys."

"Nuns serve in so many capacities. They work in hospitals, schools, they're presidents of colleges."

"Father, I'm really struggling with the idea of celibacy."

"There are so many good women religious out there who you could talk to," he said, dabbing his pointer finger into a piece of dust on his mahogany desk and then flicking it off.

"Is it hard, Father? Do you find it difficult?" desperate for him to say something consoling like, *The struggle will go away.*

"I could allow myself to think about what my wife would have looked like, my children, my house, where I'd be now, but I don't. I try not to think about what I'm missing. What would be the use?" He dabbed and flicked another piece of dust off his finger. "You know, it's a good life. You get the privilege of touching so many people's lives."

"I'm just really afraid I'll have to commit to something before I'm ready," I said, feeling the sting of tears in my nose.

"It's not like that. Discernment takes a long time. The nuns—the Sisters—they wouldn't rush you." Then, maybe because he sensed my independence, he told me that some nuns rent apartments if it's convenient to their ministry and there isn't a convent nearby, which made me feel a little relieved. He got up from his desk, walked over to his shelf where the books were in perfect size order and pulled out a royal blue, soft covered book, *A Guide to Religious Ministries for Catholic Men and Women*.

"A good person to start with is Sister Lorraine in the vocations office. Here she is," he said, marking her phone number with a highlighter and handing the book to me. "Thank you," I said, opening to a random page where the picture of a cross rose up from the New York skyline and across the top, *Sisters of Charity*.

Two nights later on Christmas Eve, I was sitting in front of the crèche after Midnight Mass when Father Infanzi, revved up from saying Mass for the largest crowd of the year, asked me to go for coffee. I had wanted to stay in front of the manger, hoping the Baby Jesus would give me the courage to finally tell him about my calling, especially given the beautiful homily he'd delivered. After his joke about how Italians know the meaning of the word "manger" from the order, "*Mangia, mangia*," which got him the big laugh he was hoping for, he explained that Christ not only humbled himself by coming as an infant, but also by being lain in a manger where animals *ate from*. He is food for the world, for *us*. It was the most precious explanation of the Incarnation I'd ever heard, and I felt the same profound warmth as when I drank Christ's blood. But then Father switched to his brother's excitement when his wife gave birth. He used the phrase, "born of love for his wife." I had been sitting in the lector's seat so close to the pulpit that if I reached out my arm, I could touch Father's garment, feel his thigh beneath it. Julie and Nick were expecting their first child in a week, the first baby in our family, which made me feel more insecure. When Father ended by explaining that Deism is the opposite of Christianity, that God couldn't get *more* involved in our lives than by taking on our human nature, something inside me broke, and a tear fell from my eye. How could God give me the gift of womanhood and then ask me to give up marriage and motherhood? Why was He taking care of every other woman but me?

"I promise not to keep you out too long," he said, looking at me like an eager boy.

"You know what, Father? Coffee sounds nice."

There was no one in the diner whom I recognized, which I was glad about, though I still told myself I wasn't doing anything wrong. Father was wearing a long, black coat that made him look so handsome, it hurt. He took it off, revealing his cleric shirt with only the tip of the white tab collar showing, and then he stuffed it in the booth and sat down. I stood at the rack near our booth with my coat in my hands so he'd get the hint. "Oh, gosh," he said, "I should be getting that for you." I said, "That's okay," as if I hadn't given it any thought.

Within minutes we were drinking coffee and exchanging the gifts we hadn't told each other we were buying. I bought him *How Houses Learn,* a book about how the character of houses develops over time. I didn't realize it, but I was implying that his character needed developing. When I'd hung around after morning Mass the day before, he admitted that he hadn't been an ideal seminarian. First, he brought up the fact that when he was walking down the stairs in the rectory to meet Janine for the first time, all he could think was: "*Whoever this girl is, she smells really nice. The seminary never smelled like that.*" It was something he'd already told me, but I pretended it was the first time. Then he told me that sometimes when he was in the seminary, he'd throw enough clothes for the weekend in a laundry bag, so the rector would think he was going home, but he was headed to Atlantic City with Matt.

"*Really?*" I said, disappointed but also a little turned on. It was something like me telling my mother I had sorority meetings on Thursday nights in college when I was really headed for the bars. Then he said, "I almost didn't make it to ordination."

"What?"

"Three priests voted me in, three didn't, and one was indecisive."

"Wow. Really?" I said, my heart sinking.

"I've never told anyone this before. I never told my mother."

"Why?" I asked, starting to feel uneasy.

"I figured once they voted me in what was the point?"

"How did they convince the indecisive one?"

"One of them said to him, 'We have a real man here, and you're going to let him get away?'" Father propped his elbow on the back of the pew, his hand so close to my face he could graze my cheek. Then he added, "The indecisive priest later told me that he pictured me in the suburbs with a wife, kids, and picket fence." He said it as if he were fishing for me to say, "I do, too," as if he were suggesting we get together. He was telling me what he'd been trying to all year. He was hungry, maybe even a little angry. A peaceful priest doesn't take a woman out and talk about how good her sister smells, doesn't repair a single woman's home and then get nervous when he's asked about it. The split vote made complete sense. It was the same ambivalence I pretended I didn't feel. Father was going to help me answer God's call. We were going to be each other's best friend and celibate significant other. He was a fulfilled priest. I wouldn't have to be alone anymore. I had no idea how much I was fooling myself. His hunger and anger mirrored mine. Despite the knot it my stomach, I said, "I'm glad you wound up here and not the suburbs."

"*How Houses Lean?*" he asked, ripping off the last bit of wrapping paper.

"*Learn*, How Houses *Learn*," I said earnestly. "You know, because you like houses? Because you would have gone into contracting?"

"Maria, this is beautiful, *just* beautiful," he said lifting it over our coffee cups, trying his best to look at it and not me. "*How Houses Learn*," he repeated slowly. Then he put it down and handed me a meticulously wrapped gift. "And this is for you." I rubbed my hands together to express *goodie*. I tore the paper, stunned to see the name of my favorite store and then a pretty soft wool turtleneck in the perfect earthy color.

"Wow, how did you know my style? I like it *so* much."

"I've been looking at you for a while now," he said his face turning rose.

I looked into my cappuccino before I raised it to my lips.

"Last year you sent me a card. This year I get to sit with you."

"I remember. It was a black and white of Shirley Temple putting an ornament on a tree."

"That's it," he said, taking a gulp of tea.

"Did you like this year's card?" I asked sheepishly. It was a picture of Raphael's cherubs. Inside I wrote: *Although I come across as very together and composed, I feel as if I'll always be working through past hurts. Meeting you and initiating the friendship has given me the chance to trust a man again. The fact that you listen and are genuinely excited by the things/stories I share is such a gift (more than you can know). I treasure you in my life. May all the good you do for others be returned hundredfold to you (as I'm confident it will).*

"Of course I did. What a blockhead I am. I *loved* it."

We were in the diner for over an hour before I asked him what time it was. He was wearing a thick, expensive-looking watch, a Rolex, though I didn't know it at the time. I asked him if it was new. "This? Just a gift from someone in the parish," he said loosening his collar from his neck. It was an awfully showy gift for a priest to accept, one that could only be from a woman, but this was a man who knew which store to shop for me in, what fabric and color and even size I liked. No man had ever zeroed in on me so quickly. I was so swept away that I didn't realize when he changed the subject. In fact, by the time he got my coat off the rack and held the door for me, I'd forgotten about the watch. Then standing beside our cars—mine a red, two-door with a spoiler on the back and his a Chevy sedan with the bumper sticker that read, *Pregnant? Call 1-800- 325-LIFE*—he said, "This has been my *best* Christmas ever," and I said, "I'm *so* glad." The next night, Christmas night, when he was leaving Janine's where he'd been invited for dessert and I was sitting on her couch wearing the turtleneck he gave me, I looked in his eyes with such longing that I knew it would excite him. Several weeks later he told me that all he'd wanted to do was hug the life out of me.

Chapter Three

Telling Father

Within a month of meeting with Father Relici, I met with Sister Lorraine and two Sisters of Charity, Erin and Teresa. Sister Lorraine was a buxom woman in her fifties who wore a large silver cross around her neck and had warm eyes and short brown hair. After some small chat about work and family in her tiny diocesan office, she told me that before I pursued a religious vocation, I should go for spiritual direction, a process of learning to trust God and discern His will. She recommended Sister Erin who worked at a Jesuit retreat house not far from me and who, a couple of weeks later, greeted me with a hug and then offered me a seat in her office. As soon as I glanced out the window at the climbing ivy, I remembered I'd been there before in sophomore year of high school and again with my mother in my early twenties before I'd started pulling away from her. I remembered how much I loved retreats—the quiet time for reflection and journaling, Confession and Mass, the talks about God's unconditional love—and how I always left feeling happy and fed.

After I answered Sister Erin's questions about my job and told her about my meetings with Father Relici and Sister Lorraine, I said what I'd never said to anyone quite as clearly before: "I'm drawn to God but *so* afraid." It was as if some closed latch in my throat finally opened. Except for telling her about Father Infanzi, I told her everything else about the previous four and a half years since I'd broken up with Dave and how ashamed I felt about not being able to pull myself together better. I was crying, and she was handing me tissues as she nodded her head with no judgment or even pity in her eyes. When she asked if I was going to therapy I said yes, though the truth was I'd stopped at the end of October. Maybe Father's attention had given me the false sense that I was doing better. I was hoping that spiritual direction could take the place of therapy.

Sister said very gently that God never forces, He only *invites,* and that the aim of discernment is to figure out *if* I have a vocation and then which religious order would be the right match, but that the underlying purpose is always to draw closer to our loving God. She described discernment as a series of conversations with a particular order that would help us learn about each other, like dating. Then she told me about her order, the Sisters of Charity, that they were founded in 1809 by St. Elizabeth Ann Seton, the first native-born American citizen to become a saint and who was a wife and mother before she became a nun.

"*Really?*" I asked, but then I remembered the book my mother had on our shelf when I was growing up, *Blessed Mother Seton*. In the first part, there were pictures of

Elizabeth with her husband and five children, and in the second part, a picture of her wearing a widow's cap, which later became part of her habit. She closed the gap between marriage and celibacy a little for me and made being a nun seem less strange, at least for the moment. Before I left, Sister Erin and I scheduled another appointment for a month later. She also gave me the name and number of Sister Teresa, the Vocation Director, adding, "You'll like Teresa. She's Italian, from Brooklyn. Call her when you feel ready." It was probably premature, but I trusted Sister Erin, who hugged me goodbye like she was trying to gather fallen leaves to her chest and was afraid one would slip. A week later I was driving north on the New Jersey Turnpike to the Convent of Our Lady in Fort Lee filled with dread. I hadn't been in a convent since high school. I didn't know anyone my age who was a nun; I hadn't even heard of anyone becoming a nun anymore. As I zipped past Newark Airport, planes descended and ascended as my mind buzzed. *Is there any turning back after tonight? How will I explain to everyone that I'm considering religious life when I don't want to, that I really want to get married?* A half mile later, as I passed a fuchsia billboard for a vacation resort with a couple lying in each other's arms on the beach, my throat tightened.

While I waited for Sister Teresa to open the door, I looked at the one-family houses across the street and then back at the enormous stucco convent. All I could see of the Blessed Mother statue a few feet away from me were her palms facing upward in surrender. Within seconds, a tall, slim woman appeared behind the screen door, her short hair completely white even though she wasn't yet fifty and perfectly tapered as if she'd just come from the beauty parlor. She was wearing gray slacks and sensible shoes and a light pink, V-neck sweater with a white blouse underneath, its collar folded over the V. I apologized for being late, and she said, "Don't worry" and "I'm so glad we're getting to meet each other." Then she hugged me generously, her shoulder blades sharp through her sweater. Inside, the quiet was like a thick blanket over the hallway, which was long and dim and bare but that had to be bustling in the 1950s with lots of young women in black habits trying to get to chapel on time like a scene from the *Sound of Music* before Maria leaves.

"We used to have a lot of Sisters in this house, every bedroom occupied, so we really needed the space. Now we're two Sisters and two novices." I wanted to ask her what happened, why she thought women weren't doing this anymore, but I was afraid to offend her. "Oh well, God always has a plan," she continued, as if reading my mind. As she showed me around, I smiled, trying to hide my unease. It felt like a museum, everything silent and placed and old like the books in their library and the 1970s television in the living room, the same kind my grandparents had until my mother and aunts, after years of trying, finally convinced them to replace with a new one. There were none of the aromas of a home like cookies in the oven or fresh-cut flowers on the table, and the kitchen had pastel tiled walls and a dumbwaiter they no longer used.

"This is my favorite room," she said smiling broadly. "On Sunday mornings, I'm usually the first awake. I get my coffee and the paper and clip my coupons, then I have a second cup. It's heavenly, the solitude."

"That sounds nice," I said, but I thought, *How lonely in this big kitchen by herself every Sunday morning.*

Afterward we met in her office where two chairs were set up facing each other in the center of the room like confession without the screen. It was an orderly and modest room with short shelves filled with books whose spines read words like *Charism, Apostolic, Contemplative* and still others that said *Praying with Vincent de Paul, Praying with Louise De Marillac, Praying with Elizabeth Ann Seton.* There was a picture of St. Elizabeth before she became a nun, with her long, curly brown tresses falling passed her shoulders, and a statue of her afterward in which she's in her habit looking attentively at two small children. Sister offered me the more comfortable chair and then sat down, her legs so long her knees extended way past the edge of the chair.

"Sister, as I was telling you on the phone, I feel like I'm supposed to be looking into this, religious life, but I don't wa—," I said crossing my legs. "I'm just not sure."

"There's no pressure. Really," she said. "But maybe we could talk a little about what makes you feel like you might have a calling."

I told her about that night in church when I was eight, how drawn I felt to prayer in high school, and that most of the time I didn't make it to a fourth date. She nodded and asked, "Is there anything going on that's making you consider religious life now?" I looked at her surprised, Father Infanzi in my head. "No, just that if I don't explore it, I'll always have this gnawing feeling." I wanted to ask her if celibacy would always feel like an interminable longing, but she looked so happy I felt silly, so I asked if it was normal that I didn't feel drawn to the poor.

"Are there students who come to you seeking more than just a job?"

"Sure." A male student came to mind whose father shamed him into being a business major when he really wanted to go into the arts. Another student was battling with a severe disability, and there were plenty of students who felt like they'd never be enough. I did my best to listen to all of them and to offer possible solutions when I could.

"In a way you're already working with the poor. In addition to the materially poor, there are so many people who are spiritually and emotionally poor, and religious Sisters work with them all."

"But I don't understand why God would pick me for this. My mother is more selfless than I could ever be, and my friend Silvia is perfect and disciplined. They'd be much more suited for religious life than me."

"Your mother has had many years to grow in virtue. And God isn't looking for perfection; after all, look at the motley twelve he chose as his apostles," she said with a grin. I nodded, but they weren't the answers I wanted or believed. Besides, if Sister was right and I was already working with the "poor" then I didn't have to become a nun to continue doing so, but I didn't say this. Instead, I asked her to tell me more about St. Elizabeth, which she did passionately for the next fifteen minutes, referring to her as "Betty" like they were old friends. Then we made an appointment for a month later, and she walked me to the door.

I couldn't tell Sister about Father Infanzi. I still hadn't told him about me, not even when we spoke during Christmas week, and he sounded depressed. He said he'd planned to open the gifts from parishioners and send thank yous, but that he didn't get around to it. I pictured him surrounded by foil covered boxes filled with scarves and chocolates and bottles of sherry. I knew that they were a reminder of his life and that I should tell him about my calling to help lessen his pain and confusion, but the prospect that I could be more appealing to him than the priesthood, than *God*, enticed me. I played dumb, "Did something come up that took you away from it?" but he evaded the question. A few days later on New Year's Eve, I was the one hurting.

My mother and Tom had Janine, Father, and me over for dinner. Phil was working, Nellie was at a party, and Nick and Julie were at the hospital where Julie was waiting to go into labor. My mother was in her glory, her first grandchild hours away from being born and a priest over for the holiday. After she gave him a tour of the house, we spent the next couple of hours talking and eating and laughing, my mother telling Father that her favorite scripture passage was the multiplication of the loaves and fishes, in part because Jesus was practical enough to save the leftovers. As I stood at the sink doing dishes, Father snuck admiring looks at me. Then after coffee and cheesecake, at about ten-thirty or eleven, he abruptly announced that he had to get going, that his sister and brother-in-law were expecting him. I assumed he was staying for midnight, that he'd sip champagne with us, that I wouldn't be alone as the ball dropped. When he hugged me goodbye, I did my best to hide how crushed I felt. An hour later waiting at the hospital where Julie was seven centimeters, I felt empty. The next day, in the midst of all the excitement—she'd given birth to a healthy baby girl, Nicole—I told Janine how sad I felt that Father left before midnight. "*I understand,*" she said.

About two weeks later on a Sunday afternoon, Father and I were upstairs visiting Nicole. He'd called Julie to ask if he could stop by to meet her. We stayed less than an hour, long enough for me to instigate Father as I held Nicole who had Nick's brown eyes and fine, brown hair. My hair was smooth and long with no wave, because I'd had it blown out straight, and I was rocking her gently, breathing in her purity and baby cream, thrilled that Father was seeing me look like a mother. Even though he was dressed in regular clothes and they knew we were going for a burger, they were too dizzy with bliss to suspect anything, at least Julie was. If Nick thought it odd, he didn't act it or say anything. But on the way out, we ran into his mother who looked at me hesitatingly. I don't know if she was trying to place Father, or if she immediately remembered him from Janine's wedding. I nervously said hello and rushed out without introducing him. It was the first time I felt caught. The second time was less than an hour later at TGI Fridays. As Father self-consciously tried to explain football to me as it played on the large screen, I saw a woman look at us, especially me, accusingly. I grew indignant, "Father, Do you know who *this* woman is?" He glanced at her quickly, loosened his collar, and said he wasn't sure if he recognized her from the parish. Then he hungrily returned to his burger and me. Fifteen minutes later she left. For the rest of lunch, I pretended her stare hadn't bothered me.

One night on the phone, he said, "Maria, my friends call me James." I clutched the receiver and said excitedly, "Okay, James." Then a few nights later, he said, "I have feelings for you." I was sitting in my kitchen where the crackling sound of baseboard heat and the ticking of the clock were suddenly amplified. When I finally opened my mouth, the only word that came out was, "Yes." He hesitated, waiting for me to say more, but I couldn't. I didn't want to say something I didn't mean. I was afraid of where I was allowing this to go, but happy, as if I'd just acquired a new boyfriend. After that, we spoke long and often. I casually told Silvia and my college friend Kara that I was becoming friends with my parish priest and how nice it was to have someone to confide in, though I said nothing about my calling. Kara said, "That's really nice, girlie," before she bounced to the next topic. Silvia was just as unfazed. In fact, she offered to go out with the two of us. I didn't realize it, but she didn't agree with mandatory celibacy. She didn't understand why a man couldn't serve the Church and a family and had been deeply perplexed when Meggie and Father de Bricassart didn't wind up happily ever after. Within a couple of weeks, I made a dinner reservation for the first Saturday in February.

When I opened my front door, Father was standing tall against the night sky, the two of us in jackets too lightweight for winter, my heart beating thickly in my chest. We hugged our waist-up hug and then got in his car. On the way to Silvia's, he played Kenny Loggins' "Return to Pooh Corner." "You have to hear the whole thing. It just gets cuter," he said, as Amy Grant's singing and the sound of children's giggling began. I wanted to laugh—I'd never known a grown man who liked such a song—but it was also sweet, and I didn't want to hurt his feelings. When he asked if I liked it, I said, "*Very much.*" Then as he braked at a red light and Loggins sang, "*...a few precious things seem to follow throughout all our lives,*" it was as if the moments of the previous fourteen months lodged in my heart. The Advent Concert when his elbow hit me right before "O Come, O Come Emmanuel"; our three hour lunch the day of my 28th birthday; exchanging our first Christmas gifts at the diner; feeling like a team on the altar when I lectored; our phone calls growing from five minutes to an hour. I ignored my conscience and misgivings as I leaned my head on his arm. He sighed, "*Oh, Maria,*" and inched closer to me.

At the restaurant it was the three of us because Silvia's fiancé Greg had to do an extra shift at the hospital. At first I was worried that he didn't approve, but then I was enjoying myself too much to care, feeling the rush of my liqueur and of being with two people whose only link to each other was their admiration of me. Halfway through dinner when James went to the bathroom, Silvia leaned in and said, "It's obvious he has feelings for you. The way he wants me to keep telling stories about you when we were younger; it's really *sweet,*" her emerald-cut diamond far less a threat than it had been. After we dropped her home, I asked James if he wanted to see the house I grew up in. It was a corner house we moved to in Dyker Heights when I was a year old, the one that made a few boys in my third grade class sing "Rich Girl" at my back, which confused me because rich, to me, meant ease, and there was always something broken in our house that my mother was left with to fix. She sold it when I was seventeen, and the new owners tore it down and started all over again. It hardly looked like the house we'd lived in, but every time I was in the neighborhood, I drove by as if I was searching for something and the answer might be there. As soon as I told James to pull over, his eyes widened. "*Wow.* Your father must have done *really* well. Were all these people around you rich?"

"No. Yes. I guess."

"*Look* at this block."

I gazed out the window to the spot where we'd had a giant fountain with a goddess at the top who was supposed to spout water but never worked, so I used it as base for hide and seek. It looked like the fountains on the Sergio Bruni and Mario Lanza album jackets that my mother had stacked in the breakfront, music I never saw her and my father dance to. That's when it hit me. *Infanzi.* The people who bought the house from my mother had the same last name as James. I touched the glass and turned to him with my hand still on it, "Their name is spelled exactly the same as yours. And it's not a common last name."

"Really?" he said, but he seemed more impressed with the house, ducking his head to stare out the window again.

I was stunned at the coincidence, certain that it was more proof that he was my destiny. There were all the other parallels too. His phone number, except for one digit, was the same number my family had when we lived in this house. He and I often wound up in the same place at the same time without knowing, like the night we were inches away in a crowd at the mall listening to the St. Stephen's children's choir sing Christmas carols. There were also our results from the Myers Briggs personality inventory, which we talked about on the phone the night before. While he put me on hold to find his scores, I moved to my bed to get *cucched*, a half Italian, half English word my mother made up that means tucked in and cozy. When he came back, he told me he was an ISFP. I was an ISFJ (the first profession on the list of recommended matches was Roman Catholic nun). We were both introverts who preferred to focus on information rather than interpretation and to consider people and circumstances over logic, but I liked to have things planned and settled, and he liked to keep his options open. All I could focus on were the first three letters. During this same conversation, I finally asked him when he felt called to the priesthood. He said he was twenty-two and in medical school feeling lost, thinking *why I am doing this?* He passed a church everyday and thought maybe that's what he was supposed to do. The school gave him a leave of absence for a year. He never went back.

"I see," I said and then I went back to our scores, "The similarity, it's strange."

"I know."

After a few more minutes in front of the house, we drove to Shore Road, parking so close to the Verrazano Bridge that the cables looked like a giant, glorious necklace over the Narrows. He asked if he could play me his favorite George Michael song, which I guessed was "Kissing a Fool." He asked flabbergasted, "How'd you know?" I said, "It just has that sound." When he opened the glove compartment to get the CD, I saw his dashboard sign that read CLERGY in large, black letters. I looked away, said nothing, but then as the long, sensual notes filled the car, the sign felt as if it had grown eyes and was staring me down through the closed compartment. I started to talk about the bridge to get James' attention off me, but it was too late. He curled one of his legs on the seat, and said, "As of tonight, Brooklyn is officially my borough. I grew up here." I looked at him crookedly and, said, "Nooo, this is *my* borough. You grew up in Queens. Claim an identity and stick with it," driving my hand playfully but pointedly into his chest, dimly aware of what I was implying. Then he looked in my eyes and said, "When I was in the seminary, I used to say to myself, 'Somewhere out there, there's a girl'... *You're her.*"

George Michael was up to the part about *kisses and lies*, but I only heard *kisses.* I turned sideways and leaned into his shoulder so that I was facing the bridge, trying to ignore the clergy sign and the sinking feeling in my gut. I was luring a priest in a parked car late at night, withholding the truth about my calling, pretending I trusted him. I knew this was terribly wrong, but there was the way he made me feel, my sense that fate had brought us together. I couldn't fathom how celibacy would ever bring me the peace that it brought the Sisters. How could God who has no body, who is all Spirit, and no longer walks the earth in the person of Jesus fill my deepest desires? I wanted to bury myself in James, believe he was everything I'd ever wanted and needed. I wanted him to rescue me from my loneliness and calling, even though I knew he couldn't. We spent the next half hour alternating between talking and being quiet, though I don't remember what we spoke about. It was all surreal, the music faint in the speakers and the tree branches, like my intentions, wobbly in the wind until he said, "*Maria?*" We moved our faces toward each other, and then, opening his mouth wide like a novice, he kissed me.

***

I didn't tell James about my calling for another two weeks. I was a wreck, afraid he might be considering leaving the priesthood but also afraid of how real telling him would make it. We said, "I love you," and spent Valentine's Day together: He presided at my mother and Tom's church wedding—their annulments had recently come through—and after the ceremony all of us, except for Nellie who was studying in Seville, went to dinner at the restaurant where James and I had first had lunch. It was decorated with red checkered table cloths, tiny white lights, and piped-in Sinatra. My mother and Tom beamed in wedding clothes that fit them more snugly than nine years earlier when they married civilly. At the end of the night, when we dropped Father off at the rectory and watched him climb the steps, Julie asked, "You think he thinks about sex?"

"I'm sure he does," I said, careful not to show any emotion.

"I feel bad for him," Nick interjected, "not the older ones, the monsignors, because they always seem, I don't know, bossy? But the young priests, I've always felt bad for them." I watched him out the window until he was safe inside. Then when we pulled away, I thought about what I wrote in his Valentine's Day card and felt overwhelming pity for us—*I am more me with you than I am with anyone else. You're a gift from God. I love you, James.*

The following night I was standing at my stove nervously waiting for the kettle to whistle. James was sitting in a chair that he'd pulled out far enough that he could cross his legs, which had made the backyard sensor light go on. Even though I knew it was far from prudent, when he asked if he could come over, I said yes, hoping that in person I'd finally have the nerve to tell him.

"Last night was so nice," he said.

"It was," I said, smiling nervously, my thoughts drifting back to Julie's question. I picked up the ceramic decanter from the center of the table even though it wasn't in the way and was about to place it down on the counter when the kettle whistled. I jumped, almost dropping the decanter. James looked at me as if he should help, but he turned red instead and then looked relieved when I steadied it. I pulled out a potholder from the utensil drawer, poured the water in the mugs, and let James walk me through his mother's secret for getting honey out of a jar without dripping it, which made him self-conscious again.

"Straight from Maria Infanzi's kitchen," he said. The sound of my name next to his made my hands shake again.

"How was your day?"

"Good. I met with a young guy who is thinking of converting."

"That must be so rewarding for you. Someone who's actually choosing the faith and not just taking it for granted, because it was handed to him."

"It is," he said, seeming surprised and grateful to have someone ask about his work. "Nice guy, too. Then I got a workout in. The stairmaster. Felt *great.*"

"Like your blood is *clean.*"

"*Exactly.*"

"I usually don't want to get on the treadmill at first, but afterwards, I feel better," I said, hoping he'd sense that I didn't mean just physically.

"Well whatever you're doing, it works. "

"James, you told me a couple of weeks ago that you first felt called to the priesthood when you were twenty-two and feeling really unsure about becoming a doctor, right?"

"Yes. Why?"

"No, no reason. Just curious."

"Maria, don't you think we should talk about *us,* about what's happening here?" he asked uncrossing his legs.

"Could you give me just a little more time? Maybe a couple of weeks? I just don't want to get into this yet."

"But why? You said you're not dating anyone."

"That's right. I'm not."

"Could we at least sit on the couch?"

"I don't think that's a good idea."

"But it would be so much more comfortable."

"What, than these dollhouse chairs?" I laughed nervously, too tangled up not to give in. We moved to the couch where we sat with space between us. I tried to get his mind on vocation again, asked him if he ever had any feelings when he was a kid about wanting to become a priest, but all he said was that his mother was very religious, and that they prayed the Rosary together every night. I'd never met anyone whose family did that. "*How* devout," I said admiringly.

"Yes, until about half way through when my oldest brother Steven would moon all of us."

"Are you kidding me?" I laughed.

"No. My mother tried her best... Why can't we talk about us?"

"Because James, there's something I have to tell you. That plays a big part in this."

"What is it?"

"Remember when I didn't want to show you my high school yearbook?"

"*You're going to show me now?*"

"Maybe later," I said, a little annoyed by his childishness. "I didn't want you to see it because in my class picture I'm wearing a cross necklace. I thought it would give me away." He looked at me quizzically, so I added quickly before I changed my mind, "I'm pretty sure I'm being called to become a nun."

"*What?*"

"The day I told you I was meeting one of my sorority sisters in Jersey for coffee, I was actually in Fort Lee at a convent meeting the vocation director for the Sisters of Charity."

"*Really?* Are you sure about this?"

"Yes," I said, placing my hand down on the pink leather between us.

"Wow," he said, shaking his head. "I've never known a beautiful nun. Does your family know?"

"No. No one knows. I wanted you to be the first, but I wanted to wait to tell you, because I don't know, I just wanted a couple of weeks after our dinner in Brooklyn to have just that night and not this conversation," I said tilting my head, looking in his eyes. I felt relieved that I'd told him, but I didn't want him to know that.

"I will never forget that night on Shore Road as long as I live. I was beginning to wonder if I should leave."

"The priesthood?" I asked, wanting to hear it.

"Yes. I even told Roger I was thinking of leaving."

"What did he say?"

"'*Oh God*, James.' There's a family who lives not far from the rectory. The husband works in Manhattan, and I see him walking to the express bus every morning when I get out of Mass. He's in pharmaceutical sales. I thought *That's what I can do. That's how I can support Maria and me.* How long have you been thinking about this?"

"I've been suspecting it for a few years now, but the first time I felt it I was about eight."

"I can only imagine how adorable you were."

"You don't seem that upset about not being able to have me," I said, annoyed. Why wasn't he crushed the way he'd been at Christmas and Easter? After the Vigil the previous year, he told me that he was hurting so much he tried to tell

Steven, but he didn't want to hear it and passed the phone to a friend who said, "Alleluia, Father James. Jesus is Risen." A few days later, still hurting, James went to see a spiritual director who told him, "As Christ died, so must you."

"I, uh," he stuttered, careful not to say the wrong thing. "I guess I just see God's hand in all of this. I've been walking around these last two weeks torn about what I was supposed to do, Maria. It seems to me that your news is our answer. Words from heaven spoken from your lips," he added ardently. "Besides, I'm still in shock that you and I have even met."

"But this is *sad*, James."

"Nope," he said, defiantly shaking his head. "It's *not*. Just the fact that someone like you wants to be friends with someone like me."

"What do you mean *someone like you?*"

"I don't know," he said, laughing nervously. I'm the luckiest man on the planet."

Pause. "*That's* my favorite song."

"Really? Do you have it? Can I hear it?"

It was seconds between the song's beginning and my return to the couch, but my steps were filled with a long and complicated history of fear and sin and longing. If becoming a nun is what God wanted, I was going to listen to Him the way an employee listens to an impossible boss, but I couldn't be alone. I'd made James fall in love with me to make sure of that, but now I'd fallen in love with him, a man who just admitted he wasn't good enough for me, whom I wasn't sure I could marry even if he wasn't a priest. Yet, I looked at him as if he were everything I felt my father and God were not —loving, attentive, crazy about me—and he looked at me like a hungry boy. Certain that we were each other's destiny, I sat back down on the couch, and with the sound of a lazy saxophone in the background, I replied, "I love you, too, James" and let him kiss me again, deeper.

Chapter Four

Courting

For the next five weeks, James and I saw each other every Saturday night. We usually went out to dinner in Manhattan where there was less chance we'd run into anyone who knew him, though a couple of times we went for coffee so he wouldn't rouse suspicion at the rectory for missing every dinner. We sat at corner tables in restaurants I chose from Zagat's and talked for hours as a small candle flickered light. We went to Little Italy where he said he always dreamt of taking the woman he loved and to St. Patrick's Cathedral where he showed me the side altar where he gave his family his first blessing on his ordination day. I took him to see *Shine* at the Angelika and to Barnes and Noble in the Village where we sat—he with a tea and books on golf and Catholicism, and me with a cappuccino and memoirs—as he looked around nervously at the college students in grunge and body piercings. Thrilled to have him to myself, I also felt a slight wave of satisfaction at his discomfort.

After our first date, we sat at my kitchen table drinking tea as I showed him all my photo albums except for the ones from my 20s. I didn't want him to see pictures of the men I dated or of me in bathing suits on vacation, but I knew showing him pictures of me as a child would provoke him too. When we were done, he said, "If I knew you when you were a little girl, I would have ridden my bike from Queens to Brooklyn," to which I responded in a little girl's voice, "I don't think you can ride a bike all the way from Queens to my part of Brooklyn." He cleared his throat and said, "I would have found a way." Then he looked in my eyes and did a chair hop, moving himself and the chair as close as possible, so he could lean in and kiss me. The fact that he did this rather than pulling me up into a seductive embrace made me feel safe, like I had this under control, but it also felt silly, and I held back a laugh as I leaned in to kiss him. Then he asked me if we could go to the couch. I tightened, said no, and he said "Okay, okay" hanging his head. When he asked again, I said, "I don't know James." In addition to all my conflicted motivations, now there was our strolling in Manhattan, eating dinner over candlelight, catching each other up on the decades before we met. When he pleaded with me a third time, "But kissing you is so wonderful, it's enough," I believed him.

At first we kissed with space between us, James' one arm on top of the couch and the other on his leg, which I nervously ran my hand over as a way to keep it there, but then he raised my hand and kissed it tenderly. I was playacting, going through the motions of what couples do on dates, of what I'd done on dates. When he put his arms around me, the feel of his warm, bulky body and musky smell made my heart beat so thickly, I pulled him close. He blew clumsily in my ear, so I raised my shoulder to nudge him away, but he didn't get it. I gave him a few more seconds before I moved his face back to my lips to show him how I liked it. I wasn't worried that Julie and Nick might hear us upstairs. Nick worked nights, and Julie fell asleep early and hard. In fact, if my family asked what I was doing for the weekend (Nellie was still away), I told them that Father and I were going for coffee. I was certain that all we'd do was kiss and only until I told them I was becoming a nun; then I'd stop. I wanted them to know *I* had someone special too. Janine was again the only one who looked a little distressed, but she didn't say a word, not even the weekend when she and Phil had Father and me over for dinner, and she caught him staring at me and the *Homes and Land* magazines littered around the kitchen. A curious, troubled look came over her face, but then she returned to talking and drying the dish in her hand, probably not wanting to believe her eyes. It was the same way I felt the following day when I was headed for a retreat for women discerning religious life, and James had walked me to my car after the early Mass.

"I wish it were a nicer day for me to make this drive," I said, looking into the dreary sky, wishing for him to say something consoling like *This calling will make sense in time* or *If this isn't the right path, you'll know and it'll be okay.* Instead, he said, "Think of the weather as appropriate. Reminding you of the slow dying process you go through for this life. All that you have to give up." What was he talking about? Ever since I told him I was becoming a nun, he seemed mesmerized and relieved. I didn't see him slowly dying. This was already eating at me as I was about to pull out and wave goodbye, and a silver Lexus pulled around in front of me beside James. Feeling slighted, I immediately retracted my arm, hoping he didn't see it. When I drove around the car, I saw a blond, forty-something woman in the driver's seat and him casually leaning in like he knew her.

At first I wasn't going to say anything, but I couldn't keep it in. He said he didn't remember saying hello to a woman, that it was a man in the driver's seat. I couldn't see how I'd mistake a man for a woman, but I also knew how insecure I could be. Besides, James noticed everything about me from when I had my eyebrows waxed to the way I held a coffee cup. He walked on the outside of the sidewalk to protect me and bought me precious gifts like the plaque of a guardian angel watching a boy and girl crossing a rickety drawbridge over tumultuous waters. He made me feel as special and giddy as I did in that home video of New Year's Eve when I was five and had my father's rapt attention. I wrote in my journal that James was able to love me the way my father couldn't, because he got to be a child and my father hadn't; he knew all the small details about me the way Jesus knows. I was idealizing him just as much as he was idealizing me. Even if it had been a woman in the driver's seat, he was just saying hello. He was going to know and talk to women. I was being ridiculous.

The following weekend we were back on my couch. It didn't take long for us to go from making out to foreplay, his hand finding my breasts through my clothes. At first I resisted, moving it back to my waist, but then he said, "Oh

Maria, you're the only girl I've ever loved." When he touched me again, I left his hand on me as I felt my insides go soft and bargained with myself, *It's not so bad as long as my clothes stay on.* I told myself that if I didn't touch his penis, I wasn't sinning as much or leading him on. I kissed his neck carefully, my lips hardly parted, afraid that if I didn't reciprocate at all, I'd seem disinterested and lose him. I was afraid he'd figure out that all I wanted was for him to make me feel good. The next time we were on my couch, after a few minutes of rubbing our bodies into each other, I took his good-looking face in my hands and moaned deliriously into his shoulder.

If we hadn't already started going to confession before this happened, we started going afterward, but neither one of us was truly sorry. If we were, we would have confessed our sins to priests we'd have to be accountable to. James would have gone to Monsignor or the spiritual director— not to one of his priest-friends—and I wouldn't have waited until the following Saturday to go to St. Agatha's where, behind the screen, I confessed that I fooled around with a man in "a committed relationship." When the priest asked if the man was married, I said "No" and repeated "But he's in a committed relationship." That night or the following week we returned to my apartment. We were using each other to try and escape our lives, rejecting the chastity we'd been called to through our baptismal vows. He was breaking his vow of obedience, which includes the promise of celibacy. I was allowing him to satisfy me without satisfying him back, letting him leave my apartment frustrated and likely to masturbate when he got back to the rectory. The next day, sometimes before he had a chance to go to confession, he was on the altar *becoming* Christ, *touching* Christ with the same hands he touched me. I sat in the congregation with my head bowed down and my knees angled to the side, so people could step over me to get to Communion. It's as if I were moving underwater, as if my sexual sins with James and the ones from my past were anesthetizing me. I didn't realize how much this was hurting me or just how much I resented him until the day of Nicole's christening.

The party was at a rustic, upscale restaurant that was filled with the aroma of artichokes and tulips. My father came but left early, before the cake, like he always did, our interactions limited to a hello and a goodbye, him brusquely brushing the side of his cheek against mine with no hug. When my sisters and I were small, he was demonstrative, holding us high in his arms, cupping our faces tightly in his hands, rolling around with us on the living room carpet like we were sons. I'd have to brace myself, but at least I had him close. Once he and my mother separated, his embraces diminished. When we were old enough to have our periods he didn't touch us at all except for the occasional headlock. Now I was lucky to get "Ciao, bella" and "How are you?" which I always answered, "Fine, Papa," even if I wasn't. I'd learned early not to say much. As soon as we tried, he cut us off, like that day I tried to explain how anxious I was about starting first grade. I was sitting on his lap in my yellow robe and Buster Brown slippers dipping a corner of my toast in his espresso. As I opened my mouth to tell him, he interrupted to complain to my mother about something—the rising price of *pignoli* nuts or the old man who came in to buy one *sflogliatella*, the most complicated and expensive pastry to make. When he was finally quiet for several seconds and I thought he might listen, I opened my mouth, but he jumped out of his chair, and I almost went flying again.

Janine and Phil were the godparents, the absolutely natural and deserving choice, since Janine was the oldest, but I felt left out even though Julie gave Nicole the middle name Maria and dressed her in my baptismal dress and bonnet. I thought having James near me would help, but it only made matters worse. The part that was most unbearable was when Julie and Nick asked him to take a picture with Nicole. He faced her to the camera scooping one arm below her and the other around her belly, as my ivory gown draped over his arm like a bride's train. Nicole's face was a squarish, dimpled version of Nick's with her small jowls plumping onto the dress, she the closest I had to a little person who shared my DNA. It was at that moment with him smiling wide and my niece's head resting in his collar that the grief shook me. I'd spent the last six weeks fantasizing the two of us married. Now to see my niece in his arms where our daughter might have been had things been different, had it not been for our callings—for God's will—was awful. It was as if I were watching a movie about everything I was giving up, and I'd just gotten to the worst part. My tears started so quickly that I ran to the bathroom where I locked myself for as long as I could get away with. When I returned to the table of honor seated next to James, the keyboardist began playing "Impossible."

Even though *I'd* wandered far from God, I blamed James.

He was a priest, the man, the older one. He was supposed to protect my honor, make the sacrifice, draw the boundaries. He was supposed to be a father-figure. How could he look so comfortable and content around my family, so flattered that they had invited him when he was lying to them, coming back to my apartment, touching me? Didn't he know what it felt like watching him happy and smiling and holding my niece in his arms? It was everything I was giving up made real. If he loved me so much, how could he be hurting me, helping me to sin in such a significant way, leading me away from *my* calling? The fact that I viewed his life as cushy worsened my resentment: a maid who cooked his meals and pleated his pants, parishioners who took him to country clubs for golf and dinner, enough single male friends, priest or otherwise, to meet for vacation.

I told him we had to stop going out, that it was making it painfully harder for me, though I said I still wanted to go out for his birthday in May. I was hoping the weeks apart would get our relationship back to what it was before my couch, and we'd be able to see each other from time to time without sinning. What it did was make me forget my resentment and idealize us more. For the next four weeks, we only saw each other after Mass, but we spoke on the phone almost every day and started writing so many cards I had to begin a bag for them. We addressed them *Dearest,* closed them with *Love always,* and declared the other person our *bestest friend.* He left me welcome-to-work messages late at night on my voicemail, one time singing "Maria" from *West Side Story* but not all the way, because he got embarrassed and started laughing at himself. When I was headed for a Holy Thursday Seder Supper that Sister Teresa was hosting, he said, "I admire you for your plans, God's watching over you as you go toward Fort Lee, you're in my thoughts and prayers," which softened my dread. He always asked about the details of my day especially when I had an important meeting or project at work and then at the end of the conversation, "You're sure I didn't forget to ask you anything?" One day he left me a message that he was doing work at "that person's" house again, the single mom whose name he never offered, and I never asked for. He sounded wearied and annoyed about it, so I believed him.

Around this time, I told my mother and older sisters I was becoming a nun. I began with my mom on the Saturday after Easter, my stomach shaky with nerves as the sun poured through the glass doors that looked out onto her small, immaculate patio. At first, she said "Okay," as if I'd just announced I was changing careers, but then the look on her face went from blank to awe struck. "Oh, *gioia*, joy. *How beautiful*," she said getting up to give me a hug. When we pulled away, she said, "How strange. I felt like I was always supposed to do something big with my life, too." When I asked her, "Bigger than going back to college at forty with four kids?" she said yes, but she wasn't able to articulate what that was. Then, with great admiration and tenderness for her mom, she added, "Grandma wanted to be a nun, but my grandparents forbade her."

"Maybe it skips a generation," I said, trying to sound light hearted, but I was being a little sarcastic. Why was she bringing up my grandmother? I didn't want her to romanticize my becoming a nun. Never mind that I'd started doing the same, imagining the day I took my first vows to be a cross between a wedding and an ordination: me in an ethereal, floor length dress with a crowd of people looking on at me admiringly while James concelebrated on the altar close to me like a groom, and then during the ceremony, me prostrating myself before the altar the way priests do. I even practiced late at night on my living room floor with "Jesu, Joy of Man's Desiring," which James had introduced me to, playing on my stereo. Didn't my mother have any sense of my hungers and limitations? I was no Grandma Giulia. I wanted her to ask me "Why are you doing this?", "Are you sure?", or "Will you be okay?" Two weeks later when she did, I told her everything would be fine.

I was driving her home when I heard a whimpering sound that I thought was coming from outside the car. It was so unlike my mother to show pain that when I realized she was crying, I was startled. "*Mom!* "*What's wrong?*" Her sobs intensified. "*Mom?*" I repeated, pulling the car over in front of a row of mother-daughters. "Mom, *tell* me." She put her hand over her mouth, and then breathed slowly to try and stop the sobs. "As a mother you know that when your child gets married there'll be some hard times, but if you're happy about the person she's marrying, you know that she won't be alone. You're not going to have anyone," she said into her lap as if she was a bad Catholic. Then she looked into my face, tears staining her cheeks, "You're going to be all *alone.*"

"Oh, Mom. I know. It'll be okay," I said, reaching for her hand, touched. She never asked about my personal life, never told me that she worried about me, which I thought meant she didn't care as much about me as she did for Janine and Nellie who were always vocal about their struggles. I felt so reassured by her worry, that her fears, which mirrored my own, had no hold on me in the moment. I didn't even cry. I just tried to comfort her. I also felt a little above her worry. Ever since I'd met James and begun discerning religious life, I'd developed a kind of superiority complex, which James helped feed by telling me that his mother always said, "God gets the best."

I told Julie in her kitchen three nights later when Nick was working. She was already showered and in her pajamas, her wet hair drying into thick curls as the sound of Nicole's soft breaths came through the baby monitor. I explained that, except for my early twenties, I'd always felt drawn to church. I wanted to say Christ, but I was embarrassed. "I'm surprised but not surprised. On the one hand, you're the sister who most gives people the benefit of the doubt," she said, unaware of the numerous grievances I harbored, including my jealousy of her (which had abated some since James). "Yet, on the other, there are so many things you enjoy like going on vacations, dancing, and your poetry readings." Then she paused as if she wanted to add *men* but didn't. I smiled. She knew me better than I gave her credit for; maybe we weren't the strangers I made us out to be. She'd acknowledged my sexuality. That's when Father Infanzi came up. I think she asked if he had anything to do with my decision. I told her that meeting him felt like a sign that this was what I was supposed to do with my life.

"Do you think the two of you will get to work together?"

"I think we're too talented to be placed in the same

ministry," I responded grandiosely, tossing the word ministry as if I had any idea what it was about. Later giving me a hug at the door, she said, "You suddenly seem so much taller than me," even though I was an inch or two shorter.

Two weeks later, Janine and I were sitting in my apartment as the early evening sun came through the windows. When I called a few days earlier to ask her to come over, there was her worried, oldest-sister pause on the other end. She didn't give me her usual, "I have to let you know." After I poured her a glass of soda, and she went on about how pretty my makeshift curtains were, I told her.

"I knew you and Father Infanzi were friends, but I didn't know what was going on. I kept having these visions of Monsignor wearing that long black dress and purple sash around his waist…"

"Cassock," offering a word that wasn't part of my vocabulary a few months ago.

"Yeah. I pictured him outside the church on a blustery day, the sash blowing in the wind as he announced to our family in front of the whole parish that we were banned from the Church because of you and Father Infanzi," she said, widening her marble-sized eyes.

"*J-a-n*, we're not going to be banned," I said, gently mocking her fears, which I sometimes did, because she could be melodramatic. Now I was doing so to save face. She *had* picked up on something when James and I had been over for dinner.

"He and I are friends, but I'm going to pursue religious life," I said looking in her face as if I'd done nothing wrong.

"He was my friend first. *I* introduced you."

"I know, Jan. It's just that he and I have so much in common," I said, incapable of empathizing with just how slighted she felt.

"You and I will still be allowed our dinner-and-a-movie nights, right?" she jumped.

"*Definitely.* The Sisters of Charity are an apostolic order not a cloistered one. They work among people and are able to see their family. Many of the Sisters see their families a lot actually," I reassured her. I also explained how long the process would take. There'd be a year or two of candidacy when I'd live with the Sisters while I continued to work followed by two years of novitiate when I'd give up my job and car and enter much more deeply into religious life. Then if I successfully completed novitiate, I'd take first vows, which lasted one to three years, before I professed perpetual vows. I hadn't asked Sister Teresa much else. All I wanted to know was where I'd be living and how old I'd be when I was done. She gave me the poem "Patient Trust" by the Ignatian priest Pierre Teilhard de Chardin. She also gave me a biography of St. Elizabeth Ann Seton, whom the more I learned about the more drawn to I felt. She lost her mother and sister when she was a child, her beloved husband William after barely ten years of marriage, and her daughters Anna and Rebecca when they were teenagers. When she left the Episcopalian faith for Catholicism, most of her family and friends disowned her, and the parents of her students withdrew their children from the school that she'd opened to help her support and educate her five children. But she continued to trust in God's will, leaning on Christ in her suffering, and going on to establish the first Catholic girls' school and the first order of nuns in America. It was the loss of William, though, when she was twenty-nine—the age I was turning—and her feelings for Antonio Filicchi, a married man, that drew me to her the most, made me feel I'd found a saint-friend who understood.

In 1803 when William became seriously ill with tuberculosis, Elizabeth took him and their oldest daughter Anna to Livorno, Italy hoping the climate would help heal him, but he died a few months later. Filippo and Antonio Filicchi, who lived in Pisa and were good friends of William, took in Elizabeth and Annina (their nickname for her). During their four month stay, both men and their wives did what they could to try to console mother and daughter and shared with them their devout Catholicism. Elizabeth was deeply stirred by their belief in the Real Presence of Christ in the Eucharist. Both brothers became her spiritual guides, but Antonio was especially taken by her beauty, and a warm, affectionate friendship quickly developed between them. When it was time for her and Annina to return to New York, it was decided that Antonio would go with them since he had business in the US. During the fifty-six day voyage, Antonio's and Elizabeth's attraction grew, and they faced the temptation to make love, but as a result of fervent prayer and fasting, they came out unscathed; their relationship remained forever chaste. I brought this up to Sister Teresa one day trying to indirectly refer to James. I had since told her and Sister Erin about him, calling him my priest-friend. Neither showed concern. Sister Erin had a dear priest-friend for most of her religious life, too, and Sister Teresa said without a trace of alarm, "Elizabeth and Antonio. It's like you and James."

A couple of weeks later on his 33rd birthday, I told myself I had enough willpower to invite him back for the cake I'd baked. After all, I had told my family I was becoming a nun; I had made it more real, but then he gave me a card—*You're my best friend, the only girl I ever loved, the only woman I would have wanted to raise a family with. Happy Mother's Day.* Within a half hour we were horizontal on my couch, erection swelling his pants, me whispering his name breathlessly, as he whispered "I love you" over and over until I collapsed from the pleasure.

When he called me the next day to apologize, I said, "You're not saying you don't love me, are you?" and he said, "No, no, of course not Maria." But this time, I felt too guilty to wait until Saturday. I went to Monday morning Mass at St. Agatha's and afterwards asked the priest if he would hear my confession, though I still didn't admit that James was a priest. In the seconds between his beginning the absolution, raising his right hand over my head, "*God, the Father of mercies, through the death and resurrection of his Son has reconciled the world to himself*" and concluding, "*I absolve you from your sins…*" it was as if something inside me cracked, as if a ray of light cut through the surface of water to the woman drowning beneath. *Christ* had just spoken to me; *he* forgave me. I didn't know until that moment just how sorry I felt as my tears made the scrim that separated the confessor and me look like a blurry sieve. It was proof that my true self exists and was trying to climb her way out. Afterward, I felt depleted for days, like I was trying to lug bricks through ocean. If foreplay could make me feel this separate from God how much worse if James and I had intercourse? But how much longer could I avoid it if we continued to see each other?

I told myself this had to stop, *would* stop at the end of May as soon as I got back from visiting Nellie during her last week in Seville. I spent the beginning and end of the trip 150 miles away on the Costa del Sol, the closest air-land package I could find, because I didn't want to stay the whole week with her host family. When the cab drove up to my hotel in Benalmàdena, I was sure I'd never seen a place so bereft. Except for the occasional sputtering moped, the silence was as large as the Calamorro Mountain in the background. Inside there was no lobby or people, just a stand near the elevator where, twenty minutes later, a bellboy appeared with my key. My room was dark and dated with peeling wall paper and frosted glass windows, so I couldn't see out. The flimsy mattress and the yellowy bathroom light I left on so I'd be less afraid kept me awake the whole night. The next morning, jet lagged and bleary eyed, I tried to find a little shop with some pretty gifts to cheer me, but all I found were near empty stores that sold beach towels with pictures of little boys holding up their middle fingers. Desperate, I called James at seven o'clock in the morning NY time, trying to explain how depressed I felt. He said, stretching and yawning luxuriously, "But you're pretty."

I didn't feel any relief until I spotted my sister's face at the train station. We crammed the next few days visiting the

Alcazàr, the Cathèdrale, a bullfight, a flamenco dance show, and Marìa Luisa Park where we posed with our arms around each other and the emerald trees bursting in the background. Over three thousand miles from home, Nellie and I weren't children competing for our mother's attention; we were friends. On our second night, she laid out on our laps a souvenir book of *Semana Santa*, Holy Week, when the streets are jammed with enormous statues of the suffering Christ and Blessed Mother. They're fastened to thick, wooden platforms covered in velvet so that all that can be seen of the people carrying them from underneath are their bare feet. I was so moved that I thought about telling Nellie my news, but I'm glad I didn't. I would have stolen her moment. I would have missed what came next: Christ stooping so far forward from the weight of his cross that he looked like he'd fall out of the book. His right leg staggered behind him as he pushed his right hand against a boulder to get himself back up. The rest of the statue looked like plaster, but his hand looked like *flesh*. I gasped. How could these beautiful, spotless hands incur such evil when all they had done was heal and love? How could I be helping to dirty the hands that became *these* hands when James was on the altar? I was moved with a sorrow and fervor I hadn't felt in years, but I still didn't grasp that my sin was helping to drive the nails into his flesh. Two days later when I was walking along the rìo Guadalquivir alone and saw bench after bench of coupled teenagers fondling each other, my loneliness and sexual frustration returned, dense and age-old like the Torre del Oro in front of me.

I let James pick up from the airport and take me to

dinner where I told him all about Seville except for the groping teenagers. He told me how he kept glancing at my pictures on my mother's shelves the night before. She had planned a small welcome-home for Nellie, forgetting that I wasn't returning until the next day, and Nellie had invited Father who she'd been writing to ever since she left for college. At first I felt elated as if James was my boyfriend and he and my family were comfortable enough to be together without me, but then when I pictured him eating pie and sipping my mother's coffee with all my sisters while I was back at the dingy hotel in Benalmàdena, I felt miserable. He gave me a card that said my absence had made me dearer to him but also helped him lean a little more on God. Again, we agreed not to see or talk to each other except at Mass. He seemed just as serious as me, though he expressed more concern over disturbing my vocation than he did his own.

Barely a week later at my cousin Sandra's wedding, I had held out through every slow song, but then toward the end, the band played "When a Man Loves a Woman" and my cousin Gino led his wife Camille to the dance floor as Camille looked over her shoulder at me and said, blissfully, "_This is our wedding song._" Before I could stop myself, I had sped walked to the pay phone and was frantically dialing James' number, devastated when I didn't reach him. I tried a second time but still no answer. I was certain it was a sign that God didn't want us to talk, which frustrated me more, even though I chose not to leave a message. I knew speaking to him would only make me feel needier. A week later he caved in and called me.

"Why didn't you leave a message," he asked when I told

him about the wedding.

"Because we made a promise we weren't going to speak."

I told him about a conversation I'd had that past week with Father Bill, a humble, prayerful man who had served at St. Stephen's years earlier and who was now taking a leave of absence from the priesthood. Janine had suggested that I talk to him. She thought that maybe if I understood why he was leaving, it would help me discern my vocation. My family's reaction to my news had made me feel so special, but it had worn off, and now my struggle showed on my face especially at family gatherings. Nellie knew something was up too. When she'd asked me how I'd gotten home from the airport and I casually said, "Father Infanzi," she was silent, the closeness we shared in Seville slipping away. A few days later I told her I was becoming a nun. Barely looking up from the socks she was folding, she said curtly, "I had a feeling it was one of four things going on with you. Either you were pregnant, becoming a nun, had a hidden boyfriend somewhere, or were picking up and moving to another part of the country." She acted like she didn't care, but I think she felt threatened and maybe betrayed. Bad enough when we were growing up, she had to hear her teachers say, "Oh, your sister, Maria. What a lovely girl." Now, I was becoming a nun *and* enjoying the attention of the family priest who was supposed to be her friend and role model. As she refolded the laundry, she reminded me that I used to get furious at her when she'd tease me that I was so good and nice I'd become a nun someday. Now it didn't bother me in the least. I walked out of her room satisfied—hidden boyfriend had made her list.

Father Bill told me about the honeymoon period, how blessed people are who enter religious life or the priesthood, and how that blessedness helps them to live their vows without much struggle. He said that when I got there myself, I'd experience God's grace so euphorically that it would move me to tell everyone about it, which made me fantasize myself floating in my floor-length dress.

"*But*," he said, drawing out his voice, "Like any other life choice, a honeymoon period wears off, and you're left with the bare, unmitigated commitment."

"Is it painful?" I asked, wincing.

"It can be."

"What can one do to diminish it?"

"Have a person who understands you. A significant other, a kindred soul. This helps tremendously. I didn't have this."

"*Really?*" James asked when I told him. I was just as surprised by Father Bill's words. A good, holy priest saying that a significant other would have helped him remain a priest? I told myself it was a sign that James and I could see each other from time to time as long as we kept it chaste, so when he asked if we could go to dinner with his friend Matt, I said yes. I would have preferred to postpone until his friend Roger was in town, because I knew James wanted me to meet him too, but he didn't want to wait. It seemed only fair, since I'd introduced him to Silvia and more recently to my high-school friend Liz. I had also since told them I was becoming a nun. Silvia said it made sense to her, since I was a lector in church and in prayer group in high school and always had jobs that involved helping people. She also said how good it was that I'd met James, since I wouldn't have to pursue religious life alone. At first Liz was happy for me too, but a few days later, she called and said, "I'm scared to death for you. You're going to be all alone," words that filled me with such dread I went to bed at nine to try and get away from them. As she, James, and I left the diner where we had breakfast, she said to me loud enough so he could hear, "Steal away with *this* one. At least for the day. Take him to Great Adventure or *something*," winking.

At dinner with Matt, James couldn't be happier—me and one of his best buddies about to kick back for a couple of hours with a steak and a drink. I uneasily wondered what Matt would think of me—a prospective nun in heels and blush allowing his priest-friend to introduce her to his friends—but he didn't seem to judge me. Halfway through dinner he lifted his chin in James' direction and said resentfully, "I didn't wind up with the life of Riley like this *one*." At first I ignored James' flirtatious glances at me, afraid that Matt would see and, among other things, feel left out, but then Matt looked away, and I flirted back. At one point when I caught James staring at my breasts, I bent my head to catch his eyes, playfully rubbing in his embarrassment. At the end of the night back from paying the bill, James looked at me sitting on the plush couch in the lounge and said, "*You look so in your element.*" Later that night kissing in my apartment, he pulled away to look at his groin. "See what you do to me?"

Half way through 9:15 Mass the following morning,

Father's Day, I was seething. I was hoping James would talk about how the mustard seed in the Gospel and the lowly, withered tree in Ezekiel became glorious trees that over shadow the ones with bigger, stronger beginnings. I wanted to hear how giving up my life would be worth it in the end. Instead, he spoke about why women are not called to the priesthood. My hand froze on my thigh, my jaw tightened. Then he said more, but I felt so outraged I only heard "God choosing a Son" and "the Institution of the Last Supper" and how the "Twelve were men." It's not that I thought he was an advocate of women's ordination, but for him to choose this topic the morning after another night when, if it wasn't for me, we would've wound up having sex? Women couldn't become priests? *I* couldn't become a priest, but men could, *he* could? It was going to take me at least four and a half years before I could take my first vows and prove to everyone there was a good reason I'd been single all these years. Then I'd have to hand over my money while James continued to keep his paycheck and be fawned over by parishioners. It felt as if God was favoring James, a man who was doing me wrong. He should have at least warned me that this is what he was going to preach about, so I could have chosen another Mass. I crossed my arms, stuck my face in his line of vision to try and call him out, but when our eyes met, he just looked away from me. At the end of the homily, continuing to look at the opposite side of the congregation, he said, "A father—as in a dad or a priest—is to act in God's image."

I wanted to get up and leave, but I didn't want people to think, *Look at the angry feminist walking out just because she can't become a priest*, as if anyone would be looking at me. I decided I'd go at the Nicene Creed, when everyone would already be standing. But first James invited the fathers to stand for applause. I saw a few rows ahead of me a husband and wife reach for each other's hands. At the same time, one of the little choir girls who was sitting rows ahead of the couple turned around to them and blew her father a kiss. As soon as I saw him gesture like he'd caught it, I had to fight back the tears. It didn't help that my mother and Tom were away for the weekend, and the rest of my family had their own plans. Janine had probably invited me, but I was too proud to spend the day with her in-laws, and I didn't want to go to my father's where he'd shovel down his dinner and disappear. James would be with his mother and father, the same father who sometimes came home early from work to surprise his kids, like the day he showed up and announced, "Forget your homework; we're going sledding." I excused myself out of the pew, fixed my eyes on the back wall, and still fighting back the tears, I prayed along with the collective voice desperately trying to hold onto the only thing that mattered: *God from God, Light from Light, True God from True God.*

***

I tried to write, but I felt too much angst and loneliness, so I went rollerblading at Gateway Park, a three mile path with the bay on the west and the ocean on the east hidden by a thick expanse of trees. As a girl, I used to love roller-skating especially with Michael Jackson turned up loud on the radio and the daffodils and four-o'clocks springing up around me. Sometimes not having a sister my age was just fine. I felt free. Now I felt trapped. *If God loved me, I'd be celebrating with my husband. I wouldn't be thinking about what I don't have with my father. I wouldn't care that I can't be a priest. I wouldn't be sinning with a priest. I'd be happily creating my private enclave with my family just like everyone else gets to do.* I started blading harder, wanting to crush the cement with all I had. *I put on a pair of roller blades for the first time in my entire life, and I'm already good at it, balanced, fast moving. Most people would be falling all over themselves. Who do you think you are, God, to limit me? Twenty-eight years old in the prime of my life, and I'm alone? In a deserted park at two o'clock on a holiday? Are you kidding me?* I suddenly wanted to hurt Him, show him how fast I could go, how self-reliant I was when a breeze began to blow even though there hadn't been one all day, releasing the sweet smell of pine trees and honey suckle into the air, forcing out the tears I'd been biting back. *Is this what every Father's Day and holiday will feel like—days that I want to end before they begin, that make me feel I've been deserted?* I pumped my legs harder, pushing to see how fast I could go without falling. *If I crashed face first, Lord, would you actually come down from heaven and save me?* But no sooner was I thinking this than I got afraid. I didn't really want to hurt myself, didn't want to distance myself from God even more, so I tried to slow my legs, but it was already too late for me to stop without falling.

Chapter Five

Confessions

I told James it was one thing to be reminded that women can't become priests, another to hear it from the priest who made out with me the night before. He lowered his head and nodded like he was genuinely annoyed with himself, "I know I know. You're right." I tried to explain what it was like to be a single woman at Mass alone on a holiday, reprimand and self-pity in my voice. When he didn't say something fast enough to comfort me, I got angrier. Desperate to make me feel better, he pleaded, "But you're not alone. You have me. I love you."

This became our pattern. I'd chastise him for not being chaste even though I was leading him on. He'd try to correct himself so he could keep my hurt and anger at bay, which is what he said he did whenever his mother was upset, because he couldn't stand to see her cry. He'd tell me he loved me or something else I needed to hear, and I'd temporarily forget my anger; I'd even playfully excuse him, *He's a man after all.* Some time would go by, and I'd ask for it again like July

Fourth weekend when I called him after getting home from the Jersey Shore with Janine. It was the same day that we'd seen a line of nuns in full-length habits walking down the street like those in the children's book *Madeline*, and then a few minutes later, when we stopped at McDonald's, two priests eating Big Macs and sipping sodas with their collars loosened. Later, when Janine and I tried to walk the busy shoreline, I blurted out, "*Why do nuns have to hide their bodies and priests don't?*" The beach was so crowded and loud that I felt disconcerted, the same way I'd started feeling at the gym where the blasting stereo and the grunting of weight lifters became overwhelming. Once home, I called James, hoping he'd tell me that when he decided to become a priest, he started to feel just as out of place as I did, or, at the very least, that it didn't sound that strange to him, but I knew he'd zero-in on my body. Sure enough, as I fumbled to explain how I felt, he asked, "What does your bathing suit look like?" I sighed into the phone like an angry mother, which made him clear his throat, "Do you think you're being called to a contemplative life?"

Convinced that my struggle was spiritual and not psychological, that God was ripping me from everything I once enjoyed in order to prepare me for a nun's sacrificial life, I wouldn't resume therapy. Meanwhile my alienation from my family worsened. One day when my mother and Tom had a barbecue for the family, I mentally disappeared. Everyone was coupled-off including Nellie whose boyfriend from Spain was visiting. Tom was at the barbecue testing the last of the acorn squash that my mother had prepared in aluminum foil pouches, and my mother, who radiated a grandmother-for-the-first time glow, was making sure everyone had enough food, getting up to serve before any of us could motion for something, her Dr. Scholl's clacking against the wood patio floor. Nicole was six months, wearing a sundress and matching bonnet, and teething so hard the drool which Julie had nicknamed "baby rain" glossed her cherry lips. I tried to pretend I was okay, smiling as I passed plates, saying, "Mom, Tom, uum this is good," and running my finger down Nicole's little nose, but after a while of taking bites and turning politely toward the person who was speaking, the grief hit me blunter than it ever had.

I'll never be here with my own family.

Then suddenly the husband, and children who would have been fifty percent me, appeared in my mind, though not any particular children or husband, not James, but vague dream figures. They felt incomplete like pencil sketches but also real, like souls who have died but can't cross over, because their loved one won't let them. I wanted to pull them into all the empty spaces inside me as the faces of my real family began to diminish, the constants in my life who knew me better than anyone, though I was convinced otherwise. Their voices grew fainter until I was looking at moving mouths. For several seconds I felt as if I'd vanished, until the firecrackers from around the corner jarred me back, and when my family's voices started to return, I looked at everyone, especially the women, and thought *Who are these people?* Later that night, convinced that my distance had something to do with Father Infanzi, my mother said with great worry,

"I'm afraid you're going to get hurt." Tom had caught the way he and I looked at each other and had told my mother that he was certain something was going on between us. "There's nothing to worry about, Mom," I said. "Father Infanzi likes me *much* more than I like him." She looked at me with doubt but didn't say more; she wanted to believe it was true. Tom, however, brought it up every couple of months when he and I met for breakfast. Over corn muffins and coffee, he'd ask, "What's new in your young life," and pulling his bifocals closer to his eyes, he'd listen. Then he'd ask, "How's Infanzi?" trying to get me to come clean. I'd say, "He's fine" or "As far as I know he's fine," and he'd let it go until the next breakfast.

It was around this time that James admitted that he slept with the single mom. I think it was the day that he had come to pick up the printer he'd bought me that I told him I couldn't keep. I'd mentioned that if I was going to become a serious writer, I'd need one, but I didn't want him to buy it for me. I just wanted to tell him my dreams. The next chance he got, he was at Best Buy. After we'd settled on a day to get together with his friend Roger, he realized he had something else scheduled. When I asked what, he turned red and told me that the single mom was taking him to dinner with her sons as a thank you.

"You *go out* to dinner with them?" Then I remembered the watch from Christmas Eve. He hadn't worn it since the day we decided to divest ourselves of some belongings. "That watch. It was from her, wasn't it?" I asked, getting hysterical. He hesitated, cleared his throat, and said neither defiantly nor apologetically, "Yes, it was."

"Is there anything *else* you do for her?"

He ran his hand down the pleat of his chinos as he explained. After he'd arrived at St. Stephen's, fresh out of seminary as a twenty-nine-year old virgin, she'd started helping him with the youth group. She had had a bad situation. Her husband had left her and the boys. She and James went out to dinner a few times in New Jersey, and then one night they had sex. "*Twenty-nine years old and a virgin, Maria, can you believe it?*" he asked, pleading with me to understand. In one respect, I did. I couldn't help but think that not having had a sexual relationship before he was ordained was a mistake. He would've known what he was giving up. He'd have "gotten it out of his system." But that would have been one thing. He was still going out to dinner with her after all these months.

"You haven't slept with her since you met me have you?" He turned redder. "Oh my God, James. All the talk that I'm the first girl you ever loved. Oh my God."

"You are."

"How could you be with her after you told me that when you were in the seminary you used to think 'somewhere out there there's a girl,' and that girl was me. How *could* you?"

"What about *you*? All those times you'd come to Mass in the beginning and not receive Communion," he said, referring to the previous summer when I'd been with Rick.

"How dare you?" I hissed. "Turning this around. I haven't even kissed anyone else since I kissed you. Besides it's none of your business what I did before I met you."

"Then why is this yours?"

"Because you were with her after we—after you opened

101

your heart to me. And because I can tell something's still lingering here."

"Not anymore," he said quickly.

"I thought there was a good chance you were faithful. You struck me as someone who might actually be faithful," I said, half deceiving myself and him. "I'm not the one who took a vow of celibacy. I'm not the one who's *ordained*." I felt scorned that he'd cheated on me and on the Church. I felt threatened by his relationship with the Church but also protected by it. Because I saw myself as a victim of God's will, I went back and forth between feeling remorseful and feeling above reproach. I considered myself superior to James and the single mom who was older than him and had teenage sons. She was the inappropriate one, not me. Theirs was the inappropriate relationship. I was the good one, the right one for him. I hadn't slept with him. I was becoming a nun.

"Besides, you said the lady was a pain."

"I said that?" he asked, looking genuinely dumbfounded.

"You most certainly did." It was the day that James and I had gone to my gym and afterward to see Julie and Nicole, requests that I caved into because I was hoping they would satisfy him and he'd stop asking. The moment we walked into the gym, I felt like I'd stepped out of a shower with no towel, like Eve trying to cover herself after the Fall. He repeated nervously, "You look just great," which I thought I wanted to hear since it was the first time he was seeing my legs in bright lights, but it felt like a step closer to sex. After fifteen minutes on the treadmills, I said "We have to go." I wanted him to drop me off at my apartment and leave, but he said he had to use the bathroom and when he heard Julie's puttering through my ceiling, he asked if we could go upstairs and see Nicole. I found it strange that he wanted to see them again; they weren't his family. I was also afraid he was going to say something childish, like the time Julie, Nick, and Nicole were at Mass, and he said to them, "I'm jealous of you." When I called Julie to ask if Father and I could stop up, it was the first time I heard her hesitate at the sound of his name. She said it couldn't be for long, because she had to get Nicole down for a nap. Upstairs, she asked if he wanted to stay for a sandwich, but he said he had to go, that he was helping paint a woman's house, which he hadn't mentioned to me. Julie said, "How nice," and he said, "Not really. I much rather stay here. The lady's a pain."

"Oh," Julie said, pulling her face back. I was mortified again. A couple of minutes later Nellie rang the bell. As soon as I heard her voice, my stomach sank. In the year since she'd found out that Father and I were spending time, my relationship with her deteriorated. She called him out every chance she got. When Julie told her what he had said to her and Nick at Mass, she complained, "Why would he ever tell parishioners he was jealous of them? What a baby." Of course she was right, but I wanted to stick my face in hers and say, *You couldn't survive one day without having some guy chase you. You try being celibate, brat,* the same way I wanted to now when she looked us up and down in our workout clothes, especially him, as if she'd just swallowed vinegar. Instead I lied quickly and pertly, "Father happened to be passing by, and Nicole hadn't gone down for her nap yet."

I couldn't see how disappointing and bizarre this scene must have looked like, especially to Nellie who, perhaps of all of us, needed a father figure the most. Too wrapped up in my own drama and illusions, I took no responsibility for the way I was distancing her and the rest of my family. My resentment toward them was a significant reason why I convinced myself James was telling the truth. I needed him too much. And who was I to judge him? As an unmarried woman, I wasn't supposed to have slept with anyone either. I was supposed to be a virgin, pure. Shouldn't I forgive this one trespass even though it had happened after he had already been ordained? I could tell from the way he kissed me that he didn't have much sexual experience. Since he was truthful about that why shouldn't I also believe him that it was over with this woman? A small, sharp pulse of instinct nagged that James was lying. I chose to believe him.

I continued to fill my journal with sublime notions especially once James left for his monthly summer vacation. I started reading the book he bought for us, *He Leadeth Me* by Father Walter J. Diszek, a Jesuit priest who wrote about the twenty-three years he endured in Soviet prisons and how prayer eased his anguish, helped him learn to rely entirely on God's will. I took a class on Christian mysticism at the local monastery with Father Dennis, a Franciscan priest in his sixties who said a Sunday Mass each week at St. Stephen's and spoke about Christ using his whole body, pleading with the congregation, "*The Lord wants to* love *you. Let him.*" I made my first retreat for young adults where I went to Mass, listened to reflections given by the priests and Brothers, and spent time outdoors with my peers. On Friday night we hiked a bumpy, dirt road in single file with only flashlights to guide us, the message being that our journeys only give answers one step at a time. We even prepared our meals together in a communal kitchen. It felt good like when I was little, and my mother, sisters, and I would clean up after dinner while Janine cajoled all of us into song and dance. I wrote in my journal that if I could turn myself over to the Keeper of the Garden—if I could give marriage up for God—my faith would have the chance to become as healthy and full as the flowers that I brought to the Blessed Mother when I was a child. It was easy to trust God on retreat where everywhere I turned there were beautiful reminders of Him, and I didn't feel lonely, left-out, or ashamed.

Three days before my birthday when my father took my sisters and me out to dinner with his cousin who was in from Italy and no one thought to sing happy birthday, I was hurt—even though Julie and Nick were having a barbecue for me in a couple of days, Janine had taken me shopping for pearl earrings, and my mother had given me a gratitude journal in which she wrote, "*I hope your 29th brings with it joy, peace, and hope and that you'll be able to see God in the simple things of everyday life. I love you.*" I wanted my father to celebrate me in front of my sisters and his male cousin whom he seemed so impressed by. He almost never remembered my or my sisters' birthdays. He'd call several days later to apologize and tell me, "Remember your eleventh birthday in Italy when I used the *pasticceria* to make you a cake?" I'd say, "Yes I remember, and that was nice and it's okay Papa," but this year when he was late again, I yelled at him on the phone. Afterward, I felt so guilty I called him back to apologize. Even if he had remembered my birthday with a cake, I'd be happy for a few hours, but then I'd be back to feeling hurt. My longing was way too deep for anyone but God to heal or satisfy.

That same month I had an important but short-lived breakthrough during a meeting with Sister Dorothy, one of the Charities (how the Sisters of Charity were referred to). She was a tall, down-to-earth nun in her fifties who was on leadership council and would help determine whether I'd be ready for candidacy the following year. We were seated in the office of her Queens convent, the late day sun peering through her half opened blinds, as she asked about my childhood: how many siblings I have, where I fall in my family, how I felt when my father moved out when I was nine. I said what I always said, that it didn't really bother me, my mother made the right choice, and I know my father loves me. When she asked how I knew, and I responded, "I just know. He has a hard time showing it," a slow burn ran up my throat surprising me. I put my hand there to stop it, but then I felt it in my eyes. I told her that after my parents separated, my father sometimes took Nellie and me to dinner. When she asked how often I saw him now, I told her every couple of months. "Sometimes a little less than th—" I corrected, a tear spilling onto my cheek. "Oh," I said brushing it away with my hand, "I didn't realize I'd react this way. I'm sorry."

"There's nothing to apologize for," she said, pulling out two tissues from the box on her desk and handing them to me. "It's just good to explore things like this while you're discerning."

"Are they that related?" I asked, trying to tuck my hair behind my ear, but it wouldn't reach. I'd recently cut it short to look more like the nuns' even though I hated it short ever since I was five, and my mother had gotten me a pixie cut the summer she took us to Disneyland. An Anaheim bus driver who saw I was having a hard time climbing the steps, said, "Step up, young man." When James saw my hair, he said emphatically, "You look so beautiful." "*Really?*" I asked touching my neck in relief.

"Our parents are our first introduction to God. I don't mean just that they're the first ones to teach or not teach us about God. I mean we develop an image of God based very closely on the relationship we had with our parents."

"So if you have a parent who's emotionally unavailable you might see God as absent or indifferent?"

"Yes."

It was as if a pin-prick of truth penetrated my heart: God isn't emotionally distant. He hadn't forgotten me. He cherishes women. I felt something ease in my chest, but I didn't know exactly why. By the time Sister was showing me around the convent I felt the most lighthearted I'd had in months, until we got to commons area, and I saw the pictures of the Sisters on the wall. They were all fifty, sixty, or older. Except for one other woman Frances who was a year ahead of me, the order had no new vocations. Then in their library, a long shelf of Danielle Steele romance novels struck me as terribly sad even as I heard the Sisters' laughter from the kitchen. They were finishing up their dinner, joking and enjoying themselves like five was a good number, and they'd been matched well. One of them made a cute joke when I said where I'd gone to high school: "Oh, those Sisters of St. Joseph; they're not so bad." Earlier in the day, being fitted for my maid-of-honor dress for Silvia's wedding, I felt just as detached among the bridal gowns as I did now. When the Sisters asked if I wanted to have something to eat, I said, "No, thank you. I have to get going."

A couple of weeks later, I finally told my father I was becoming a nun. As I waited for him to finish ringing up a customer's espresso and cannoli, my heart was beating in my ears. The last time I tried to tell him something important I was six. I was worried he'd think I wasn't getting married because of him and that he wouldn't believe I had a calling or accept it. I knew how much he distrusted the Church and its priests, though, at the time, I didn't know why: when he was an altar boy in San Andreo's, he'd seen a priest passionately kissing a woman.

"What is it?" he asked coming out from around the counter, his thick eyebrows knitting tightly across the wide bridge of his nose. At sixty, his hair was still jet black and course with fewer greys than most forty year olds, and he looked tanned even though he never took the sun. The only sign of his age was his belly, which made him look eight months pregnant.

"I have good news for you Papa, *but-*"

"You have a *buoyfriend?*" Forty years since emigrating, and he still had an accent.

"No, Papa. I have good news," trying again. "It's hard for me to explain. Do you remember when we were in Rome the summer I turned eleven?"

"Sure, it was so hot and you wanted to see the Pope, and I said, '*Ma*,' but, 'it's too hot to stand in the Vatican' and you said, 'But Papa we came all this way' so I took you and then I had to go back and forth and get you Coca Colas in the heat all afternoon."

"Yes," I said smiling at his narration, which made him a hero. "Something about that has to do with what I'm going to tell you. You're always asking me if anything is new, if I have a boyfriend. But I don't have one," I said quickly. "I'm going to become a nun."

"Oh, Papa, *why* are you going to do this?" he said lowering and shaking his head, addressing me the way I did him, a sign of endearment. "Oh, Papa, why?"

"Because, I just know," my eyes filling with tears at the sound of his dismay. "You know? I've gone out with guys, and it's never been right with any of them."

"Did someone hurt you? Did something hap—" I shook my head, "—pen?" Are you in trouble?"

"No," I said keeping my eyes on him, so he'd believe me. "Nobody hurt me." James and I were hurting each other. I was letting him.

"Are you sure?"

"I'm sure."

"You telling me the truth?"

"Yes. I understand your questions. But no one hurt me. I actually met some nice guys along the way."

"Papa, answer me. Is it because your mother and me? The divorce."

"No, you did the best you could then," I said, because it's what I needed to believe. but also what I would, eventually, come to understand as true. My father had never healed from his childhood, from parents who expected him to be a man when he was still a baby. From the time he was two until he was eight, while my grandfather was at war, my grandmother took him and Uncle Frank to bed with her from four in the afternoon to escape their hunger. When my father was five, she brought him into the night to help her catch food that was parachuted from the sky. He was afraid, but he adored her; she was his everything. Every time she showed him and Uncle Frank the picture of their handsome, imposing father and she flushed a deep pink, my father felt pride but also the stab of jealousy. When his father returned, battered from having been a POW on three continents, he sent him and Uncle Frank back to their own cot. My father was so devastated that he started giving his mother a hard time. The next thing he learned was his father's large, calloused hand slapped hard across his olive skin. He cried even harder. But even this wasn't as horrible as watching his scared mother return his father's cruelty with adoration. Except for those two or three years when his father pulled him out of school at ten to work with him as a blacksmith and endearingly called him *Maestro Nino*, they were always at war.

At eighteen, my father carried his conflicted resentment of family, especially women, across the Atlantic. A year and a half later in a Brooklyn pastry shoppe, he saw my beautiful, fair-haired, sixteen-year-old mother who loved school and swept the floor with no *faccia brutta*. He was break-your-heart handsome, an Italian James Dean with washboard abs and a hot temper, but also an odd, boyish charm that made her ignore the knot in her stomach the way her mother had with her father, also a Nino, who was a good, courageous provider but who, except for Sundays, expected their lives to be an endless round of chores, and belittled their mother, "Be quiet. You don't know anything." When my mother was sixteen, and her father caught her wearing lipstick, he slapped her face. At seventeen, she tried running away, but she couldn't bear to hurt her mother. Later that year, still trying to run, she got engaged to my father, who had already become something like his own father.

"Because you know I respect your mother."

"Of course I know that, Papa." What I knew was that now that he was beginning to age and have regrets, he respected her. He was realizing all she was, and all he'd done. Whenever he was in her neighborhood making a restaurant delivery, he brought her more bread and pastries than she could use or need. I think it was his way of saying *I'm so sorry for all those years ago. You're a good woman. I loved you.* But it didn't erase the past; I still couldn't face it.

What followed were a lot of questions, more than he'd ever asked me. I explained that at first my mother felt very blessed, but now she was worried, though I didn't explain it was because I was unhappy. If everything went as planned, I'd move in with the Sisters the following September for a year of candidacy. Then if I was accepted to novitiate, I'd quit my job and give away my car to begin the life of a nun. I'd probably live in a convent in Brooklyn, Queens, or north Jersey. During my two years of novitiate, I'd learn Church history. I didn't know how to explain pastoral counseling to him. I was also resisting it, convinced that I wanted the hard-core theology that priests study, not the "soft" education that women in religious orders receive, as if I knew anything about either. I told him in a falsely confident voice that I'd work with the poor or the sick and that, after I took my first vows and resumed working, "The order would take care of me." I left out that my salary would be shared evenly with the order and that I'd get a hundred dollars a month. Money was how my father had always measured his worth, so I couldn't help but think it's how he measured mine. I explained that I didn't want a lot of possessions or excess, which was true, but I also didn't want to give up my yearly Caribbean vacation, getting my hair done, or treating myself to some new clothes every once in a while. I talked fast, afraid I'd lose his attention, but except for one brief interruption to show a well-dressed couple to the best table, he listened. It was the first time in my life. I was so happy.

"If you were younger, I'd tell you no. I wouldn't let you," he said, wagging his finger. "But you're a *womon*. If I tell you something and then you do it, because I'm your father," he said not finishing his thought, "and now I'm old. And then I'm going to die."

"*Papa.*"

"What about the man you introduced me to last year?"

"No." I'd only introduced him to Rick, because he hadn't seen me with a man in four years.

"You never met the right one?" he tried one last time. I looked out onto *Cristoforo Colombo* Boulevard where a thirty-something couple walked by hand-in-hand, the woman with dark brown hair like mine. My father was the last person I'd ever tell. He'd distrust Catholicism and priests even more than he already did. He'd call James all kinds of names. He might even call me *puttana*. He definitely wouldn't believe I had a calling.

"N..no, I haven't, Papa," I said shaking my head, dropping my eyes from his.

***

After Silvia's wedding the following month, my depression deepened, even though God had been very good. My hair had grown just enough that the hairdresser, armed with a basket full of bobby pins, managed to give me an up-do. The two best men were so tall and strapping that during the processional with my arm linked in each of theirs, I had to hold myself as upright as possible otherwise they would've swept me off the floor. During the kiss of peace, instead of shaking my hand, the groom's brother kissed it. And the best friend asked me to dance throughout the reception, which I obliged happily. I'm pretty sure both men knew I was becoming a nun, and they treated me accordingly, like a woman they admired but who was spoken for. I was having a good time in spite of myself until I started comparing my life to Silvia's. Sometime after I'd given the toast—how marriage is the only sacrament performed by those receiving it, which I'd heard the priest say during the rehearsal—I walked into the botanic gardens where the sweet scents made me feel miserable as I played over and over how James and I would never be. My misery sharpened when I got home and found the red rose and love note he'd left me: *You're the only woman I would have ever wanted to marry.*

I called to thank him and to say again, *James, please we can't talk. It's too painful.* At first the separation was awful. I woke up every morning wishing I could be anyone but me. But as time went on, the pain began to dull. I started going to daily Mass at St. Agatha's, because it was early enough to get me to work almost on time. It was a small, baby-blue chapel with a statue of the Risen Christ suspended by a cord behind the altar and a statue of a plump Mary and baby Jesus blissfully gazing at each other. There was also a small Infant of Prague in a glass box and his words, "*The More You Honor Me the More I Will Bless You.*" I stared at it every day, hoping it was true. I prayed hard, *Lord please help me to want what you're asking of me.* I was also writing five things I had to be grateful for every day like baby Nicole, daily Mass, feeling connected to any of my sisters, success at work, reading a good book, witnessing humility in someone. For the first time in seven months, James and I didn't go out or talk on the phone, though we still sent cards. It was all I wanted, a male admirer and spiritual companion who I didn't owe anything to, though I was still looking forward to hearing from him and getting together for coffee from time to time. Then one night in November he called.

He sounded frustrated, but I pretended he didn't. I happily told him about that morning's homily at St Agatha's and then about a couple of students who were struggling because their parents wanted them to go into one career, and they wanted to go into another. When I rebelliously added, "It's *their* lives," James' voice brightened, "It's amazing Maria how just talking to you can fill me."

Before we hung up, he asked if he could see me, that he missed me, and, I said yes. I was certain that all the time apart meant I was strong enough to resist him. But I wound up in his arms on my couch one night and then again a second night not too long after. The first night when he pleaded, "Maria, please let's go to your bed," I said no, that we should stop. He asked me if my father ever hurt me when I was little.

"What do you mean 'ever hurt me'?"

"You know. Like that. Sexually."

"*What?* No, of course not," I said pulling my face back in disgust. Why would you ask me such a thing?"

"Because you're so resistant to being intimate."

"I'm resistant, because if you haven't noticed, you're a priest." This was the only reason he could think of why I wouldn't sleep with him? I stifled my outrage. I was afraid he'd start to figure out that it wasn't just my conscience that was keeping me from having sex with him but also my will. I was afraid that if he sensed for one moment that I didn't want him, I'd send him to the arms of the woman who did.

On the second night together, he said it again, more impatiently than ever, "*Maria, please, let's go to your bed.*" Even though I was angry at his ugly, arrogant insinuation about my father, in my blind mix of needs, I pushed it away.

I knew sex with him wouldn't satisfy my hunger and that if I wanted and leaned on God's grace, I could resist him. But I also knew that if I didn't sleep with him, I'd probably lose him, maybe not at first, but eventually, which I couldn't bear to do especially to another woman. I told myself that since I couldn't marry him and give him children, that maybe this one time would satisfy him, secure and bond us to each other, and prevent him from going back to the other woman, to any woman. From when we'd first met, I had the staggering feeling that I'd known him my whole life. In retrospect, I understand that was true, for he was my mirror image, the both of us incapable of seeing anything but our own need.

I got up from the couch and led him to my bedroom where the only light was the one that crept in from the kitchen until I told him he had to shut it off. I was afraid the neighbors would see our silhouettes through my shades and that James might see a glint of my body, especially my thighs. Maybe I even hoped the darkness would erase what I was about to do. As he lay me on my bed, I felt more numb than anything else until, as I'd always dreamed, I heard the whisper, "*I love you, Maria.*"

Chapter Six

Mystic

It was as if I'd hurled myself over a great chasm, and my spirit ached from the exertion. I couldn't write a word of what I'd done in my journal. When James called me the next morning to tell me how sorry he was, but that he really loved me and felt like the most privileged man in the world, I was so relieved. There was a part of me that was afraid he might be done with me, because he'd gotten what he wanted or thought I wasn't good in bed. In confession—where I confessed what'd I'd done but still not with whom I'd done it—the priest, for my penance, impatiently told me to pray for an infertile couple in the parish who desperately wanted a baby. The irony devastated me. The last thing I would've wanted was to be pregnant with a priest's baby, and thanks be to God I wasn't, but having had sex with him made it infinitely more painful to let go. After a cozy, pre-Christmas dinner in Little Italy where we talked for hours and made best-friend-forever promises in front of the crèche at Most Precious Blood Church, waving goodbye to him in the snowy night cut my heart in two.

Again, we pledged not to see or speak to each other. I even asked him to give me a copy of the priests' schedule of Masses, so I wouldn't run into him. By the time January was up, we'd made one addendum: we could see each other for special religious excursions. The March for Life in DC on the 25th commemoration of Roe v. Wade was coming up, and James asked me to go on the bus trip he was leading for another parish. I was excited. I'd never been to a march before, and I believe strongly that life begins at conception and must be protected, another kind of irony given my indiscretion. Except for when he stood up to lead the Rosary on the bus, which he did fast so he could get back to me, we hardly left each other's side or worried much what people thought. If anyone was listening closely as the film about life in the womb played, they would have heard James say, "That's what you looked like. That's how precious you were."

Less than two months later, I thought, *I can't stand you James*. It was a First Friday during Lent; he was leading a holy hour and saying Mass at a nearby church. He started his homily with a joke about how St. Stephen's was a better parish than theirs, but he didn't get many laughs. I felt bad for him but also annoyed. Why would he think insulting people was funny? Then he told the congregation that St. John Vianney is the patron saint of "*us* priests" as he pressed his thumb into his chest. Why couldn't he be more like the cantor whom I hadn't been able to take my eyes off since the procession? He had his head bowed so reverently he looked completely lost in Christ like a mystic. Now he had his eyes closed like he was absorbing the homily with his heart. When James explained that Satan appealed directly to Christ's pride, and then backed away from the microphone as if Satan was headed for *him*, I softened. Pride was one of my biggest sins as a single woman. I associated having a husband with having a kind of power and edge: I'd be able to hold my own with happily married people, tout stories about my husband's accomplishments and our family life. I wouldn't have to be the embarrassed single on the perimeter or sitting in the backseat of some couple's car like a giant child. I wouldn't have to rely on anyone's mercy. I clung to the archaic fantasy of a knight-and-shining-armor-husband taking care of everything for me. Even James had started to correct my neediness, "How could I ever take care of you as well as the Creator of the *Universe*?" I wasn't humble and unselfconscious like the cantor either. That's why what happened after Communion was miraculous.

I had folded back the kneeler and was sitting down with my eyes closed, the lapping sound of water from the baptismal font giving me chills as the church resounded with the cantor's refrain, "*Here I am Lord. Is it I Lord? I have heard You calling in the night. I will go Lord if You lead me. I will hold Your people in my...*" It was when the cantor lifted "*h...e... a...r...t*" into the air that it happened, when I felt as if the Holy Spirit had stepped into my body, like I was parched land and He was a clear fresh stream flowing through every inch of me: satisfying my thirsts, healing my wounds, delivering me from my fears and insecurities, filling my emptiness. He reached that part of me that still had nightmares about my family abandoning me and that felt plain and invisible, that mourned my father's absence and the husband I'd never have—that part of me trying to make James that man and that believed God was calling me to a life I didn't want, asking the impossible, because He didn't really love me. He washed through every grief I'd ever felt and every sin I'd ever committed, and then suddenly it was as if every person in the church, including James and the cantor, had vanished, but I wasn't alone. I felt love, not isolation. I felt the past and the future collapse into one, like the I AM of Yahweh's name. Then, as mystically as He'd entered, He withdrew, leaving me spent like after a night of making holy love.

The next day I felt more out of sorts than ever, as if God had carved out a big space in me for Him and then left. I had gotten together a few girlfriends for dinner and a Broadway show, the *Diary of Anne Frank*. I'd always preferred drama to musicals, but now I purposely avoided anything happy or romantic, because it only made me feel worse. At least with drama, I could cry for someone other than myself, which is what I did during the dimly lit annex scene when the Frank's and Van Daan's fought over a small piece of two-month-old bread. The horror they endured didn't obliterate my misery or make me feel sudden gratitude for just how blessed I was. I just felt sadder and more drained.

Afterward, while we waited for our entrees and sipped our drinks with little pieces of fruit clinging to the rims, Silvia told us that the night before, a chief surgeon who was interviewing Greg for a position as an ER surgeon had taken them out to dinner at a country club that overlooked a golf course.

She spoke like a newlywed, swirling "my husband" into her dialogue as often as she could, while Liz, whose husband sat in front of a computer all night every night, pulled her face back as if shielding herself from Silvia's euphoria. I disappeared from the conversation, thinking about the previous night. For the first couple of miles after we'd left the church, James had followed behind me in his car. I hadn't told him what happened. It felt too intimate and precious to speak of, and I was certain he wouldn't understand. I also sensed it was a turning point that separated me from him, which I didn't want to accept. At the fork where we went in two different directions, I watched his car until I had no choice, and he was gone. When I heard Silvia say, "Golf's my husband's *favorite*," I snapped back to the present. James loved golf. James was excellent at golf. *James would beat Greg to a pulp at golf.*

Weeks later I told Sister Erin how out of sorts I'd felt after that First Friday Mass. She explained that because my experience of God was so *other* worldly, and seeing a show and going to dinner are so *this* world, it made complete sense that I felt misplaced. If that had been the only time, she would've been right, but I felt this way more and more often. One day when Julie and Nick had us all over, and the conversation had turned to interest rates on credit cards, I drifted away. Later, Julie told me with frustration, "It's like the things we talk about don't matter to you anymore. It's like you're not *here*." She was right. Most conversations felt mundane in comparison to my grief. I also felt increasingly torn between the secular and the spiritual like the weekend my sisters and I went to see *The Lion King*. The night before,

Sister Teresa had led a retreat for four of us who were considering religious life, and one of the retreatants who worked with incarcerated women spoke about their struggles. The following night sitting in the limo that Julie had reserved for us, I felt shamefully out of place. I hadn't felt at home in the convent either, but then Sister Teresa played "On Eagle's Wings," and I got goosebumps up my back. I felt them again when the costumed-cast paraded down the side aisles of the New Amsterdam Theatre inches away from us. While God wanted me to live simply and share generously, He wasn't trying to rip me from the world. He wanted me to enjoy and savor its beauty, including the talent He'd given to everyone onstage and behind. He wanted me to be healed, but he wasn't going to magically get me the help I needed. I had to do that for myself, which I finally did after I found out I'd failed the psychological test for the convent.

The psychologist Dr. Togres had asked me to interpret a drawing of a man, a woman, and a gun, and I said that one of them would shoot the other. She looked startled again when she asked if I'd ever been sexually active, and if so, how long ago had it been, and I answered, "I don't think that's something I should have to discuss." It had been four months since I'd been intimate with James. I was certain it wouldn't happen again and that it wasn't the order's business. Of course it was. They needed to evaluate whether I was healthy enough to embrace a celibate life. During my follow up, Dr. Togres told me that the results showed unresolved anger and a tendency to look on the dark side of things. She didn't have to say I failed; I knew. I nodded numbly, and then asked her to send the results to RF, whom I hadn't seen in almost a year and a half, so I could talk them over with her. I felt as if I was being punished for something I didn't have complete control over. I felt like a failure, but I held my tears until I got to my car. By the time I was on the Brooklyn Gowanus headed home, I'd convinced myself that maybe if I resumed weekly therapy, I could still be accepted for candidacy in September, anything not to be in horrible limbo for another year. I got home and called my mother to tell her the results, sounding like I had everything under control. She said with concern, "Try to go to bed early tonight. You must be *so* tired." Then I dialed Sister Dorothy, but she wasn't home. When she returned my call and missed me, she said I should call her on Mother's Day, which I knew meant bad news since she would've otherwise left the results on my machine.

We had just finished Nick's roast beef dinner and were all staring at sixteen-month-old Nicole who was dancing to Selena, her chubby little thighs accentuated by the elastic hems of her short, pink onesie. I was pretending I was okay, because I didn't want to ruin the day for my mother, who, ever since Nicole had been born, was the happiest she'd ever been. In his homily that morning, Father Dennis said that we must look directly at Christ's wounds on the cross, not for morbidity's sake, but to remember just *how* much he loves each of us. This comforted me, but then at the end of Mass he asked all the mothers to stand for a blessing, and I was the only female seated who wasn't a teenager. When I went into Julie's bedroom to call Sister, she and I exchanged hellos and how are yous, and then she gently repeated Dr. Togres' evaluation. I looked at the picture on the nightstand of Julie, Nick, and Nicole on vacation in Cape Cod and pleaded, "Sister, I'm already *twenty-nine* years old."

"It's very difficult to move into a convent and be in therapy at the same time, Maria," she said, reading my mind. "I've been doing formation work for six years now, and there have been women, who had they had therapy first, would have found formation more productive. We're recommending a one year delay, just one year. Instead of this September, you'll enter the following September. Besides, this is not about doing this in a certain amount of time. It's not a race. It's an important, life changing decision that's about your happiness and peace. You should be proud of yourself for coming so far. This is probably just not God's time." "Yeah, God's time," I said sarcastically. I could express exactly what I felt to the Sisters without having to apologize or worry. They didn't take everything personally like so many people I knew did, like I did.

"I know you don't see it now, but His time is so much better than what we come up with, and yes, you're right to feel frustrated."

"Sister, at this rate when am I actually going to become a nun? If I don't start until next September, then there's a year or two of candidacy, then four years of novitiate. I'm going to be thirty-six, almost thirty-seven."

"You say that as if it's elderly," she said trying to get me to laugh.

"I feel old now."

"That's probably the depression."

"But I've been going to Mass almost every day for the last year, and I exercise five days a week. I'm doing everything I can."

"So much about a process like this, not just religious discernment but the spiritual life in general, is not about doing. It's about trust and letting go. I know it's difficult, but the answers will come to you. You don't have to chase so hard after them."

I couldn't believe what I was hearing. The seminary had admitted twenty-three-year old James who had never held a job and who told the rector he was going home on Friday nights when he was really headed to Atlantic City, but the Sisters weren't admitting twenty-nine-year old, independent, responsible me? I'd just spent a year and a half discerning a vocation I didn't want, and they were rejecting me? I couldn't see what a blessing this was. I shouldn't have been entering a convent. I was doing it for the wrong reasons, thinking it was my only choice, hoping it would legitimize my relationship with James and make my mother proud. When Julie had announced she was pregnant, my mother admitted that until that point she thought that God had been punishing her for something —after all, a daughter married for ten years and no grandchildren? What source of punishment must she have thought I, the daughter who was never going to marry, was? As a nun, my unmarriedness wouldn't be the sign of a scourge.

Back in the kitchen, I felt so bereft that I asked Julie and my mother if I could talk to them in private. At first I tried to explain what Sister said without mentioning my anger for fear my mother would ask me whom and what I was so angry at. Julie tried to encourage me, but my mother looked at me with silent confusion, which made me angrier. Why couldn't she take me in her arms and embrace me with the same adoring love she had for Nicole, love me like I was her little girl? I was still stuck at eight years old. Maybe I did want to ruin her Mother's Day, snap her out of her grandmother-for-the-first-time trance, so she'd see what was really going on with me and James. Even though I'd rebelliously started referring to Father Infanzi as James to my mother—which she rolled her eyes at disgustedly—she still never brought us up again. She didn't want to believe that I could succumb to sleeping with a priest, to shaming the family and hurting myself so profoundly. She was also really afraid to say anything to me. Anytime she tried to tell me that maybe religious life wasn't my calling, I snapped back condescendingly, "God's will isn't always *our* will, *Ma.*" I wanted her to love the lies out of me, but if she tried, I would've angrily denied them. I wanted to say, *Mom, I'm so unhappy, it's killing me,* but I was too afraid. I finally blurted, "The results also show I'm angry."

"I think it's *me* you're angry at," she said wincing.

Overwhelmed with guilt, I said, "*Oh no, Mom, it's not you at all.*"

***

I resumed therapy with RF, but I don't remember talking in depth about the sources of my anger. I told her I was afraid I'd never be at peace and couldn't imagine what that would feel like, that I didn't see Christ as victor, only as victim, and that I constantly had the desire to put James in his place. I didn't tell her that he and I had slept together and that there was another woman who I suspected was still in the picture. I was afraid she'd tell me to stop seeing him or, worse, that she thought we were perfect for each other. After several weeks of still feeling depressed, I finally agreed to a mild anti-depressant. I was certain I wouldn't have to take it if God had called me to a natural life, but I also could no longer deny that I needed help. I hesitated whether or not to tell James, afraid he would say something insensitive. When I did, he said that had we been married, we would've faced my depression together; he wouldn't have held it against me.

By the end of July Fourth weekend, I felt temporarily better. I made a retreat with the Sisters of Life, a young, vibrant pro-life order that Cardinal John O'Connor had founded. I wasn't interested in entering, but when I read his column in the *Catholic New York* inviting professional women who had figured out what they wanted and were now trying to discern what God wanted, I felt he was speaking to me. I went with a new friend Barbara and a friend of hers. On our way there, I couldn't help but think bitterly, *Three cute, single women headed for a religious retreat on July Fourth weekend instead of the Jersey Shore,* but as the weekend went on, I experienced a religious fervor I had never before as an adult. Forty-one women my age in full, navy-blue habits prayed four hours a day every day in front of the Blessed Sacrament and spent the rest of the day serving women in crisis. They were living out what the Cardinal spoke about in his conference on obedience. They were surrendering their wills to God. How else could they lead such radically sacrificial, generous lives with such joy and peace? Celibacy wasn't supposed to be as chronically painful and conflicted as I was making it. It could be a way to work out my sanctity. I also reflected on the wisdom I'd received in the previous six weeks from Dr. Togres, Sister Dorothy, RF, even the author-teacher Julia Cameron. I felt blessed. When I got home, I excitedly began writing the three daily Morning Pages that Cameron calls "the bedrock of a writing life." I started visiting a Perpetual Adoration chapel where the Real Presence of Jesus is exposed in a monstrance every hour of every day. I asked out a man who was unhappily considering the priesthood.

His name was Dominick, a Eucharistic minister at St. Stephen's who had asked me out the previous year. I'd told him I was in a relationship and then avoided him, afraid he'd ask about my boyfriend. About a year later after Mass one day I saw him shrug his shoulders when James asked him if he ever thought about becoming a priest. Two weeks later, still on high from my retreat, "Maybe we can go for coffee sometime" spilled out of my mouth. I was certain the Holy Spirit had made me say it, that since he might have a vocation, maybe we were supposed to get to know each other, and he, James, and I could be friends. Maybe I could even be of some help. A few days later he asked me to dinner instead. I was concerned it was too date-like, but I felt bad to say no. By the time we got our pasta, he told me that he'd been struggling for ten years with the idea of becoming a priest and that more recently had almost been baptized into another church. I took a sip of my drink and said, a touch flirtatiously, "I'm happy *we* kept you" but still nothing about my vocation. The following week he asked me to go to

Lincoln Center to hear a Cuban band. I said yes, but then I asked God to help me out of it. There was so much traffic on the FDR Drive that it didn't look like we'd make it in time. I think he also sensed my trepidation, so he turned around and we headed to a downtown restaurant where the rest of the night was a strain. After I asked about his father who I saw at morning Mass, he grumbled bitterly that Mass was his father's way of making up for all his wrongs. "I'm sorry, Dominick," I said, unaware that his angers resembled mine, acting like I didn't struggle. That's when he brought up James.

"I look at Father Infanzi and think, he's young. He must be attracted to women."

I took a forkful of food, enjoying my secret but also feeling its sting.

"It must be so difficult to control all your urges, and then you wonder if suppressing them can cause psychological problems," he said furrowing his brow.

"Men who have psychological problems might be drawn to celibacy, but celibacy doesn't cause psychological problems. It's a supernatural calling."

"But we're *not* supernatural. We're *human*. About a year ago, you said you were in a relationship. What happened with that?" he asked as if he knew the answer.

"It was an indirect way of telling you something." I scanned the restaurant, and then lowered my head and whispered, "I'm going into a convent next year."

"I saw you praying in church a lot and thought, *Maybe she's becoming a nun.*" He added sarcastically, "The harvest is full. The laborers are few." I wanted to tell him that he didn't have to become a priest if he didn't want to, but I didn't believe it enough, so I said, "I suppose." A couple of weeks later, when James called me in Italy where I was visiting my father's hometown in Basilicata, Dominick showed up at the rectory to talk to him. "Isn't it ironic that he'd come see me when I was on the phone with *you?*" he asked excitedly. Why did he have to sound so happy about it? Why did God have to remind me again that James belonged to the Church and not to me? Wasn't it enough that I was four thousand miles away? I'd recently read Sister Marie Schneiders' "The Special Friendship in the Celibate Life," which she describes as a relationship with an erotic tone but no genital expression, where neither person feels threatened by the other's celibate commitment. Threatened is all I felt. While in Italy, I had a dream that James left the priesthood. Instead of saying Mass, he was dancing like a hippie up and down the aisles of St. Stephen's with the rest of the congregation. Even though I was upset, I joined in because I was afraid I'd lose him if I didn't. During the consecration, one of the other men pulled the host from a camping bag while James took off his clear-rimmed glasses and placed them on me and then removed his father's thick, black-rimmed glasses and put them on himself. He was handing me his celibate role and taking on his father's role as a husband. When I woke up, I was still upset.

All I wanted was to see him for a little while, tell him about my trip. My father's family had taken me to the major sites: the 15th-century castle and abbey built on the ruins of an ancient city, Piazza Orazio Flacco dedicated to the

poet Horace who was born in the town, and the churches—
Trinita, San Andreo, and San Rocco where I knelt at the
life-size, supine Christ looking into his ripped-open chest
and prayed, *May I want my vocation as much as You want
to give it to me.* I saw the apartments where my father and
uncles grew up and *Fontana di San Marco* where they made
mischief. Nearly everywhere I went, someone exclaimed, "*E
figlia di Nino, nipotina di Vincenzo!*", she's Nino's daughter,
Vincenzo's granddaughter, which delighted me. But it was
so ruthlessly hot, I couldn't sleep. At the end of the week,
I had to share a bed with a cousin we visited in Corsica
who was a chain smoker and snorer. I broke down in tears.
The following day my cousins were taking me to the beach
where I prayed I might sleep for an hour or two, but at ten
o'clock when I stood in their living room with my beach
bag looped over my wrist and sunglasses on my head, they
were still in their pajamas drinking espresso and smoking
cigarettes, saying *Piano, piano* and *Piu tardi.* As I told James
the details, I pretended he wasn't struggling to keep his eyes
off my breasts. Then we ran out of words and locked eyes.
We wound up where we were the first nine months: me dizzy
with orgasm and he hard and untouched.

Two days later, on the morning of my thirtieth birthday,
I was in the Perpetual Adoration Chapel at 8:45 despairing,
reading Sister Josefa Menendez' *I Wait for You: Jesus' Lament
Over Man's Indifference.* I wrote in my journal, *The weight
of my sin holds me down.* After everything God had done
for me, how could I do this to Him? He had allowed me
to *feel* Him. He had arranged my random upgrade to first

class on the way home, consolation for my sleep deprivation—I was sure of it. I still wouldn't tell the whole truth in confession; I still couldn't let go, especially now that James was leaving the parish to begin a hospital chaplaincy. He was moving only a few miles away and would still be saying Mass at St. Stephen's, including an early daily Mass that he'd convinced Monsignor to add, but he'd be meeting a whole new set of people, of women. A few days after he moved, I had another dream about him leaving the Church. We were at Mass together again, this time at my childhood church, St. Bernadette's. Instead of getting in the pew that a man had exited to let us in, James hid behind the man, so the priest on the altar couldn't see him. Eventually he sat down, but during the consecration he got up and left. I was about to follow him, but then, right before the door, I saw Janine and sat back down. RF asked me what I thought this and the other dream meant. I told her I was nervous his new ministry was going to distance us. If I admitted what I really suspected, I'd help make it come true. Besides, I had to stop looking on the dark side of things.

In late September, when a morning show aired a conversation between President Lyndon Johnson and Jackie Kennedy, and one of the hosts suggested they sounded like they were flirting, I looked up from the shirt I was ironing and yelled at the TV, "*Get a life!*" How dare they listen to an innocent, private conversation between two adults and make judgments? It was also around the time of the Clinton-Lewinsky scandal, which in my mind bared no resemblance to James and me. Clinton was using her. He didn't love her.

He was almost thirty years older than her. A few weeks later at the farewell party that St. Stephen's had for James, used is exactly how I felt. After Monsignor toasted him, James told the room of one-hundred plus guests how grateful he was for the chance to have served them. To make matters worse, his sister Marion looked me up and down when James introduced us. I wanted to say, *You try being in love with a man you can't have, sweetheart,* but I shook her hand and said, "Nice to meet you, Marion," and then spent the rest of the night at my mother and Tom's table knotted with self-pity. When James showed up at my door afterwards, I relished sending him away in my silky, short, chartreuse robe. He was going to continue being fawned over by parishioners, telling them, "I'd do it all over again for you," and I was going to continue getting incriminating once-overs? I almost wanted him to look me in the eye and tell me he didn't love me, because then I'd be forced to let him go, but just the thought of it shattered me. The following month I had intercourse with him a second time.

I don't remember if he invited himself or if I invited him, but once there, he was shoeless on my parquet floor, cajoling. The next day my mother and I were going to Rhode Island for a mother-daughter weekend. I thought about how I wouldn't be able to get to confession before we left and the shame I'd feel sharing a bed with her after having shared one with him. It wasn't enough for me to say no. I felt so guilty afterwards that all I could do was pretend that it hadn't happened, but then my mother woke up on Sunday morning violently ill. I was certain it was my sin, not the glass of wine she had on an empty stomach the previous night followed by the Mediterranean stew. As I knelt at the bowl with her, my palm glued to her forehead, I thought, *I've done this to my mother.* I was sure God was making me see how my ugly sin affected others. Once I got her back to bed, I asked her if she'd be okay long enough for me to go to Mass. I was dying for confession, but once I got to the church, the priest was already vested and in the sacristy with the lector and cantor. I could've asked him after Mass, but I was so embarrassed I decided I'd wait until I could hide behind a screen at home. During the homily when a visiting nun explained that her order might be bankrupt within nine years with nothing left for their retired Sisters, I thought, *After all they've done and given up, this was the thanks they'd be getting?* I immediately thought of my mother back at the B&B who had to have a migraine by then.

Later that night when she was feeling better, I was back to pretending. She was sitting up in the four-poster canopy bed with the quilted floral bedspread pulled up to her armpits and her prescription sunglasses on because her indoor ones had broken. She was reading *The Awakening Heart,* the sequel to *Embraced by the Light,* by Betty J. Eadie, a woman who had died and came back to life after glimpsing heaven. We had just called Tom who told me that Father Infanzi had called him the previous night to make sure we'd gotten there okay. I already knew because I had called James on the way home from church to tell him how horrible I felt. He said, "Me too, me too," but for the first time, he sounded like he didn't mean it.

"Father Infanzi checked in with Tom to see if we got here okay," I said. I wanted my mother to know how much he

loved me, that I wasn't alone, that we'd always be each other's special someone, that I was just as desirable as her other
daughters. I was trying to wake her, make her see the real me
and not the angel she was making me into again. One day,
Nicole, staring into the large Norway maple in the backyard,
said, "*God*" with a dreamy smile on her face. Afterward my
mother said to me, "I'm not surprised she saw God; she lives
in the same house as *you*." She still hadn't brought my and
James' relationship up again, though one night when she and
Tom took him out to dinner, she asked him if he had been
as unhappy as a seminarian as I was about becoming a nun.
Over their martinis, he told her that while he hadn't liked
being bounced from one parish to another or being under
the thumb of a head priest, once he was ordained, it got
much better. "Not to worry," he added, "Once Maria takes
final vows, she'll be as settled and happy as I am."

"Father's Infanzi's too cute!" she said laughing.

"He knew we were coming. *I* told him."

She nodded and smiled, her mouth closed as if she were
holding back the question she knew she should ask. "I don't
know what it is about our family he likes so much. He truly,
truly likes us. I mean when Nellie was in St. Stephen's, Sister
Patricia and Monsignor never took such a liking to us. Sister
Patricia hardly paid any attention to Nellie. She—"

"That's because with Father Infanzi, it's *not* a clergy-parishioner relationship, Mom. For him, it's truly about all of
us. From Janine on."

"I know, but I can understand him taking to Janine and"
looking away from me for a second, "to you, but me? He

really likes Tom and me. It's genuine."

"It is. He'd actually call Janine and you more, but he holds back, because he doesn't want to seem too eager."

"I can tell. When he does call, I feel like I should be reciprocating more. But I don't have time for all these wonderful people. I have my kids, my husband, my granddaughter, my work. God has really blessed me. I think this is the most blessed period of my life. And I guess I think, why does a young, handsome, intelligent priest who has a family and friends of his own want to be our friend so much?"

"*Because it's not a clergy-parishioner relationship, Mom,*" I repeated, growing frustrated. Didn't she see the way he looked at me?

"He's humble in his own way like a little boy. A good person."

"He is," I said brightly disguising my ambivalence. When he recently showed me that he still had a baby tooth, I rejoiced as if it was symbolic of his innocence. I ignored the ugly black enamel on the front of the gum where the adult tooth had tried to break through. "He is a good person," I repeated. He cleaned the throw-up off of nervous altar boys and comforted them. He went to his unmarried aunt's every Christmas Eve to sing carols in the courtyard with her neighbors. I glanced at the TV where *Touched by an Angel* had come on, a weekly drama about a set of angels who help humans face what they don't want to. Maybe one day when my mother got closer to the end of her life, she'd finally understand how special James and I were to each other, that we were each other's lifelong significant other.

It wasn't until the following day when she and I got home, and Silvia stopped by to see me that I finally collapsed from the weight of my delusion. Her white doctor-jacket and the glow on her face gleamed so brilliantly, it hurt to look at her. It was not unlike the glow I'd seen on the Sisters of Life, the deep-down kind that comes from living a pure, authentic life. "Are you okay?" she asked, my eyes so small and swollen from tears they looked like they'd been bitten. "Yes, just tired," I said. Then after walking her to the door, I returned to my couch, where I curled myself as small as I possibly could, hoping I'd disappear.

Chapter Seven

Nellie

Over the next ten months my family went from having one child to having five. Janine gave birth to triplets at thirty-three weeks: my niece Amanda at 4 pounds, 6 ounces, and my nephews Robert at 4 pounds, 4 ounces and Luke at 2 pounds, 13 ounces. Initially it was Robert the doctors were most worried about, because he was born with so much water in his lungs that he had to be intubated, but it was Luke, my godson, the tiniest, who had to stay in the neonatal intensive care unit for two months. In one picture, Janine is bowed down over his incubator as if she can pray the weight into him, his tiny fingers curled around her index finger, hanging onto her for life. During the two months, our prayers were answered as all three babies grew healthy and plump. In addition, Julie was expecting her second child in the fall, and Nellie had gotten engaged to Brendan, whom she'd met in grad school. One January night they rang my bell to tell me. Brendan was on one end of the couch with his hand on Nellie's leg, and I was on the other end. "We told Janine and Julie and Mom and Tom," she said, and then Brendan added, taking her hand in his, "And now we wanted to tell you."

"Oh, wow," I said, "How wonderful," trying to down play my hurt and surprise. They'd been going out for less than a year. I told them they had all my love and support, but I thought, *Why did she tell me last? Why am I the one who's always excluded?* I should have been concerned about whether or not she really loved Brendan, or if she was marrying him to fill a void. This was my baby sister who had always looked up to me, who wanted to be everywhere I was, a human doll waiting for me on the front stoop with her chin in her hands whenever I went out. She didn't see the beautiful, smart twenty-two-year-old in the mirror. She saw a chubby, awkward twelve- year-old with braces. She struggled. One day, she asked something that revealed just how much: "If everything's vanity, even work, then why should we bother doing anything with our lives?" I responded, "If we give work its proper place, then it's not vanity." Maybe she would've talked to me more if I didn't act as if I had all the answers, if I wasn't playing couple with the family priest. He hadn't been to my apartment since that November night, but I was still pretending to trust him even though his friend had recently told me, "Don't."

It was after I'd gotten home from Rhode Island. James had suggested that we go to confession to his friend Father Sean. They'd graduated the seminary together, and their mothers were friends too, *mops*, mothers of priests as they called them. Father Sean had just been named pastor of a

140

parish and was living in the rectory by himself. I thought going to him for confession was strange, a cop-out—after all how hard would a friend of James' be on me—but I agreed. At least this time I wouldn't be withholding the truth that the man I slept with was a priest. Father Sean told me that God forgives me, but that I had to know and accept that, with most men, the burden to be chaste would always be on me. With the violet stole around his neck and one end sliding off his thick thigh, he absolved me with the sign of the cross over my bowed head. Then he took his stole off, looked at me, and said, "Maria, I don't want to hurt you, but you need to know something about James—you're only special until the next woman comes along."

By the time I walked down the rectory steps, I'd repressed it. James was so dedicated, awake every morning to say seven o'clock Mass, and then off to the hospital for a full-day of ministry. When a parish called him for an extra Mass or a family asked him to be the attending priest at a wake, he was there. Whenever there was a story about nuns in the *Times*, he cut out the article and sent it to me with a note: *A little reminder of how noble your plans are.* There was no way he didn't value celibacy, that he didn't want to be a priest. I couldn't see that he was burying himself in his work, running from the truth, growing anxious and miserable. A couple of months after he began his new job, one of the priests he lived with told James that he made all the other priests nervous, that none of them liked him. James developed insomnia, sleeping at most four hours with the help of pills he got off a pharmacist-friend. The only time he slept without them was on Friday nights when he stayed at his sister and brother-in-law's to avoid the rectory. I told myself that he was adjusting, that the other priest was mean, and didn't know what he was talking about. I wrote in my journal, *When you love someone, you worry about him.* Yet, there was a part of me that was relieved he was suffering, that he'd have some idea how hard things were for me. I was hoping it'd make him turn to Christ.

Nellie called me one night to tell me she was asking Father Infanzi to officiate at their wedding. She added, "But only because Mommy wants me to, because you know I *don't* like him."

"Why do you have to be so biting like that? I can be biting with you, but I refrain."

"It's not biting. In the beginning I didn't know what he was doing with you. And then that time when he was over for dinner, he acted so pompous. I felt like he was saying those things about Madonna just to annoy me, because he knows I like her. He's so judgmental."

"He's not *that* judgmental. You and I are more judgmental."

"The way he criticizes Madonna like he's holier than thou."

"He's a priest, Nellie. He's going to criticize Madonna."

"I know, but there's something about him."

"Still, you don't have to be nasty. He's my *friend*." She drew in her breath and then was silent. I don't think she or my other sisters would've imagined that I'd slept with him, that my conscience would have allowed it. Nevertheless, I was calling him a friend? A man who I let pick me up from the airport, go to the gym with me, send me a romantic box of souvenirs from the Venetian in Las Vegas when he was on vacation the previous summer. She'd been at my apartment the day it arrived and asked who it was from. "Father Infanzi," I said, a wave of satisfaction washing over me. *You can't stand me half the time, but there's a man who'll love me forever.* She said, not meanly, "Leave it to you to have a priest fall in love with you." I didn't know what she meant, and I didn't probe, afraid she'd ask me exactly what was going on. When she and I were younger, and I'd tell her, "Don't step in the dirt" while I was sweeping the kitchen floor, she'd bite back, "*You are the dirt.*" Maybe I had been assuming she'd mess everything up. I was thinking it now: If she wasn't rushing into marriage, I wouldn't be the only unmarried daughter left, at least not this soon.

A couple of weeks later I found out that my mother gave Nellie the engagement ring my father had given her without first asking if I wanted it. "Why wouldn't you have asked me first?" I demanded, the three of us standing in her kitchen. I had kept my feelings in way too long; I was going to fix them both, remind them I was the older one not the other way around.

"Because you're planning on becoming a nun," my mother answered.

"But I'm older than her. And nuns wear rings too, *Mom,* to symbolize the vows *they* take. Didn't it dawn on you that at the very least I deserved to be asked if I wanted the ring? That I'm the third born, not the last born. That she's the last born. Or does the fact that I'm not getting married take me out of the line of respect in this family entirely?" I continued.

I don't remember if or how my mother answered, just that she looked at me more confused and intimidated than ever while Nellie glared at me. Even if my mother had offered me the ring, I would've still felt inadequate and insecure, less a woman than she and my sisters. My romantic fantasies would've continued to distort my view of celibacy and family life and intensified my grief. Around this time there was a black and white commercial of an attractive thirty-something couple getting engaged in a church courtyard that looked like it was in Italy. The man yelled "*I LOVE THIS WOMAN*" as the church bells tolled and pigeons burst into the air. Then he gave her the ring, and stunned, she whispered into his ear, "*I LOVE THIS MAN. I LOVE HIM, I LOVE HIM, I LOVE HIM.*" Every time I saw it, I felt like I was in a boxing ring with the devil. I wondered if God might even be laughing at me: not just a proposal, not just a couple my age, but, of all places, Italy. I'd shut the TV off for three minutes to make sure it was over before turning it back on. I couldn't do that with the jewelry billboard that stared me down every day on the way to work, a blown-up engagement ring with the words *Rock Her* in letters so large, I could almost hear them.

I had no idea of the enormous responsibility and burden that my mother and sisters carried. When I helped Janine with the babies, I saw up close just how much she sacrificed, how exhausted and sleep deprived she was all the time, how just getting to shower was a luxury. I told myself it was because she had triplets. I compared my life to Julie's, like the day she and Nick took two-year-old Nicole to the city for a horse and buggy ride, then to FAO Schwarz, a stop at Bloomingdale's, and, to cap off the day, Serendipity for ice cream where Julie snapped Nicole's Christmas photo. I pictured their day shiny and happy in comparison to mine in my apartment alone working on a fifteen-page paper for a Christian Apologetics course that I was taking through the seminary James had attended. (If I couldn't get the same education as he did, I could at least take graduate classes.) The reality was Julie wound up packing much more into a day than a toddler without a nap could handle. Who knows, maybe she was trying to make up for our childhood, trying to keep some emptiness at bay. Even if she wasn't, the picture of Nicole dressed in red with her locks of hair up in a small loose bun and sitting at a table with a luscious sundae made an exquisite Christmas picture, but it wasn't easy to get.

A couple of weeks later when Nellie chose Julie to be her matron-of-honor, I felt betrayed. Even though it'd be less awkward this way—I wouldn't have to be on the altar near James—it didn't make me feel better. I was the one who had visited Nellie in Spain, who had driven the three and a half hours to her college when she felt depressed, who stayed on the phone with her encouraging her to receive the Eucharist and get to the fitness center. I was the one who wrote her love letters when she was born, helped her write letters to Santa, dressed up as a clown for her fifth birthday, ran her baths and made her pastina. I'm the one who worried when there was a milk strike, turning to Silvia one day as we walked home from school, *"How is my mother going to feed Nellie?"* I'm the one who went to bed every night at eight, so she wouldn't be afraid of the dark in the back of the house by herself as I twisted and turned, listening to Janine and Julie watching TV. After everything I'd done for her, this was the thanks I was getting? Julie and Janine were good older sisters too, and of course it was Nellie's prerogative, but all I could think was, *The stupid, pathetic single sister.*

***

RF said that my tendency to see things darker than they were could be manifesting itself in my dreams. If she called me paranoid, she wouldn't have been completely wrong. I was jealous that motherhood bonded my mother and older sisters and that babies and the wedding were all they talked about. The fact that my mother had a hard time accepting gifts and appreciating the untraditional didn't help. When I wrote her a seventy-line ode for Mother's Day celebrating her, she uncomfortably hung it in a corner of her bedroom with the bow still on it. I felt like she was hiding me and my work, that we weren't as worthy as my sisters and their children whose photographs she had displayed throughout the house. Hurt, but embarrassed to sound like a child again, I nursed my anger. It was the same thing I'd done with Sister Teresa whom I hadn't seen or heard from in seven months.

I felt that it was her and the order's job to keep in touch with me, to let me know they were still interested, so I never reached out to her even though in the previous year she'd moved and started a new ministry. When she and I finally saw each other at a vows ceremony that Sister Erin had invited me to, she asked if I felt badly that she hadn't called. Instead of owning my feelings like an adult, I was embarrassed and said no. She told me that if I didn't hear from her by mid- December, I should call her. I had no intention of doing so, even though the Charities were still the only order I could imagine entering. They didn't have an intense prayer schedule, and they didn't wear habits, legitimate reasons for some to choose an order, but in my case, additional indicators that I didn't want to be a nun. The biggest telltale, though, was my "sense" that I was only supposed to make first vows and not final ones, so that I could leave to start some kind of ministry with James. Not only was I delusional, I didn't understand that making first vows without intending to make them final would be as hurtful as getting engaged to someone you're not going to marry. I'd be using the order. When I didn't hear from Sister Teresa again, I wrote her an angry letter that I didn't mail. I complained to Sister Dorothy. Within a week I heard from Sister Teresa. She was sorry. Did I want to go to dinner? It felt almost as good as the day of the triplets' christening when Janine's girlfriends saw James sitting close to me on my mother's couch and told me, "Father's in love with you."

A month later I was reevaluated by Dr. Togres. I made sure none of my darkness or anger seeped out. Becoming a nun still felt like God's choice for me, not mine, but candidacy did feel like the right next step. Sharing daily prayer and chores with the Sisters as I learned more about the order was appealing to me. I looked forward to it. I yearned to belong to something bigger than myself. Yet, I wanted it on my terms. When Sister told me she'd like me to attend a discernment event in Pittsburgh at the end of April with her and Frances, the candidate who I'd gotten to know a little in the previous year, I asked if we could fly. I liked Fran, but she gave one word answers to everything, and I didn't want to be stuck in a car for six hours trying to pull conversation. But the plane turned out to be a puddle jumper, and I got sick. As I looked up from my aluminum bag, Sister was chatting obliviously with Fran several rows ahead of me. Even in religious life, I was going to wind up alone, I thought bitterly. It was only when the woman who picked us up at the airport took us to see a church, and we pulled in the lot, that I lightened up. I'd never seen a prettier one. Built with large, pale colored stones, it looked part castle, part cave. I walked around in awe, feeling humbled, whispering to St. Louise de Marillac, "I'm sorry. I wouldn't have wanted to miss you." The following day when I had eight fellow aspirants to break bread and window shop with, I felt content and at peace.

At Sunday's closing ceremony, we were asked to write one thing we needed to relinquish in order to draw closer to God. The altar was spare except for one long sunflower, a lit candle encased in glass, and a metal bowl. Erica, a candidate from the Kansas province, was leading a guided meditation and had asked us to close our eyes and imagine Saints Louise de Marillac, Elizabeth Ann Seton, and Vincent de Paul approaching us in our favorite place, speaking to us the quotations we'd read before the meditation. Louise: "*If you wish to satisfy God you must not stop to consider what you would like to do, but rather what He wishes you to do.*" Elizabeth:

"*There is no road. The road is made by walking.*" And Vincent: "*Although I am 79, I do not feel excused from the responsibility of working for the salvation of the poor.*" As the three of them stood in front of me, I only made eye contact with Elizabeth, because I was afraid of Louise's words, and felt it was less rude if I didn't look at her *and* Vincent. After a few minutes, Erica asked us to let the three saints go and to slowly, when we were ready, open our eyes, approach the altar, and take a pencil and piece of paper. I touched my pocket, felt the outline of the phone message from James that was taped to my door when I arrived wishing me a good retreat. It was one thing that I raised the eyebrows of *his* secretary when I sent him postcards, but I didn't like being called out when I admitted to Sister Teresa that the message was from him and she, for the first time, rolled her eyes at me.

I looked around the room and imagined what the Sisters might have a hard time letting go of: good health, esteem, a particular ministry, a deceased loved one. None of the ones I'd met seemed to pine for sex or marriage, and neither did my peers, except maybe Fran. I was embarrassed to ask anyone if they did but also afraid to accept that I wasn't that different than them. Failing the psychological exam would've been a perfect excuse to walk away from the prospect of a celibate life. Yet I hadn't. I'd passed the retest and was beginning candidacy in September. And I wasn't only doing it for the wrong reasons. When I'd gone on retreat for the Triduum, a Jesuit priest reminded us that during the agony in the garden, Jesus felt all of our human sin and suffering. He felt utterly abandoned. He sweat blood, begged, "*My Father, if it is possible, let this cup pass from me; yet, not as I will, but as you will.*" I'd heard it before, but this time it pierced my heart. He poured himself out on the cross like a bridegroom for the world, for *me*. Without him, it made no sense for me not to marry and have children, but with him it did. It was a way to follow closely in his celibate footsteps, to be intimately joined to him like a bride. When I'd first arrived on retreat, I wanted to go home, but the image of Jesus chained in the dank darkness of Caiaphas' dungeon—an innocent on death row—made me go back to my room and quietly hang my clothes in the closet.

As the women were finishing and dropping their folded papers into the steel bowl at the foot of the altar, I melodramatically touched my pocket again and felt James' message. If I wrote his name, I'd no longer be saying *I think I know what You're asking of me*, but instead *Here he is*. Earlier in the month, I'd come across Sister Wendy Beckett's "Absolute Trust": if Abraham didn't intimately know God, and if Isaac didn't intimately know his father, their trust would have been madness. Surrounded by celibate women who didn't make me feel threatened, who were now singing, "Eye has not seen, ear has not heard what God has ready for those whose love Him," I thought I trusted God, but not yet. A month earlier upstairs at Julie's where she and Nellie were addressing the wedding invitations, Nellie had said spitefully to me, "I'm not inviting you with a guest." She was probably thinking, *You've made the priest your guest*, but I heard, *Haha, You're becoming a nun; you can't be invited with a guest; you'll always be alone.* I couldn't accept that Sister Wendy's words also applied to James and me. "There can be no love without... intelligent trust. Love is *not* blind despite the saying...we cannot truly give our hearts to the unknown." Picking up the pencil, I wrote only half of what I needed to: *Marriage and children in the earthly sense, Jesus, I offer these up to you.*

Chapter Eight

Candidacy

A few weeks after my thirty-first birthday, I moved in with Sisters Teresa, Arlene, and Louise to begin candidacy. We lived in an old two-story that Sister Arlene had fallen in love with a year earlier when she was looking for a place closer to her ministry, and there were no convents nearby. It was located on Cardoman Road, a major thoroughfare that was a quarter mile from the college—the shortest commute I'd ever had—and two houses in from the traffic light where we could hear engines idling and accelerating day and night. It had plenty of rooms but little space, windows that Arlene had to doctor in the winter to keep the cold out, and wiring so ancient we couldn't plug in two appliances without blowing a fuse. The first time I saw it, I thought, *Glad to know you think this much of me, God.*

Tall and stout and in her late 40s—one of the youngest women in the congregation—Arlene had short hair that was more pepper than salt. Her bedroom was on the first floor between the living and dining rooms with a full-size bed that was too big for it and a plaque on the wall that read in pink curlicue letters, *I Have Called You Each By Name.* The rest of our bedrooms were upstairs. Teresa's room was pristine and sparse with nothing left out for others to see and a twin bed with an eyelet spread and crisp hospital corners. Louise's was smaller with a bed and a bureau on which she left everything out—change, IDs, antidepressants, fragrant lotions. She was in her mid-fifties, a pastoral associate for a parish in Bed Sty, Brooklyn. She had wavy, dyed brown hair and was heavy in the middle. The first time I met her, she leaned to the side to get herself off the couch and winking at me, said in her Canadian accent, "Welcome to our *humble* abode, darling." Then she came at me with wide open arms and a huge, soft hug.

My room was rectangular shaped with just enough space for my desk, hutch, and twin bed, the latter which Arlene helped me put on risers so it'd look less childish. She also helped me paint, and I bought a new bedspread—a fresh start in a bed where I wouldn't wind up with a man, though I'd given my queen size to Kara along with my other furniture in case I didn't make it to novitiate. I'd finally told her I was becoming a nun the day JFK Jr.'s plane crashed into the Atlantic, and he, Carolyn Bessette Kennedy, and Lauren Bessette died. I thought that since three stunning, successful people in their prime had just lost their lives, Kara might understand. Swiping her auburn bangs off her face, she said, "I'm surprised, but I'm not" and "Wow, girlie" when she realized I was entering the same order that her father's cousin was in. Then she got quiet. Maybe she wanted to ask me how the Church could allow her unfaithful ex-husband to get an annulment, or why I, who was at the bars every Thursday night in college, was choosing celibacy. Maybe she was thinking about what I'd said—I didn't think everyone was meant to get married—and was scared that included her. But she didn't say any of this. She didn't even mention Father James as she called him. Instead, she brought out a beautiful, glossy book on Elizabeth Ann Seton that her father's cousin had published. I flipped through it, joyfully stunned by the *God*-incidence, coincidence that God had facilitated. Then we went into her Florida room, sat on the couch, and shook our heads as we watched the Coast Guard on TV trying to find some sign of John's plane.

Despite my grumbling about the house, the Sisters were so welcoming and down-to-earth that within a few weeks I felt at home. I liked that it was just the four of us and that I didn't have to adjust to a lot of women or compete for attention the way I did in my family. Here we were all unmarried, all hungry for prayer, and I was the youngest, the special one, especially in Teresa's eyes. She did everything she could to make sure I had an easy transition, allowing me to get away with cleaning the bathrooms once a month instead of twice and cooking one night a week instead of two. She ordered two daily prayer devotionals so I had a choice and made sure, with my input, that my Rite of Candidacy ceremony was lovely. She even organized a welcoming committee for me. Once a month, she, Louise and I, and three other Sisters got together for dinner and an informal talk on some facet of the order or community life. It was like watching sorority sisters at a reunion. They were so different from one another—from

Teresa who sat in the high-backed winged chair in her accordion skirted dresses and her notes neatly on her lap to Matylda who sat cross-legged on the floor in sweats and sneakers and spoke extemporaneously—but they all made me feel like I was a niece they'd been waiting a long time for. With the numbers of women going into religious life anemically low, my being there resembled something like new life.

Every weekday morning at seven, we gathered in the living room for prayer. Arlene and Teresa would light the candle and wait for Louise and me who came down at the last minute (unless it was our week to lead). We used the Companion to the Breviary, the official set of daily Catholic prayer, and prayed for all the individuals we knew needed our prayers. At night we gathered for dinner around the blonde-wood table with another candle in the middle. Unlike the standard grace we prayed in my family, the Sisters prayed for the poor, the suffering, and for all those who had helped get the food to our table, and they ended with *We ask all of this in Jesus' name.* At first, I felt too self-conscious to pray this way, but as the year went on I began to imitate them. Even though they weren't cloistered, they closed off the world when it was time to, which helped feed my hunger for quiet, for God.

What I didn't like about community life was how it forced me to face my selfishness, like the time Teresa and I went to a wake for the father of one of the nuns. After an hour or so, when she had signaled that we could leave, a woman and her husband who knew Sister stopped her. A few weeks earlier, the woman had been close to death, but there'd been a miracle. She was cured and overjoyed. I tried to listen and care the way Teresa was, but after a few minutes, I got that same racing feeling in my veins that I felt whenever I had to wait on an impossibly long line. All I could think about were my pajamas. Later that night, with the smell of our pork chop-dinner still vivid in the air, Teresa was setting up the automatic pot for the next day's coffee. I had followed her into the kitchen, pretending I had something to do, but I really wanted to ask her the question that had been taxing me all night. She pulled her glasses up the bridge of her nose, so she could see the numbers on the side of the coffee maker.

"How do you do it, Teresa?" The night I'd moved in, she told me, "You don't have to call me Sister anymore; you're one of us."

"Do what?"

"Listen. How do you listen to people all the time? Listen to all these different people who need so much to talk, who talk *at* you, not with you. How do you stand there and care so much?"

She put down the carafe of water, looked at me the same compassionate way she'd looked at the woman, and said something like, "You don't know any of these people. You're just meeting all of them. You have to give yourself more time."

There was also the Sunday afternoon when Arlene got home from a conference she'd attended and excitedly sat us down for a half hour to give us the details. Within minutes I was crossing and uncrossing my legs under the table, annoyed that she had to share so much, ranting silently about how if I had a husband, I'd *want* to hear about *his* conference. I was also annoyed that my writing time had gotten interrupted, though the truth was I could barely sit down for three hours. I didn't have the hunger or discipline to wrestle with sentences and meaning. I wasn't self-aware or mature enough to write real memoir, to tell the truth about myself and my relationship with James. When he'd shown up uninvited my first week at Cardoman to wish me "Good luck," I matter-of-factly introduced him to Arlene and Louise as "my friend, Father James." They fought not to give him and his collar a double take, but they shook his hand heartily and didn't act suspicious. At the end of October, I asked Teresa if we could invite him to our Open House, ignoring the still small voice that told me, *Don't.* She hesitated but said yes. I wanted my family, who was also coming, to understand that James wasn't going away. I was going to do everything to make our relationship seem as natural as possible. Everyone was cordial to him even Nellie, but it was so awkward, I tried to camouflage it by attempting to serve food every few minutes.

Now that I was living with Sisters, I was certain I had enough willpower to go out with James from time to time. A few weeks before Christmas after having gone to dinner with Matt and Roger, I let him in. The Sisters weren't going to be home for another hour or two, but I knew it was a bad idea. Within minutes, we were fooling around on the couch. Horrified, realizing what I was doing and where, I yelled "*No!*" I pushed him away. Surprised, he said, "*You're good.*"

I was living with *nuns.* If this were a traditional convent, there'd be a tabernacle holding the Body of Christ. I would be living in a house with the *Body of Christ.* I was supposed to be pure, the temple of the Holy Spirit. Just a month earlier, in the very same room, in front of the Sisters, my mother, Tom, Janine, and my friend Barbara, I pledged to be a candidate, to learn more about the order and religious life, to be honest and true. Now I was lying to two families. I let James have it, and then, with him still sitting on the couch, I called Roger on the phone as I glared at James, "Your friend James is using me." Roger listened but didn't say much. He was probably thinking, *Yeah, Maria, you're letting it happen.* What kind of woman was I? Certainly not the kind Monsignor Brennan saw looking into my face six months earlier when I went to him for a recommendation for the convent. He widened his brown eyes and said, "You'll be happy. *You're going to f-l-y.*" I stayed quiet in case he said anything more about happiness. Then he compared me to one of the second graders whose father had recently left the family.

"I can't believe the father wasn't there to see this magnificent child on his First Holy Communion day," Monsignor said choking up. "The boy's face was so filled with God, he lit up like a light bulb. His face was like *your* face is right now," he said, reaching his hand to touch my cheek, but then thinking twice, he brought it back to his lap. "That smile, your face. It's wholesome."

I felt numb, the way I often felt at the end of confession when the priest spoke the words of absolution. What would he think of me if he knew I'd had sex with one of his priests, brought scandal onto his parish? What would my father or my grandfathers, if they were still alive, think? What did God think of me? I had finally started taking baby steps towards his Son. Every morning after community prayer, I tried *lectio divina.* I spent most of the time vacillating between scripture passages and inundated with distracting thoughts, but every so often, I'd be still enough to feel God lovingly whisper to my heart. Now I went and did this, separated myself from Him again? No wonder that a couple of days before Christmas my back gave out.

It was close to five on the last day before the week-long break, and everyone was gone. I was killing time, dusting my office. If I went home, I wouldn't be able to write much before dinner, and what would I do sitting in my room? Louise would be in the living room watching crime shows. As much as I enjoyed joining her at night, I didn't want to start from five. I had come around my desk and was facing the view of the Narrows. During the summer, Career Development had moved to a renovated suite of glass offices in the Student Union. It was lovely, but I always felt on display especially when Admissions' tours came through, or the Board of Trustees walked by in their suits and snowy hair. All I wanted to do was hide, afraid my cross necklace might give me away. I was waiting until the end of May when the students and faculty were gone to tell my Dean that I was leaving to become a nun. I didn't want anyone to stop taking me seriously or to feel bad for me. I didn't want to have to defend a choice I was still unhappy about. Whenever Teresa and I attended congregational events, I wanted to leave as soon as Mass was over. I didn't want to meet more Sisters. It was a step closer to commitment like meeting a boyfriend's family. The fact that there wasn't anyone else entering the New York province—Fran had left half way through novitiate—made matters worse. So did receiving round-robin calls all the time about Sisters passing away. As I put the dust cloth down on my desk, I felt excruciating pain rip through my lower back.

"*Aaahh!*" I screamed, clutching my spine with one hand and the corner of my desk with the other. Terrified to move, I waited several seconds, and then gingerly lowered myself onto the edge of the chair with my eyes closed tight and my back as still as possible as tears leaked onto my cheeks. I sat for a few seconds worrying how I'd get home. Then I remembered: *Louise*. I hooked my arm around the phone, dragged it closer to me. Not only did she take me to the emergency room and stay with me for the three hours, when we got home, Nellie was waiting in the living room with concerned eyes. I was so grateful, especially since she'd recently given birth to a baby boy, Zack, but my thankfulness didn't last. All I'd done was put a dust cloth to my desk. Why did my body do this? Why did God? Was He trying to tell me something? If so, I didn't want to know what. Wasn't I hurting enough? Julie and Nellie had just chosen each other to be godmother to their sons Daniel and Zack. I hadn't expected Nellie to pick me, but I thought there was a good chance Julie would. I was the next oldest and the natural choice, the one who was giving up her life for God and wouldn't have children of her own. I felt humiliated again. I told myself there was no way I was going to Daniel's baptism. I didn't care how much it hurt Julie or my mother.

James said he was sorry, that he'd do better, and that I deserved better. On New Year's Eve, after I had dinner at Janine's, he and I met at the monastery for an eleven o'clock

Holy Hour and a midnight toast and breakfast with the monks. A good way, I thought, to be together without the risk of becoming intimate. He sat on one side of me, and Barbara, who'd been in love with a priest years earlier, sat on the other, but a parishioner from St. Stephen's who was considering the priesthood spotted James and took the seat next to him. I ate my fruit cocktail and talked to Barbara, but I steamed. Why did this guy have to show up and ruin my New Year's Eve, take James away from me? When he asked James if he was happy, James said again, "I'd do the priesthood all over again, haven't regretted a moment."

A month later I asked him to go with me to Kara's for the afternoon, so he could help me move a bookshelf to her house, even though it was light enough for me to do myself. I told Teresa, and she said, "Oh" with a raised eyebrow, but that was all. He came in for the bookshelf, the two of them said hello, I said something about Sunday afternoon traffic on the Belt Parkway, and we were gone. Then on the car ride there, I made some comment about women's rights, maybe to get back at him, and he put his hand over my mouth. I ripped it off and glared at him. "I didn't mean anything by it," he pleaded for several seconds. After a few minutes, I thought maybe I had made a bigger deal of it than necessary, or maybe I just didn't want to ruin the nice afternoon ahead of us. Kara made dinner and invited her neighbor. Afterward, she took out her college photo albums, and James excitedly spotted our pictures from Singfest. There I was on stage dressed in a silk nightie with the rest of my sorority singing and dancing to bedtime songs. At the end of the day as James and I walked to the car, Kara's neighbor, who was a non-practicing Protestant, said to her, "The two of them are good together." Kara responded, "*No. No.* They're *friends*. He's a priest. She's becoming *a nun.*" When we got back, I allowed him to feel my breasts on a dark street, but as soon as he moved his hand to the inside of my thigh, I said, "I better get home now."

I wrote him a letter to try and explain how much it hurt me whenever we were intimate, that we could only go out during the day, and that the only way I'd find happiness is if I lived the life that God was giving me. I thought if I wasn't barking at him on the phone he might listen. One time when we'd had another fight whose details I don't remember, he said to me, "If we were married, I'd hug you, and it would all melt away." I snapped back, "First of all, a hug cannot melt everything away, and second we're not married," but I was fooling myself just as much as he was. I thought that married, I'd be able to heal him of his ills, make him happy. His insomnia hadn't gotten any better. He even stopped sleeping at his sister's, because he said he felt lonely around her and her husband. Yet, I continued to fantasize the two of us starting our own order one day and that the younger nuns and priests would be our "kids." I sponsored us a child from Thailand, a tall ten-year-old girl with short, shiny black hair to whom I explained in a letter that Father James was a Catholic priest and I was becoming a Catholic nun, and we were each other's best friend. I also signed us up to pray for a baby who was in danger of being aborted. I sent James a note: "Why will I not be surprised when we meet this child in heaven and know immediately that he or she is the one we prayed for?"

Around this time, Julie asked me if there was another way I could give my life to God without the confines of religious life. I had gone to Daniel's christening—I couldn't bring myself not to. When Monsignor poured holy water over his dark-haired, angel head, I felt joy and healing. Afterward, I explained to Julie that I was hurt that unless I was visiting the kids, I never saw or heard from her. She apologized, we went to dinner twice in two months, and she asked for a book on Elizabeth Ann Seton, which I delightedly shared with her. I told her single people can also give their lives to God, but I said it as if it wasn't good enough for me. I prayed for single people all the time especially around holidays but in the third person. I had no idea of Henri Nouwen's book, *The Wounded Healer,* a phrase he borrowed from Carl Jung: recognizing your own wounds can help you figure out how you're supposed to serve and whom, but when united with Christ's death and resurrection, can also help heal *you.* Even if I had, I would've still thought being single was inferior to being married or a nun.

One night in March during dinner, Teresa was talking about Sister Eileen Rancher, the oldest Sister in the community. I listened interestedly as I took a bite of Arlene's pot roast when she added, "You'll get to meet Sister Eileen in July at the Motherhouse for annual assembly." "That's good," I said, swallowing hard. Visiting the Motherhouse not only signaled the last step before entering novitiate, it was where most of the elderly sisters lived. I'd finally be confronted with the reality I had been trying to ignore all year. It was also a Jubilee Year for the Church, which meant a crowd of two hundred. Teresa wasn't going, because she was giving a retreat, but she was in charge of making the travel arrangements. I asked again if we could fly instead of drive, and, with Louise's help, I also bargained the trip down from two weeks to one. I told Teresa I had a lot to do before novitiate. How could I admit that I didn't want to spend a lot of time with sick, elderly nuns without sounding like a monster and offending Teresa and the order? The only aspect of my unhappiness that I had let on about had to do with work. I started to feel as if I was phasing out and didn't belong there anymore. Teresa said it was normal and would help me make the transition when it was time to leave. Then she hugged me tight the way she did at the end of all our monthly meetings.

In early May I had a dream that upset me so much, I wrote for forty minutes straight when I woke up. James and I were in a building that was a cross between a Catholic hall auditorium and a house in Connecticut. He was socializing with two of his priest friends, one of whom was named Iman, and their female companions. Meanwhile I was upstairs preparing a three course Italian meal for him—the kind my mother used to serve my father who'd never tolerate a simple American meal. James came upstairs and sat down to eat, his legs spread wide, his fists planted firmly on the table with a knife and fork in each like a Neanderthal. I served him the meal like a doting Mrs. Brady, rewarding him after a trying day of priestly duties, but then I sat down and asked him, trying not to sound too needy, "How come you couldn't find even fifteen minutes to spend with me tonight?" He looked at me as if he had no idea what I was talking about and continued to stuff his face. I went berserk. I screamed and poured each course into one big heap on his plate. He started saying hateful things back. When I ran out of the place, I was on the Brooklyn street I grew up on headed toward my childhood home, but then the scenery changed again, and I was headed for Cardoman Road. Before I got there, James ran up behind me, put his hand on my back, and yelled, "Tag!"

"What the hell are you doing? You think you can play, and that'll make me forget?"

He reddened and yelled, "It's so like you to blow everything out of proportion."

I was playing out a similar dynamic with James that had existed between my mother and father. I was looking to him to fill the need my father should have met. I was using the convent, in part, to try and run away from it all. I'm sure RF tried to point out the blatantly chauvinistic *Iman* and the multiple inappropriate priest-female relationships, but I didn't want to understand or give up my fantasy. One day before I'd moved into the convent my mother and I were driving home from a day together in Manhattan for my birthday. She had just treated me to a facial and lunch, but I was annoyed because she was going on about the grandkids, calling them *bambinidittu* and *shaditittu*, Sicilian for beautiful and delicious babies, the *ittu* sound grating on my nerves. I started sighing loudly, pretending I was upset because I couldn't find the sign for the FDR South. After going another couple of streets, I started crying forced tears.

She didn't notice, which irritated me more, so I yelled, "Why is it that everyone, including God, thinks I can get along without a man?"

"Live without a man, Maria?! Live without a man?!What are you talking about? After a fourteen hour day in the bakery, who would have to run out and get formula for you kids if we didn't have any left, or if you were sick and needed medicine? I would. Not your father. I'd have to walk to the pharmacy in the dark even though I'd worked just as hard as him, harder because I had everything to care for in the house. Your father's better now, but he was an Italian *autocrat*. He'd tell me how all the young girls in the bakery were beautiful, and I was a *Strega*," witch.

"He called you that?"

"No, but after hearing him call all the other girls beautiful, what else was I supposed to believe?"

I was quiet for the rest of the ride of home, mortified. Yet, I still vacillated between anger and adoration of my father like the time he visited each of my sisters but didn't come to see me. I blasted him over the phone, "What, they matter and I don't?! How dare you not acknowledge me, not come and see me? I don't deserve the same attention as they do?" At first he was furious, "How dare you talk to your father like that?" I started crying, and he apologized. For the next few weeks he called me. I wouldn't call him. Then one day, he and Nonna visited. Ever since Nonno had passed away, the two of them had become inseparable like a couple, the way they'd been when my father was a boy and Nonno was off at war. He called her *Waninna* in their dialect. She limped around Cardoman Road in her knee length dress and wool sweater smiling like she couldn't be more pleased with the plain accommodations and my becoming a nun, while my father looked around the house uneasily. After everything he and my mother had worked so hard for, I was living *here*, choosing *this* life? I'd never invited him, because I was embarrassed. But now I was so happy to have him over that it didn't matter. Later when I spoke to Julie, my voice was lit up like a school girl with a crush. "I couldn't tell if Papa was imagining himself being alone or if he felt bad for me." "Probably both," she said quietly as if she felt the same but was afraid to tell me.

I wrote, *I have to live the life God is offering me. I don't want to serve a man three course meals, and then he gets all the credit for the work he does. I have to move forward towards God and being betrothed to his Son. Only then can I enjoy whatever deep relationships come from being centered in Christ,* the loophole I gave myself. A week later, I was having dinner at James' parents' house for his 36th birthday. They were moving to the Midwest, and he wanted me to meet them and see the house he grew up in before it was sold. I'm sure Mrs. Infanzi gave in only because I was becoming a nun. She was a tall, broad shouldered, Irish woman in her early sixties with smooth skin and light blue eyes who cooked a delicious three course Italian meal and did most of the talking—about religion. "In grammar school, I purposely did things wrong so that the nuns would call me up. It's like a sanctifying smell came off them. They smelled *holy*," she said dreamily from across the table as James uncomfortably tugged on his shirt collar.

Mr. Infanzi, who was shorter and darker than his wife and fifteen years older, involved himself in eating, except when Mrs. I. mentioned that an acquaintance of theirs had named their child Daisy. "It must have been the circumstances in which the child was conceived. You know they must have gotten *romantic* in a park or something," he said catching James' eye, the two men bursting out laughing. She ignored them, told me that in her part of the South Bronx in the 50s, there had been a lot of vocations especially from Irish families. The prettiest, most intelligent girls became nuns. Those who didn't at least consider it were considered "slouches." "Really?" I asked excitedly, looking at James, who nodded rigorously at me as if he were saying, *Told you so.*

We could have stayed another hour without overstaying, but James was itchy to leave. Mrs. I. said to me, "If there's any way I can ever help you, please let me know." She was talking about the work I told her I wanted to do with children, the only part of novitiate that I was possibly looking forward to. I thanked her and Mr. I. who smiled broadly at me and shook his son's hand like he was pleased. Kissing them goodbye, I felt irony sting. They would've made great in-laws. I based it on one night. I told James in the car, "I wished we could have stayed longer." I couldn't see the connection: the piousness that James was attracted to in me was the same quality in his mother that he felt guilty admitting turned him off. When he and his brothers were growing up, she had a pew, not a couch, in the parlor to discourage watching TV, and she had James receive First Holy Communion a year early, so that the Mass would still be offered in the Latin rite. For his fifth birthday, she took him to church instead of having cake; at least that's what he told me. When he spoke about his father, he grinned, the fun parent who always swooped in to give him a "boodle" of cash so he'd never have to pay a toll. When he spoke about his mother, he often looked uncomfortable and torn. Maybe he became a priest to make her happy. Maybe he was looking for a mother-figure and trying to get back at her at the same time. If he and I got married, he'd eventually be itching to leave me.

Back at Cardoman Road, I kissed him on the cheek and dashed out of the car. For all I knew, Teresa could be looking out the window. I'd told her where I was going. She paused longer than usual but didn't say anything then or the following week when James and I had dinner at my mother's, and she saw me make a chocolate trifle. Did she really think I was an Elizabeth Ann Seton and James was an Antonio Filichhi, that the two of us were as innocent and short-lived as Teresa and her priest-friend had been? Months earlier I'd finally asked her if she had ever struggled with being celibate, and she told me that when she was a young nun, she had fallen in love with a priest. She even played hooky to spend a day in the country with him. Her eyes lit up with the same excited disbelief she must have felt that day calling in sick to work. It had been painful for them to part, but they both knew where they belonged. All I could think was, *they went out* one *time*. James and I were more like Father Browne and Flavia Alaya whose secret, tumultuous love affair I read about in Alaya's memoir, *Under the Rose: A Confession*. I read it in one day and then locked myself in the bathroom to call

James and demand he tell me why he wasn't leaving Holy Mother Church for me like Browne had done for Alaya. Actually Browne had not left. The Church ousted him once they found out he and Alaya were living together and had a family, but it felt the same to me.

"Because we've talked about this, you know I love you but we've decided this together, that there's peace here."

"Funny, peace is not what I'm feeling."

"Well, uh, this book didn't help," he said trying to stand up to me. He was right. I'd cracked the door for Satan. When I didn't see or talk to James for long periods, when I cooperated with God's grace and trusted Him, I did feel peace. I was one more day chaste, sober, closer to clearing a space in my heart for His Son. I began to resemble the woman I was meant to be. I started getting a glimpse of the life-giving freedom celibacy could bring when it's someone's true calling, the way Brother Frank explained at one of the monthly formation weekends that Teresa and I attended. If six or seven years from now living celibately is painful, then it's probably not for us, but during these early phases of discernment, it was normal. We have to learn how to handle the loss that comes with it, to say an authentic "no" to everything else. However, we must not deny or repress our sexuality; we must see God as alive and mystical, gentle, loving, and passionate—not punitive and moral—and to try and see ourselves as His *delight*. Prayer is as critical to being happily celibate as sex and communication are to being happily married. Maybe Teresa hadn't expressed concern because she was confused. She saw in me what I wasn't fully facing in myself. I wanted the same peace and freedom that she and Brother Frank and the other Sisters had. She heard it in my prayer and in our monthly meetings and in the reflection questions I had to complete for my novitiate application. It's true that I didn't talk about novitiate with much excitement, but she thought it was because of my strain of leading a double life at work. She was hoping that once I told the college, I'd be happy.

At first I was. Even our internship coordinator, Stanley, a cynical economics professor in his seventies was encouraging. "Planning another year of Career Development is not going to matter down the road. What you're doing? *That* probably will." I felt deeply humbled and grateful by my coworkers' faith, but as the days went on, I grew ill at ease. When our assistant said, "We have to start calling you *Sister Maria,*" I blurted out, "That sounds wrong. I can't imagine it." When the director of student activities gave me an incredibly thoughtful card, "As you enter the Lord's service…" I didn't want it. But what really upset me were the few people who openly expressed pity for me: the Catholic secretary from Academic Advisement who stared at me as if she just found out I had cancer and said, "I thought they were going to tell me you were leaving to make *real* money" and the woman in HR who told me she once felt called to become a nun, but added, "It's such a hard life" like she'd escaped something. Then there was President Davis who, I heard through the grapevine, told my Dean, "*What a waste.*"

At my farewell party a month later, a group of about twenty-five of us, mostly support staff and my career development colleagues were standing in an awkward circle in the basement dining hall with Robert the Provost officiating for the President who had an "emergency appointment." I liked Robert. He was the only male VP I'd felt comfortable sharing my news with. But I couldn't help but think that if I were leaving for something prestigious, my guests and I would be milling around *President* Davis' scenic fourth floor office as my former directors toasted my many accomplishments. Instead when Robert said, "Let's go around the room and give anyone a chance who wants to toast Maria," Sister Kelly, a small, zealous campus minister who had known me less than a year, piped up, "What Maria's doing, becoming a nun, following Christ in such a radical way is a sign for all of *you* to get closer to God."

I dropped my hand holding the champagne glass down by my side. I knew religious life would come up as it did in Robert's opening joke, which made all of us chuckle: "When people leave Westerly, they usually leave to make more money. Maria's the first to leave to make *less*." But I had no idea my party would become a case for God. Where was the Dean of Admissions, or the Business Professor who had hired me for Placement Director, or Doris who I diligently reported to for ten years? True, I had pulled away from her especially in recent months, but that was because I knew she didn't understand. When I tried to explain that I was more spiritual than I let on, she said, "Yes, but you're also *pretty* secular." I smiled as hard as I could for the rest of the party, but I felt humiliated and lonely. Even my former assistant ran out of the room embarrassed for me. God was trying to make me into a real Christian, divesting me of the trappings I tried to lean on for happiness and self-esteem. He was trying to transform me into a humble woman who was not embarrassed of His Son, who didn't need people, especially men in power, to tell her how well she had done. It was God who had endowed me with my talents and opportunities, God who made up for my many weaknesses. The college didn't have to give me a party at all, and what about all my lovely, supportive coworkers who had shown up? My worth wasn't tied to which directors were or weren't there and whether or not they praised me. It was and is tied to the reality that I'm a child of God, His beloved daughter, but beloved was the last thing I felt.

When I told Marie how furious I was that Sister Kelly used my party as a soapbox, she looked genuinely concerned. She already knew something was wrong two weeks earlier. I had taken a day off to rent bikes with James in Central Park and lied to her. She and the other Sisters always left for work before me, so I was certain I could get away with it, but at 8:15, she came out of the bathroom in her pink robe and told me she was going in a little later. I panicked but feigned calm as I told her that I was taking a personal day. "For anything in particular?" she asked with a raised eyebrow. "Not really," I said, afraid the lie was all over my face. I spent the next forty-five minutes hiding in my room. At 9:05, I ran downstairs and when I saw James walking toward the house, I slipped out the door. He had parked a few houses away, not to conceal himself but because he had a surprise for me. On the back of his car was a brand new, shining, royal blue man's bike.

"That's a surprise for me?"

"You're the one who inspired it."

A few blocks away from the house, I made the mistake of mentioning I'd forgotten the picnic blanket in my trunk. The moment I said it, I regretted it. He insisted we go back. I pleaded with him to let it go, that if Sister Teresa hadn't already seen us through her bedroom window, then she'd certainly see us now, but he kept insisting. I finally said okay to shut him up. Even if she hadn't looked out the window at the exact moment—which is hard to believe—she had to know something was up. At home later that day, she still didn't say anything. Maybe she was waiting for me to grow up and talk to her, or maybe she didn't want to find out for sure that I was a liar. Even if she had confronted me, I would've never admitted that I didn't want to be a nun, especially now that I'd given my notice. If I didn't enter novitiate, I'd have no plan. I'd look like a fool. God was going to lead me somewhere else after my first vows anyway; I was sure of it.

A few weeks later on a steaming July Saturday, I came down the stairs dressed up for a cousin's wedding. Teresa was sitting in the straight, high-back chair like she'd been waiting for me. "You look nice," she said stiffly.

"Thank you."

"You know the toilet's clogged?"

"No, I didn't," I lied.

"It's going to have to be fixed."

"Uh-huh." Bad enough there was no lover waiting for me at the bottom of the stairs and that in a few minutes I'd be sitting in the back seat of Nellie and Brendan's SUV. If she was upset, why not come out and say it instead of playing passive-aggressive? (I was one to talk.) I was too knotted and self-absorbed to realize that she was hurt and probably found it as difficult to talk to me as my mother did. She'd invested three and a half years in trying to help me discern God's will without ever imposing hers. We were friends, yet I was acting like a stranger and teenager, pretending everything was okay. The broken toilet might've been her way of bringing it up. Later that night trying to fall asleep in my eighty-degree bedroom, a hellish monologue took over my mind: *You're going to keep going to these weddings alone year after year, watching other people your age and younger get married? He'll leave in a second for you. All he needs is more prodding, a woman who knows what she wants, who doesn't go on about not feeling "called" to marriage. You don't even want to be a nun. Trying to be celibate only brings out the worst in you. You'll be a much better human being married. Just imagine yours and James' kids. You'll finally have something of your own to be proud of and brag about. Your kids—not your sisters' kids—yours. How are you going to pass all that up? If you live until eighty, that's forty-eight more years without sex. Why would you subject yourself to that? It's not natural. You're no angel. Your purity is long gone.*

For the next three nights, I twisted and turned. On the morning Arlene, Louise, and I left for the annual assembly, I woke with a sore throat, which the flight worsened. When we arrived in Nova Scotia, and the Motherhouse's 350,000 grey square feet came into view, I put my hand over my neck and swallowed. Then as I reached to get my luggage out of the trunk, I fantasized a porter reaching for my and my husband's luggage, the two of us having just arrived at our honeymoon. I shook my head, pulled out my bag, and got out of the way, so Arlene and Louise could get theirs. A dozen elderly Sisters were sitting at the top of the lawn overlooking Jipugtug Harbor with their backs to us, their thin, white tufts of hair like shoots growing out of the chairs, their canes and walkers resting beside them. I stared at them, and then followed Arlene and Louise inside where I gaped at the humongous entranceway and a hallway so long I couldn't see the end. When Arlene turned to tell me that they didn't have a room for me, I walked over to the receptionist. She had the same list in front of her that each of us had received in the mail a week earlier. I was the last one, number 201, the only candidate and one of only eight women with an Italian last name, the list filled with Donovans, McNeils, Schmidts, Walshs, O'Briens. Even though they were apologetic and at work readying a room, I turned to Louise, "You got to be kidding me. There's *like* a million rooms in this place, and they don't have one for me?"

While I waited, I tried to pray, but the chapel was so gothic-like I couldn't get comfortable, so I changed into shorts and went outside where the Sisters were sitting. Some were reading, others were praying with their eyes fixed on the harbor. I chose a chair several feet away. A couple of the Sisters looked at me as I smiled nervously and went back and forth between *Living Faith* and *Living with Christ* until I finally chose *Living Faith*. At the top of the page was *Learning To Trust God,* St. Bonaventure's name, and an excerpt from the day's Gospel: *Even the hairs of your head have all been counted. Do not be afraid.* Jesus couldn't be plainer or more compassionate, yet when I closed my eyes, I started yelling at His Father. *I don't know if you've noticed, but I'm* thirty-one. In my prime. *I don't belong here. What am I doing here? Do you even care? You sent every one of your disciples out in pairs. Where's my other half? No husband, now this? You lead me to this foreign place where there's only one of me, where they don't even have a room ready for me. Trust You?* Instead of praying to the Blessed Mother or St. Michael, Satan's chief opponents, I continued my silent ranting. Maybe if I'd gotten quiet, I might have heard God ask, *<u>What</u> are <u>you</u> doing here, Maria?*

The following day before the main assembly, about a hundred twenty five Sisters milled around the courtyard. Louise hadn't come down from her room yet, and Arlene was involved in behind-the-scenes preparations. I was feeling a disguised-kind-of-better: showered, changed, my throat sprayed with an analgesic. I talked to all the Sisters I recognized, but soon there was no one I knew left. I moved through the crowd feeling like I was at someone' else family reunion, comparing myself to all the happy Sisters. I fantasized my husband and I hosting a lovely party, the two of us mingling with our closest friends over cocktails and conversation about mortgages, and then at some point flirtatiously catching each other's eyes from across the room. A small elderly nun sitting in a chair not far from me said, "You must be Maria."

"Oh, Sister Eileen. I've heard so much about you," I said, recognizing her immediately, pulling up a chair. She had long, white hair and a soft, thin body and was wearing a blouse and shin-length skirt that were too big for her.

"The Sisters are going to think you're a journalist and not the candidate," she said, which made me smile. "How are you?"

"Actually, I'm pretty sure I'm getting strep throat," I said putting my hand there.

"I'd never know looking at you."

"It started right before we left. Probably just the stress of a new situation," I said waving my hand casually.

"Even some of the Sisters find assembly overwhelming," she said trying to make me feel better. We spoke a few more minutes until a middle-age Sister in a lovely bouclè skirt suit came over to tell us that assembly was about to start. She helped Sister Eileen up, cupping her elbow so tenderly that I paused in admiration before following them into the large auditorium where everyone was buzzing as they took their seats. At my table, one of the Sisters asked what stage of the process I was in. I told her I was entering novitiate in a month, though I wasn't sure where. Before I'd left, Teresa said that novitiate may not be held at Fort Lee after all. She didn't tell me that the parish was closing it because there weren't enough nuns.

After a series of welcomes, thank yous, and an opening prayer, the Superior General introduced the guest speaker, a laywoman who founded a residential community for women survivors of prostitution and trafficking. Within minutes, she had the Sisters' rapt attention. I tried my best to listen, but out of the corner of my eye, I saw a Sister in a wheelchair at the next table dropping her head and struggling to bring it back up again. Her face looked like a tired flower, and her hair was so thin I could see the veins through her pinkish scalp. I stared at her, and for the next half hour, table by table, at the other elderly sisters in the room. They weren't all frail, but they had no family of their own to cheer them in their infirmity, no one to carry on their name when they were gone. I was in the presence of interesting, brave, holy women who had helped thousands of people, but all I could focus on was that they were old and celibate. I clutched my throat. *I'm giving up my youth, stepping into something that looks like it's going to die.*

A burst of applause invaded the auditorium, and everyone who could stand did. I automatically joined them, clapping my hands rigorously, but as soon as the Superior General finished thanking the speaker, I got up and explained to my table, "My throat is getting worse." Before I could get away, the Sister who had asked me about novitiate said, "I'll keep you in my prayers." I smiled, forgetting my dread for a moment, but then she added, "Be prepared. There's going to be a lot of dark nights."

I ran out of the room and to the pay phone where I dialed the airline. Then I hung up. An earlier flight home was going to cost an extra two hundred dollars. I'd have to explain to Teresa. I didn't want to disappoint Louise whose family we were visiting the next day. I wanted to be obedient and see the week out. But I needed to talk to someone. I needed James. I ran back to my room and frantically clawed through my bag for the cell phone he had bought me. Except for one digit, it was the same number as his. He was on his summer vacation, this year for five weeks instead of four. When I complained about the extra week, he said, "I'll miss you even more," but he couldn't hide his excitement. I didn't know what motel he was staying in, because I'd told him not to give me his itinerary, though I knew he was stopping by the Hotel *Bellagio,* beautiful ease. In the card he'd given me before he left, he wrote, "While you're making this next important step toward becoming a nun, I'll be in Vegas thinking of you."

I dialed the area code and then remembered I needed a country code that I didn't have. I kept dialing, pretending it would work without it. When I got a ringing tone, I said, "*Thank you, God,*" but after the second ring, "The number you are trying to reach is out of service. Please check the number and try again." I banged my foot on the floor, dialed zero for an operator, but again nothing. I was going to get him on the phone. He was going to walk me through, tell me there's a light at the end, that things will work out and I'd find my place. I dialed two, three, five times, the same message replaying: I can't do this alone. I won't do this alone. He loves me. As I was about to dial his number a sixth time, something popped and clicked at the base of my throat. I tried to say something, but nothing came out. I dropped the phone, heard it crash to the floor.

When I'd tried to tell James how miserable I'd grown these last couple of months, all he could say was, "It'll be better once you start novitiate." All these months pretending it would improve, that the fact that I wasn't happy didn't mean I wasn't supposed to become a nun, that I could become one if I had James. I stared at the small, white sink jutting out of the wall, heard a bathroom door closing down a distant hall. I was becoming a nun *for* him. What an idiot I was: three and a half years adamant that I was following God's will. All it did was get me here, sick in a place I didn't belong. This couldn't be the door that God was holding open, could it? If being a nun were really my calling, I'd be at peace, wouldn't I? God can't want only some people to be happy, can He? How could I ever accomplish anything good if I'm so unhappy, living a life that's not meant for me? What does a man like James do when he's finally thousands of miles away from home, with no rectory or ministry or collar to rein him in? How could I believe that he was spending his vacation in Lake Tahoe reading his *Times* and riding his bike alone and not in Vegas at blackjack tables with glasses of scotch and a woman servicing him? What would ever make me think there'd be a connection between a Motherhouse and the *Bellagio*?

I fell back onto the bed, curled myself into a ball. I tried to say "HELP," but it wouldn't come out. Then a knock at the door. Louise. "I lo—," I mustered, holding the door open with one hand and pointing to my throat with the other.

"*You lost your voice?*"

I nodded. "I'm going to—" She finished my sentence, "go to bed?" I nodded again, collapsing into tears.

"*Oh, honey, what's wrong?*" she asked, covering me with her eyes and arms. That's when I finally pushed the words through my shattered voice, "*Lu, I can't be here anymore.*"

Chapter Nine

Novitiate

When Teresa asked how the visit to the Motherhouse went, I told her how lovely and hospitable Louise's family had been. The day after assembly I'd gotten an antibiotic, and my voice started coming back before our visit ended. I was afraid if I said anything else, I'd insult her and the order and be barred from novitiate. I was back to convincing myself that things would be fine once I got there, and that I was someone who got less choice about her life than others. I did ask, however, if we could postpone my entrance ceremony until after my retreat in August, which I was scheduled to go on with James, though she didn't know that. I also finally told her about the trip to the Bahamas that I'd booked for a week with Kara, which made her look at me with a mixture of surprise and hurt. Knitting her eyebrows worriedly, she said yes, we could postpone, but then a few days later—probably after she'd had a chance to talk to Louise and Arlene—she told me it couldn't wait: we had to talk. She took the small, utilitarian chair and gave me the roomy rocking chair the way she always did. She asked me what really happened. I told her that it wasn't the Sisters of Charity in particular but the fact that religious orders in general were aging that frightened me. She said that if I was happy about becoming a nun, my desire would override my worry. I'd feel as joyful as an engaged woman. "At this point you haven't formally entered the convent, so you're not leaving anything, but if you enter novitiate and leave there's…"

"Shame?"

"Well, not exactly shame, but it just becomes more difficult for everyone involved, especially *you*." Then she added gently, "Maria, I can't with good conscience recommend you for novitiate."

The sound of a rattling car engine rose through her bedroom window as I nodded. She was turning me away, granting me permission. I felt numb and then relieved. I blurted out, "Teresa, I felt so depressed around the elderly Sisters." As soon as I saw her face, I wanted to take it back.

"Be careful what you say to me, Maria. This is what *I've* given my life to."

"On no, Sister. I'm so sorry. I didn't mean it that way."

A week later, I was on Paradise Island with Kara. We were staying on Cabbage Beach, a three-mile stretch that was still healing from Hurricanes Dennis and Floyd that had hit the year before, though you'd never know it from the calm sea and level sand. One day walking back from the bathroom fixing the tie on my sarong, I stopped to absorb the scene—the Caribbean a beautiful blue-green mirror, bright red hibiscus and groves of casuarina trees growing in the sand, and a few yards away, my friend of thirteen years in a bright, coral bikini applying more lotion to her long runner's legs. I closed my eyes, lifted my face to the sun as I listened to the sound of children yelping as a winding slide spit them out like right angles into the pool. I was standing on billions of grains of sand that, although whipped by storms, had survived. Suddenly, a feeling of well- being and gratitude sprung up inside me. For the first time in years, I didn't dread my life.

Back from vacation and sitting in my room with the window open and the sun beating on me, I panicked: *I don't have a plan.* The day after I'd returned from the Motherhouse, I had called my mother and broke down, "*I don't know that I can go through with this, Mom.*" I could hear the oil bubbling in a pan on the stove, her hand probably suspended in mid-air with a spatula in it. She paused, and then said, "*Then don't.*" She told me I could move back home, a selfless offer given that she and Tom finally had the house to themselves. It'd be a huge step backward for me, not to mention that everyday I'd have to face her bulletin board packed with almost as many baby pictures as my gynecologist's office—everyone we knew was having babies. Yet, it'd give me time to figure things out. Teresa had told me that I could do another year of candidacy while I volunteered in a ministry, and, then reapply for novitiate, but I knew another year wasn't going to change my heart. I told her I'd think about it, because I didn't know what else I'd do. In the meantime, I called Father Dennis to ask him if I could make a retreat at the Monastery for a few days to help me decide. I knew they didn't offer overnight stays, but I thought he might make an exception. If he said yes, that would be my "sign" to cancel my retreat with James on Long Island; if he said no, it was my "sign" it was okay to go. I pretended I never had the harrowing breakthrough at the Motherhouse. When Father Dennis said, "No," I asked desperately, "What will I do with my life now, Father?"

"This is good."

"That novitiate's *not* working out?" I asked, naively surprised to hear it from a priest.

"Yes. Because it leaves you open to the next thing, which will be better for you. This is a very good thing. You should be happy."

It was similar to what Father Brian, a Redemptorist priest in his sixties, said when I met with him on the retreat I wound up on with James: God leads us *through* us. Fifty percent of discernment is figuring out what God wants us to do; the other fifty is a combination of our dreams and what our closest family and friends think. Everyone, except for James, said they couldn't envision me a nun. When I'd told James what happened at the Motherhouse, he winced, and then kept asking if I'd be ready to enter in a few months. He even asked Sister Erin, whom he knew from the hospital, if she could talk me into applying for another year of candidacy. "No," she said, "This is Maria's life." But I still felt called to celibacy and had a sense I was supposed to start some kind of religious order for unmarried people my age. The truth was I wanted to surround myself with people like me, so I wouldn't be alone. I felt drawn to the Holy Family and I thought a special devotion to them could help me and other unmarried people be chaste and happy. God was planting a seed for the ministry He had in mind for me, but He still had a long way to go. On this same retreat, James and I went to the beach twice in five days. We swam out to the deep where I wrapped my arms around his neck to hold me up, the both of us dewy and salty with ocean, he like a wet Adonis. He said, "If heaven is even half of what this feels like, I need nothing else." I stayed quiet, hiding just how turned on I was. That evening when he knocked on my door for dinner, he walked straight to my bed and lay down. "*James,*" I nagged. French kissing in the middle of the Atlantic was one thing. I wasn't about to upset my peace of mind more.

While he slept soundly four nights in a row, I was awake reading *The Unwilling Celibates*. It had found me in the reading room in an upright holder. The author Jean Sheridan borrowed the phrase from Dorothy Day's *Long Loneliness*. When Sheridan divorced in her forties, she found herself in a no-man's land. The invitations she used to receive when she was married stopped, or friends felt it necessary to invite a single male friend to their dinner parties, so she didn't create an uneven number at the table. It wasn't any better at church. Her parish no longer knew what to do with her, how to make her fit, so they did nothing. She termed it "benign neglect." I knew exactly what she meant. On the rare occasion when a parish did advertise something geared toward singles, it was one of those incredibly awkward dances meant to marry people off. Over the years, I'd gone to a couple and walked out as soon as I'd had a look around. Sheridan didn't wallow in self-pity, though. She cultivated what she calls "focused living," making single life meaningful by living it with intention: praying or meditating daily, developing a community of other single people, extending hospitality to others, living a balanced life. One evening turning excitedly to James who was holding the *New York Times* so high I couldn't see his face, I said, "This is a *really* important book."

Someone who knew what I struggled with, who was rising above it. It felt like some kind of answer. So did the note Sister Arlene left for me the day I went on retreat: Whatever choice I made—religious life, marriage, or single life—should be made freely, not by default. It *has to be* a fit, and it *has to* bring joy. There are sacrifices attached to every choice we make, yet we choose one over the others because we believe the benefits will outweigh the things we're giving up. After I returned from retreat, I knew what to do. I told Teresa, Arlene, and Louise that I'd decided to move back home. I hugged and thanked them for being so incredibly good to me. I told Teresa how afraid I was of the nothingness in front of me. She said, "When we're left with no answers, the richest, most significant things can happen." It was similar to what my mother said to me later that day over cappuccino. I told her that if the offer still stood, yes, please, I'd like to move home.

"How will I fill my days, Mom?"

"When you find what you're looking for, *that* will fill your days."

As we walked out of the pizzeria, she tripped and fell on a crack in the sidewalk just like she had one day when I was four and we'd been walking on 13th Avenue. As I bent down to kiss her and help her up, I asked her if she was okay, and she said yes, just a little embarrassed, and then, *"At least this time, you didn't walk away from me."*

***

I asked Father Dennis if the single life was really my only other option to becoming a nun. He told me about Secular Institutes, groups whose members are unmarried and take vows of obedience and chastity but not poverty. They live on their own, keep their paychecks, and meet with fellow members once a month to pray, study, and eat. It sounded similar to the kind of order I wanted to start that would bring single Catholics my age together to hear guest speakers on relevant topics, have some coffee together, and learn to be at peace. If I struggled, and Sheridan struggled enough to write a book, then there had to be other single Catholics who struggled too. I went from sharing my idea with Father to showing up to his office one day with statistics. Based on the US Census, 31% of men and women between the ages of 30-44 were single or single again, nearly a third. The figure was even higher for single people of all ages. More people were divorcing or marrying later, including Catholics; 40% of the U.S. Catholic population was single. There were groups in the Church for young adults and retirees but nothing for those of us in our thirties and forties. Sitting across from me in his black cassock with the fluorescent light waxing a glow on his bald spot, Father listened carefully, jotting notes on the agenda I'd prepared, a yes forming in his green eyes, but with one correction, "What you're describing isn't an order but a singles ministry. Besides, you don't want to exclude people who *do* want to get married."

I spent the next several weeks reading everything I could on Christian singlehood, but it wasn't until I got to Dr. Susan Muto's *Celebrating the Single Life* that I found someone who had chosen the single vocation. Other than the few unmarried female teachers I had in school—who were likely celibate but never said whether or not they'd chosen it—I didn't know anyone who had. Here was another Catholic woman who had written a book about it and was both fulfilled and honest about the struggle. It was more confirmation that, if lived for God and others, the single life is a vibrant and worthy path. I couldn't deny it; I was excited. I started drafting the mission statement for the Singles group and lining up guest speakers with Father's direction in mind, though I was still hoping most members would remain single. I also accepted an adjunct position teaching literature at the local Catholic university. I didn't want to teach, had no experience and was scared, but it fell into my lap, and I needed to make some money. Saints Vincent de Paul, Louise de Marillac, and Elizabeth Ann Seton followed me around the hallways in their long plaster habits as I pushed my queasy, over-prepared self through classroom doors, trying to look confident. I imagined "Betty" winking at me, cheering, *I didn't leave you*. I also started teaching C.C.D., religious education, to adorable second graders who would be receiving First Holy Communion. My life started to resemble Muto's, except I was still lying.

I told my mother that Father Infanzi and I were going to go out from time to time as friends, that we were going to the San Gennaro Feast in Little Italy. She stopped sweeping, looked at me as if she wanted to say something but was at odds with herself, and then resumed as I casually wiped my sweaty palms on the front of my jeans. The night we went, James waited outside for me the way I'd directed as I said good bye to Aunts Rose and Anna, who were over for dinner and whom I'd told I was going out with a friend. "Have a great time, *gioia*!" they called out as I waved to my mother and avoided Tom's eyes. At the feast, James zigzagged me by the waist through the huge crowd as we happily screamed over the noise. Then we ate dinner at a sidewalk restaurant where we ran into a priest he knew. He looked at us curiously but not unkindly as we sat and had a cappuccino with him pretending it was natural. Afterward James and I visited Most Precious Blood Church where we made our best-friends promise almost three years earlier. I watched as he played the strongman game, trying to tear my eyes from his bulging muscles as he hammered the lever, and it rose swiftly to the top and rang the bell. He reddened as I teased, "My, what strong arms you have!" Stuck at the top of the Ferris wheel, I kissed him on the mouth, and he pulled away nervously, which surprised and offended me. It was okay that a month earlier he'd shown up uninvited to Zack's 1st birthday party and embarrassed me in front of my family, but I couldn't kiss him fifty feet in the air where no one, including his priest-friend, could see?

A month and half later, James told his brother Steven

about us, and Steven called Monsignor Brennan to warn him.

"I'm calling Monsignor to clear my name," I said to James.

"No, Maria, don't do that." He sounded alarmed and intrigued.

"Oh, no that's exactly what I'm doing." All we'd done in the last ten months was kiss. Now his brother and Monsignor might think we were having sex.

"Who is Father Infanzi's brother to call you, a fellow priest, and malign my name?" I boldly demanded of Monsignor.

"James is not just a fellow priest, Maria. He's a friend. And his brother wasn't calling to malign your name. He was calling to warn me," he said calmly, which made me realize my foolishness. Before we hung up, he told me, firmly, "*You need to terminate the friendship.*"

After three years of doing everything I could to protect our lie, James gave us away in one phone call. He had to have suspected his brother would do something like this. He wanted to get caught. He was trying to tell the truth that he was unhappy and didn't want to be a priest, and I couldn't accept it. Yet, I knew Monsignor's words were God's and that they were for my good. I was determined to do better, be stronger. If James called, I was going to tell him I couldn't talk to him and mean it, but I wasn't going to yell or hang up on him. I was going to be a calm, cool adult. I was relying on my own willpower and trying to punish him. If I were serious about letting him go, I would have changed my number, switched churches, or at the very least taken a break from lectoring. I would've made a more complete confession the day my mother and I went on a pilgrimage to a Marian Shrine. The Pope had decreed that any Catholic who did so during the Jubilee year and went to confession within the octave was granted a plenary indulgence, which reduces a person's time in purgatory. I finally confessed that I had sex with a priest, but not that I was still in love and hate with him or that I felt jealous and insecure. Once I stepped out of the confessional, instead of the joy I saw etched into the stained glass windows, I still felt guilty and sorry for myself.

On Christmas night, I was at it with James again. Earlier that day after Mass I'd spotted a woman touching his elbow suggestively and him smiling at her. At least that's what I thought I saw. It could have been the state I was in, but it brought up all the suspicions I was trying to pretend I didn't have. When he called me that night to say hello, he didn't know what woman I was talking about, which only made me angrier. I hung up on him. He didn't call me back or pick up when I called him. He'd never gotten angry at me before not even for a second, let alone not call me back. I was so desperate that the next night I called him in Utah where he'd flown out for a few days to help Roger paint his house. He accepted my apology, but he still sounded cool, as if he'd decided he didn't need this from me anymore. I wrote him a letter asking him to please imagine switching places with me: he the single, inconsequential man in the pews on Christmas morning in love with me, the priest on the altar whom he cannot have, all the while surrounded by a congregation of families our age. Then after Mass he sees a parishioner flirting with me. "Add to this the sensitive makeup of a woman's heart and psyche, James, and that's how devastated I felt."

One night I dreamt that a group of people and I were hanging onto a kind of motorized monkey bars with our legs in a harness. I called out to James, "Join us!" He boarded the ride, but within the first minute, he let himself fall and got badly hurt. When we got off to make sure he was okay, he yelled at me, "I would have never fallen if *you* didn't push me!" There was a woman by his side who looked like me and was comforting him. Maybe those of us on the monkey bars were trying to let go of our wills in order to be serious Christians. If so, I was both them and the woman on the side. I felt terribly guilty for helping to defile James, afraid that all my nagging over the years helped him dislike women. The previous day at a Knicks game, which I agreed to go to because it wasn't at night, he said to me like he was talking to a two year old, "Now, basketball is that game where they get the round ball into the basket." Maybe he was trying to get back at me. In the parking garage, he took a big swig of mouthwash, which he kept in his glove compartment, and spit it out in a corner. Then he kept popping one breath mint after another like he was trying to cover something up. I thought the whole afternoon bizarre, but, except for giving him a couple of side glances, I kept my mouth shut, afraid if he knew what I really thought of him, I'd push him back into the arms of some other woman.

Even our phone conversations became more unsatisfying. I couldn't stand hearing about his insomnia anymore. I knew it meant he wasn't at peace. He told me that to try and relax, he'd imagine walking up and down the strip in Vegas looking at all the hotels. He tried to persuade me to go out west with him on vacation. "C'mon," he said like I was a drag. I brushed him off, but in my Valentine's card I wrote, *Dearest James, Until we're able to be in Las Vegas together, I hope this card will do.*

Then one night he asked me what I was wearing.

"What are *you* wearing?" I replied, shocked and hoping to make him uncomfortable, so he'd stop. It was the last thing I needed. Whenever a *"Do You Want Better Sex More Often?"* commercial came on, if I didn't change the station immediately, I'd have an all-out scene in my head.

"I'm wearing shorts. It's hot in the room. And a dress shirt pulled out and over my shorts. I don't wear pajamas," he said all in one breath.

"It's patronizing to be asked, right, as if you're being treated like an object?" I said my pulse thickening at the image of his loosened shorts.

"No. Yes," he caught himself. "But I asked you."

"I'm wearing pajamas," I said as flatly as I could.

"You must look cute," he said, and then gave up.

I started returning his calls by writing notes and asked him to do the same, which he did until the night of my first meeting of the Singles group in March. I looked out nervously at the sixty people and thought *I wanted a lot of people to show, Lord, but not quite* this *many.* The audience was mostly divorced women in their forties, but there were also men, as well as those who had never married, and a handful of people in their fifties who had disregarded the age cut off, because they were just as hungry as the rest of us. I explained that while I'd spent my twenties dating, I'd always had the feeling I was supposed to be doing something else. At first, I thought it was to become a nun, but then I felt the tug to start a group to help validate and inspire single Catholics. A few people looked at their watches, but most listened and nodded. I told them, "Our best shot at being happy single is to get closer to Christ. God is closer to us than we are to ourselves," as the picture of a stunned Mary at the Annunciation looked back at me. Then I opened the floor to hear what kinds of speakers and topics they wanted to have. An hour before everyone had arrived, while I was in the storeroom among the containers of salt and sugar packets, a gnawing sense of unease came over me. *You're going to confirm your singleness, take a step closer to God and the Church and further away from marriage? How mortifying. No one's even here to help or encourage you. You're alone again.* That's when Brenda, the Assistant Director who had helped me set up the cheese platters and wine, called over the intercom, "Maria, Father Infanzi's on line 1."

"I just called to wish you good luck. What you're doing tonight is heroic."

"*Thanks, James.*" It's what I'd wanted my mother to say. When I'd told her I was announcing the Singles group at all the Masses one weekend, she bunched up her face as if she were the one doing it and said, "You're really going to put yourself out there, aren't you?"

I continued doing things for him that I didn't want to

do like drive him to Kennedy Airport the weekend he was flying out to baptize his brother's daughter. The last place I wanted to be at five thirty on a Friday evening was the Gowanus, especially to help him get to one of his sibling's. Maybe if they flew out to visit him every once in a while, and didn't forget the anniversary of his ordination, he wouldn't be so needy and lusty. I resented him and them especially after I dropped him off and got so lost that I almost missed the exhibit I was headed to. An artist had painted a picture for each of the thirty-four cantos of Dante's *Inferno*, which was being displayed at a high school. It was my "Artist Date," a once weekly solo art expedition that Julia Cameron recommended to help kindle and sustain a writing life. I was bringing my copy of *The Divine Comedy* and was excited to take notes in the margins, but I'd never been on the Jackie Robinson before, and when I reached for my glasses in the dark, they were broken. Once I got off the exit, I couldn't read any of the street signs. I had no idea where I was going, kept taking random turns, panicking that I'd never find my way until finally I spotted the street I needed, and there in the middle waiting for me was *Christ the King*.

One day James was telling me about one of his friends he said I'd met before, but I didn't remember. "You know, the guy who looks like Jesus Christ." He said it as if Jesus were some far off stranger, not his friend and Savior, like he was taking his name in vain. It upset me so much especially given what was happening to me in prayer. I'd recently read that fifteen minutes of silence in front of the Blessed Sacrament after receiving the Eucharist is the most effective way to commune with God, so I started doing it five days a week. I also became a Eucharistic Guardian, someone who keeps Jesus company in the Blessed Sacrament one hour a week. When Monsignor told my second graders that they should go back to their seats after Holy Communion to listen for Jesus, their Prince in Disguise, the hair on my arms stood straight up. Then one day I heard Jesus whisper to my heart, *Please don't let this be in vain.* I looked up, startled but not afraid. I heard him twice more, the day the second graders received Communion and the following day when I brought four-year-old Nicole to Mass so she could see the children in their Communion outfits. As Jesus cleaved to the roof of my mouth, I heard him say, *Thank you for helping bring these children to me. Don't let this be in vain. Trust me. Thank you. Trust me.*

The Saturday of Mother's Day weekend when James and I went to lunch, and I kissed him goodbye on the cheek, I felt like someone was tearing off one of my limbs. Afterward on a walk with Kara, I wanted to tell her how much I was hurting, but by the time I got the nerve, she remembered that she'd put a bottle of iced tea in her mother's freezer and was afraid it would explode. I could have said, "Kah, no, wait, this is important, I need you," but I didn't. I'd never told her the whole truth about James. I'd have to explain the last four years. It was too complicated and painful. Later that night, lying on the living room floor watching *Return to Me,* tears slid down the side of my face making wet spots on the carpet while my mother and Tom were sitting on the couch behind me. It was one of ten movies I had to watch for a Christian screenwriting class I was taking in June. Bob, played by David Duchovny, loses his wife, whose heart is donated to Grace, played by Minnie Driver. Bob feels inexplicably drawn to her, and they fall in love. It was so beautiful that I felt lonelier and weepier. I called James. He was kind for the first fifteen minutes, but then he got tired and said, "I don't know what to say to you."

The next day my mother and Tom went to the eight o'clock Mass, which James was celebrating. I went to the 9:15, and when the priest asked all the mothers to stand for applause, I cried again. After Mass I picked up Grandma Giulia in New Jersey to bring her to Julie's for dinner. As soon as I saw her waiting eagerly at the kitchen table with her white beauty parlor hair and wide, childlike smile, I started crying again. Aunt Anna who knew I was struggling with my calling, but who was on her way out, gave me an enormous hug and told me she loved me and would say a prayer. Then she added, because she was worried I'd upset my family, especially my mother, "You're going to pull yourself together before you get to your sister's, right *gioia*?" Meanwhile, Grandma's face had turned from joy to sorrow. She looked at the plaque of the Holy Family on the wall and then at me and said tenderly and urgently, "*Vai sempre alla Sagra Famigia e il tuo angelo custode,*" always go to the Holy Family and to your guardian angel. I nodded my head, wiped my tears, and took a deep breath. At the end of the day, I looked at Grandma and said "*Mille grazie, Grandma. Ti voglio bene.*" She whispered in my ear again, "*Vai sempre alla Sagra Famigia e il tuo angelo custode.*"

The following day my mother asked worriedly if someone

had done something to me. I said no, explaining that Mother's Day without my own family was a little hard, and then I corrected myself, "It's *a lot* hard, but I also realize, Mom, how needy I am, and I'm trying to be stron—" I broke up in tears again. She didn't bring up James even though she was struggling with her feelings for him. A month earlier, she'd said, "I wish *all* priests were like Father O'Brien." He was conducting a Lenten mission at St. Stephen's, a tall, skinny man who wore a black cassock and long gold crucifix, and encouraged the congregation to develop a devotion to the Sacred Heart of Jesus. I don't think she fully realized that she was comparing James to him, but I defended him anyway.

"The priesthood is just like any other path or profession. You have some really good priests and some mediocre ones."

"I can understand having mediocre or ordinary priests but terrible ones?"

"You make it sound like you've known so many terrible priests," I said egging on.

"No, I guess just ones who aren't inspirational. You'd think the graces they received at ordina—"

"But grace only builds on nature, Mom, and if you have a weak nature then that's all grace has to work with," I said, making a ludicrous excuse. "Married people get graces from their sacrament too, and look at how many of them are doing such a great job."

Later that week at the mission, as my mother, Tom, and I were on line for confession James showed up to help Father O'Brien. As soon as he saw me, he turned bright red and kissed me. He didn't notice my family at all. I was so embarrassed, I said, "*I came with <u>my family</u>.*" He turned redder, apologized, and kissed them. After he walked away, my mother asked, "Is Father Infanzi annoyed with me and Tom?"

"No, actually he thinks you're annoyed with him." He'd recently told me that my mother had stopped kissing him hello after Mass. She rolled her eyes. "Don't get mad."

"I'm not getting mad. It's just that the last time we saw him he was abrupt with *us.*"

"Really? I think he just gets nervous. I'll talk to you more in the car, Mom," but then neither of us brought it up again.

A few days later, Nellie and I had the blow out of our lives. She, Brendan, and baby Zack had been living at my mother's since February and were leaving the end of May when they were moving to Maryland for Brendan's job. Zack was a year and a half, a replica of Nellie with the same *fungita* and mischievous blue eyes. If my mother wasn't first to get him in the morning, I'd go in, change his diaper, and bring him in bed with me where I spooned his warm body for as long as he'd let me. Nellie appreciated the extra sleep and the love. On the surface everything was fine, but I still thought of myself as the good, older sister and she the Prodigal daughter. Combined with the embarrassment I felt being thirty-two and living with my mother, especially with Nellie there, made matters worse. To compensate, I'd become something of a *mammarell'*, little mother, looking for small ways to be in control, to feel worthy. One day when she got home from visiting Janine, I asked "Is Brendan still at Janine's?" She was on one side of the counter, and I was on the other. My mother was at the stove, Tom was sitting at the table, and Zack was toddling around. I wanted to know how many to set the table for, but I also felt insecure that my sisters had husbands that brought them together.

"Why do you want to know? What are you going to do, write about it in your book?"

"What are you talking about? I want to know how many to set the table for. Why do you have to be so mean?"

"Ms. Holy, Ms. Holy, Ms Holy," she chanted.

"You want to see *fucking* Ms. Holy?" I'll show you *fucking* Ms. Holy, *bitch!*" I reached across the counter and slapped her face. She touched her cheek, stunned but smirking, which only enraged me more. I flew around the counter for her throat when my mother and Tom, coming from opposite sides of the kitchen, lunged in to hold me back. Nellie picked up Zack to make sure he didn't get caught in the crossfire and then looked me straight in the eye like she was using him as a prop, and said, "We're all supposed to suffer, because you're not going to have a family."

There it was: the truth. I had let my misery become a burden for everyone else. I couldn't handle it. The more I tried to break free, the more my mother and Tom tightened their grip on me, their faces puffed and strained with effort. I don't remember how they got me to calm down just that I was still waiting for my mother to defend me, but she didn't take either side nor did she get angry with me for my rage.

I couldn't help but think that my prayer and faithfulness to the Eucharist in the previous months had been a waste, as if I had accomplished it on my own, as if it wasn't all gift, all grace. If only I had kept my cool, I wouldn't have let Nellie win. If only I had kept my mouth shut and my hands to myself, if only I had said, "I'm sorry you feel that way," my voice perfectly calm and controlled, I would have won. I wouldn't be the wrong one. I wouldn't have to go to confession. It was her meanness and taunting that had brought out the ugly in me. She was the one who was wrong. For nights afterwards, I didn't sleep not even for a few hours. I'd slapped my sister's face. I'd yelled and cursed in front of my mother and stepfather and baby nephew. I let my anger and rage take hold of me. I harbored hate toward my sister. I couldn't see the wooden beam in my own eye. Deep down I wanted to be part of the bundle of sticks that Alvin Straight spoke about in the movie *The Straight Story*. When his children were young, he gave each one of them a stick and asked them to break it in two; then he asked them to take all their sticks, bundle them, and try to break them in half, but they couldn't do it. He said that family is like a bundle of sticks. Each member is broken, but if they love one another and stay together they're stronger than they can ever be individually.

At the end of June, Grandma Giulia died. Two days before, God and the devil had fought for her soul, and God won. One moment she looked so petrified—like evil was headed for her—that Tom jumped out of his chair and said, "*Ma, ma, what's wrong?*" which got my mother to notice. She wrapped Grandma's rosary beads around her hands, and we all began praying the Rosary. Within seconds, a joyful calm came over Grandma's face and remained there as she passed from this life. When James didn't acknowledge our loss, especially my mother's, I was furious. He once told me that he felt silly saying "I'm sorry," which I understood felt inadequate, but it wasn't an excuse to ignore someone's loss. What was the use of holding onto him if he wasn't even capable of saying, *I'm sorry that the most lovable person in your life died?* I prayed, "Lord, please keep my hand down when I'm about to call him. *You're* my best friend." I ignored his calls for several days trying to punish him until finally one day I picked up. The more he spoke, the more aggravated I grew. I didn't want to hear that he played "The Way You Look Tonight" forty times driving from Illinois to Kansas thinking of me, or what a wonderful time he had with his brother's family, or how difficult it was for him not to have his own. He was slipping further away from the priesthood. After I hung up, I wanted to throw something at the window. I begged, "Lord, please tell me what to do to have peace of mind. I'd do anything for it. I'd give up all my clothes in my closet for one dress, my habit."

I wondered again if I was supposed to become a nun even though I ruled out Secular Institutes, because I didn't want to be tied to a formal community. One day sitting with Sister Catherine, a diocesan Vicar of Religious, she told me, "Maria, you don't need a title to serve God. There are several women and men who have privately chosen the lay single life for the 'sake of the Kingdom.'" She was quoting Matthew's gospel where Jesus says, *Some... have renounced marriage for the sake of the kingdom of heaven. Whoever can accept this ought to accept this.* The only right reason to choose celibacy is to make a complete gift of self, as St. Pope John Paul II coined it. By renouncing earthly marriage, celibate persons can be a sign that the ultimate "marriage" and complete fulfillment of the human person come from union with God and service to others. It results from a person's free choice *and* from a special *grace* from God. In the truest part of myself, I wanted to give myself away, but I was selfish and looking for a way to legitimize my unmarriedness. It was as if Sister read my mind when she added that taking a public vow of celibacy has to be for the right reason. I asked with knitted eyebrows, "But is there a church document somewhere, Sister, that states that the single life can be a real, official way to give your life to God?" A week later, she sent me a copy of *Sharing the Light of Faith: The National Catechetical Directory for the Catholics of the U. S*: there are three vocations—marriage, religious life or the priesthood, and the single life—and their foundations are "laid and nurtured from early childhood on, though vocational choices are imminent in adolescence." She attached a note, "Maria, *please* be at peace with your single life."

In mid-July, my back went out again. This time a herniated disk was pressing on two nerves. The pain was so excruciating, I couldn't move, not even to the bathroom. The orthopedic surgeon said it was due to moisture loss, but I knew it had more to do with what Dr. Edward Bach said about illness: its presence can imply that a person is refusing to do what the soul wants it to do. It was similar to what my mother tried to tell me after she helped me move to her bed. She sat down on the edge of it, made her voice as tender as she could so I wouldn't snap, and said, "I think you're pulling yourself in too many directions. You're writing children's stories and now this screenplay when you really want to write memoir." I was lying on my right side to lessen the pain as a tear slid down my face. She was right. I was writing pieces I could finish faster, that I hoped would sell and make people admire me, but they weren't going anywhere and felt contrived. My poetry mentor had recently told me about an English PhD program that would allow me to write my memoir for the dissertation. I'd have assignments and deadlines and serious classmates to help hold me accountable. I'd finally be doing what I was meant to do, but I couldn't think about it. Why would I go through all the trouble of getting a PhD when I wasn't even sure I wanted to continue teaching? It would mean moving two hundred miles away from James and the prospect of a traditional life. What would happen when he didn't see my face from time to time? Who would he turn to then?

On vacation with his parents in August where his sexual frustration and insomnia were terrible, he punched a hole in the hotel headboard. His mother and Steven coaxed him into therapy and a priest-support group. They also told him to wear a scapular, a sacramental necklace with a picture of Mary and Jesus' divine hearts, which protects the wearer from the devil. He was eager and hopeful, but I knew he wouldn't be able to stick with it. Once he was home, I told him that except for written correspondence he couldn't be in touch with me. At first he got angry, "Have a nice life," but then he called back, "I want this to end on a better note, Maria. I look forward to spending heaven with you." For the first time in all the years I'd known him, he listened to me and didn't call. The next two times we spoke, *I* was the one to cave in.

The first time was the day after 9/11. Didn't he want to make sure I was nowhere near the Trade Center? (I was almost never near the Trade Center.) The day before, I'd called retreat houses, hospitals, and the high school where they'd taken in children who had been displaced from lower Manhattan schools, but they either weren't ready for volunteers or they had too many. I wanted someone of my own to force me to turn off the TV, which I watched for almost twelve hours as broadcasters interviewed people who held up pictures of missing loved ones. The story that most haunted me was that of a missing mother who was a paraplegic. The reality of a disabled woman struggling to get out of a building that was turning to ash made the tears pour from my eyes as did watching Father Mychal Judge's body being tenderly carried out by his firemen. James said that seeing couples jumping from the Towers with their hands held, he imagined that we would've done the same. Two weeks later driving up the driveway of the retreat house to meet with Sister Erin, I saw a long line of people holding sandwich bags with their loved one's tooth brushes and hair strands. It had become a center for the American Red Cross to test for DNA that could be matched up with the remains. As I passed them to get to Sister's office, I felt embarrassed to be headed for spiritual direction. After speaking for a while about the tragedy, she said, twice, "*If James loved you, he would have left the priesthood.*"

Did she know something I didn't? Was there another woman? I didn't want to know. As Sister and I continued to meet over the next several months, I didn't bring his name up at all. She advised me to pray, "Jesus, unbind me, set me free. Lord, show me *your* desire for me; help me to know *my* heart's desire," which I did. I took a hiatus from lectoring, so I wouldn't run into him. I stopped bringing a ton of books to prayer and prayed with just a few lines from daily Scripture. I went to my first healing Mass where I told the three ministers who were about to pray over me that I was recuperating from back pain and depression and trying to get over someone I was in love with for years. After they anointed my head and palms with oil and began praying over me, first in recognizable words and then in tongues, I dropped into their arms as if they were Jesus' and felt a warmth spread over my body. After this, I went back on the antidepressant that I'd come off of again two months earlier. I did the back exercises every day that my mother told me I must do in order to make a complete recovery. I started going out with friends more: brunches and musicals and pedicures. I called my father and asked him if he, Nonna, and I could go to dinner for my birthday. When the waiter took a picture of the three of us, and my father put his hand on my shoulder, I grabbed his hand, and he squeezed mine. Back at his house at the end of the night, he put out his arms and embraced me, said, "*Bella, Bella.*"

I rediscovered just how joyful and secure my childhood was—the bouts of uncontrollable, after-dinner laughter as my mother, sisters, and I sang and danced; my loving, colorful extended family gathered around our dining room table for my mother's lavish, five course Sunday meals, and, then, when he got home, my father's animated story-telling; the trips to Manhattan Beach all summer long packed with my cousins in the backseat of Aunt Anna and Uncle Dom's Cadillac, Carole King on the radio, then swimming in the salty ocean from 9 – 5 like it was a career. I reflected on how much I relished school and sports and Church: the echoing of hymns, the sweet smoke of candles, the running spring near Bernadette, the warm burn of Christ's blood in mine.

Sister wanted me to date, go out and have fun, make up for lost time. She told me that if I dated with my mind already made up that the single life is my calling, I'd never give marriage a fair chance. And she added that I had to be open to dating men who weren't as "prim and polished" as James. I nodded, thinking bitterly, *I know what my calling is, Sister, thank you.* I'd reacted similarly the day of Grandma's funeral when my older cousin John asked, "Are you pursuing a religious calling because you don't trust men, and your father wasn't there for you?" He might have seen me kneeling at Grandma's casket by myself and felt sorry and worried for me, but having to defend celibacy, especially that day, felt like more than I could bear. I shot back, *"Absolutely not,"* and then spitefully, because John had left Catholicism years earlier for a Protestant church, I added: "It's funny how many Christians don't understand the nature of a call." As the weeks went by, though, I wondered about Sister's and John's comments. Maybe I did have to make sure I wasn't afraid of men or intimacy. I let a friend set me up on a blind date, but when the guy didn't show, I couldn't be more relieved. I curled up on the couch to watch *It's a Wonderful Life* and longed for James.

I called him a second time. I had just gotten a month-long writing internship with a Catholic TV station, and I was thrilled. After three months of not talking at length, we spoke and laughed for close to an hour. A few days later he called to ask if we could go to lunch. The day after Christmas, sitting in a restaurant decked with garland, I buzzed about the TV station and brought him a book I wanted him to read, *God Underneath* by Father Ed Beck. It's a collection of memoir essays, including one about him fighting off the advances of a female parishioner and his reflection on how he contributed to it. I didn't tell James that I'd applied to the PhD program that would help me write my own memoir. One day at a reading, my mother had overheard a poet say to me, "*Apply with me.*" On the way home with the autumn sun shimmering through the Greenbelt, my mother said, "This would be the perfect time." I couldn't deny it. The chance of the internship becoming a job was incredibly slim, and there was no reason for me to stick around for an adjunct position. At first I was going to wait to find out if I was accepted before I said anything, but a couple of months later James and I went to see *A Beautiful Mind* in Manhattan, and I brought it up over dinner hoping he'd ask me not to go. I told him that if I was admitted, the scholarship would require I teach two sections of freshman English a semester but that I'd have Fridays off to write. I was careful not to show too much excitement as he chewed his Shepherd's pie. His eyes widened, and then when he was done swallowing, he busted out, "*A Phd*, Maria, a PhD, that's just great*!*"

"Is there any reason you can think of why I shouldn't do this?"

"Not at all," he said, shaking his head. "My uncle really regrets not going all the way to a doctorate. That's great. *That's just great,*" he repeated.

I nodded, put my fork down, and looked at the elderly couple sitting next to us whose silence I couldn't tell meant they were happy or unhappy. He was going to let me move two hundred miles away without putting up a fight? A few weeks later, I got the letter: a full scholarship and a teaching assistantship that would cover at least half my living expenses. It was the answer to a prayer I hadn't prayed, a blessing and push to move toward the future. How could I say no? I didn't tell anyone for a week, didn't sleep for days. In addition to having to move, I was afraid of all the work, anxious about what would be expected of me during and after the four years. I'd be leaving when Tom was dying.

He'd come home sick from a wedding in April and never got better. His doctor told him it was allergies. There were two malignant tumors on his lung, and the cancer had spread to his spine and right hip. When he and my mother got the results in May, and I saw the look on their faces, I pretended I didn't. At first, he went into the office for a few hours every morning and came home to the living room floor—because it hurt less than the bed—but soon he couldn't leave the house. By early June the cancer had spread to most of his bones. He lost thirty pounds, slept a lot, and was angry about his life, thought he'd been a failure. I felt terrible that he was dying this way and guilty that I hadn't been a better step-daughter. Whenever he'd gotten on his soapbox about politics or real estate, I stopped listening. I might have even walked out of the room a couple of times. For Father's Day I wrote him a letter telling him everything he meant to me. I reminded him of that night ten years earlier when I'd sliced open my finger cutting a Christmas tree trunk with a steak knife, and he drove over with a first aid kit. He nursed my wound, sawed the trunk to fit the stand, let me cry on his shoulder. I told him it was a great gift, a metaphor for our relationship. Anytime I was down, he tried to bring me up. "So, what's new in your young life?" Whenever I needed him, he was right there, the man who always made me feel treasured, and the only person who consistently tried to get me to come clean.

When James sent me flowers that Mother's Day, my mother had finally had it. "*What* is *going on with the two of you?*"

"We're just friends; he admires me," I said quickly, mustering nonchalance as my heart raced. After all these years of thinking I wanted her to catch me, now that she did, I felt stupid. She had a sickened look on her face, but she didn't say more. Maybe because she knew I'd soon be three hours away from him. And her husband was dying.

I taught a summer class and organized a fundraising-party for the Singles Group 1st anniversary. I dated two men for less than two months: Larry who I was attracted to even though he asked me to drive on the second date and Alex who I talked myself into being attracted to, because he did three hours of Eucharistic Adoration in the middle of the night. I still didn't know why I was about to pursue a PhD, but I couldn't argue that it was a God-send. Everyone was happy for me, especially my mother who, in the midst of her heartache, went around the house saying, "My daughter, the Professor." Nellie was happy for me, too. As ugly as our fight had been, it burst my decades-long resentment and forced me to look hard at myself. We apologized and started to move beyond it. I drove up to see the university and look for an apartment. I registered for my courses, including an autobiography class with a professor named Dale. She wrote a memoir about her troubled relationship with her mother, her struggle as a Division I athlete in the years prior to Title IX, and the sexual relationship she had with her coach. I started writing the first chapter of my book at the desk that Tom had assembled for me when I'd first moved home. Meanwhile he got smaller and sicker: the same man who had managed his sailboat with vigor, had served in the US Navy in Mine Warfare during World War II, who drank Herbal Life and cod liver oil straight from the bottle, and told me, "Your mother and you girls *made* my life."

A couple of days before I left for school, he said softly, "Your feelings for God are starting to rub off on me," grace and morphine flowing through his veins.

"Oh, yeah?" I said uneasily as I squeezed his hand through the bars of the Hospice bed. Where was the man who didn't understand why anyone would choose celibacy, who had once told me years earlier at a family party with two or three martinis in him, "You're too much woman to become a nun"? My mother had found him a good, kind psychologist, had made sure Monsignor brought him Communion every week, and had his sons over so they could make peace. He had abandoned and alienated them when they were young, because he thought their stepfather was a worthier father than he. "You seem different," I added.

"Tell me," he said straining his head off the pillow. A toothless smile spread across his face like a baby's.

"You seem more peaceful than even a couple of weeks ago. Dare I say, in case it hurts your male pride a bit; you're *softer*. Of course in a manly way!" I teased. I apologized for not being a better listener, more patient. He gave me the baby-smile again, and said, "Don't you worry about that." I reread to him the letter I'd written him for Father's Day, because I still wasn't sure that it had sunk in.

"Tom, I'm going to miss you so m—," I started to cry.

"I'm going to be with you. I'm going to be with you *more*," he said, bringing his head up only a half inch before he had to bring it back down. "When you call on me, I'll always be there. *Call* on me."

I nodded as the tears fell down my face. There was a part of me that wanted to die with him, that was still dreading my life, despite the beautiful revelation I'd had three months earlier. During a guided meditation for the Singles group, Sister Erin had asked us to imagine Jesus taking us up a high mountain and putting our hands out over our futures to bless them. Then she told us to picture Jesus giving us something to take with us before we left. The stone I'd had in my jewelry box since I was nine popped into my head. It had washed up besides my toes at my neighbors' country house one summer. When I bent down to pick it up, I couldn't believe it. Except for a tiny dent, it was a perfect little heart. I felt like God was telling me he loved me, that my future was love. Now I imagined Christ giving me back the heart of my youth. Then Sister told us to imagine Jesus putting his hand over our hearts and whispering, "The scars show where you've been but not where you're going."

I had the eternal love and protection of the Creator of the *Universe*, yet I was hanging onto a man I disliked more and more. A week earlier he'd been at my mother's to see Tom. He'd asked to come over. She wasn't going to tell a priest, even this one, that he couldn't visit her dying husband. Sitting in a rocking chair in the kitchen, Tom looked smaller than ever. He no longer wanted the shakes my mother tried giving him. The four of us prayed the Our Father holding hands, but James paid more attention to my red toe nail polish. When he playfully teased, "Not very nun-like," I replied, spitefully bobbing my sandaled-foot, "Yeah well, I *didn't* become a nun." We were infants in the presence of real adult love. My mother was God's instrument, and James felt it. When I saw him to the door, he said, crinkling his forehead, "From the moment I stepped into the house, I felt peace. That says everything about your mother."

"I feel the opposite of peaceful with you here," I said, trying to hide my anger.

"I know. I felt something similar when you were at my parents' for my birthday."

A week and a half later on a day that was overcast and

cool, as if summer had forgotten who it was, I left for school. I packed up my car and tinkered with my voicemail for a half hour until I got it the way I wanted. When I was done, I went into my mother and Tom's room to say goodbye. He was sitting up in bed, half lucid as my mother stood by his side, and Tara, the music therapist, sat on the upholstered chair holding a guitar on her thigh. I leaned my head against the door frame and watched silently, trying to hold onto the moment. Tara asked if Tom had any requests, but he couldn't answer. I said, "He's always liked show tunes. So maybe something upbeat?" As she began a lyric from *Showboat*, Tom strained his head off the pillow, looked at me, and smiled, *Thank you*. I looked at my mother and back at him, their holy love breaking my heart. Then, choking back tears, I walked over to Tom, and kissing his forehead, whispered, "*I'll always love you.*"

Chapter Ten

Exit Interviews

I.

Less than a month later, on an early Sunday morning, I got the phone call. "*Oh, Mommy. I'm so sorry,*" I cried into the phone. She had woken at three-thirty to check on Tom, his breaths shallower than ever. A half hour later, he was gone. Nellie was with her, and Janine and Julie were at the house by five. The four of them sounded like angels as they took turns comforting me over the phone and I them. When I hung up, I emailed my professors, packed a bag, and cried for the first hour of the drive home. I told myself that I wasn't allowed to cry for the rest of the trip, which I listened to until I got to the Poconos and saw a billboard for Herbal Life.

At the funeral Mass, Monsignor Brennan spoke about the deep look of peace on Tom's face the last time he brought him Communion. I gave the eulogy, a litany of all the people and things Tom loved. At the burial, an honor guard folded and presented the US flag to my mother while another sounded "Taps." My mother hadn't asked James to concelebrate, but he'd been at the wake where he sat on a love seat with my friend Liz, quizzing her about whether any men had tried to pick the two of us up on a Caribbean vacation we'd taken years earlier. It wasn't until Aunt Anna approached him and said, "Father, you *need to lead* the Rosary for the repose of Tom's soul," that he finally did so, but he recited it like an annoyed teenager antsy to get back to Liz. When Liz told him about her impending divorce and the new man she'd met, he excitedly suggested that the four of us go to dinner. I gave an obligatory closed lip smile—no way I was agreeing to that—and excused myself to greet family. Thank goodness my father hadn't shown up until after James had left. Bad enough my grieving mother and sisters had to see him act that way. The last thing I wanted was to have to introduce him to my father especially now in light of the Church sex abuse scandal, which the *Boston Globe* had brought to light in the past year. I was devastated that so many young people had been gravely harmed over the decades and that so many more could have been spared if the priests in charge had been the God-like men they were supposed to be. I was also really upset that a lot of people blamed celibacy for pedophilia.

Home again one weekend in October to run the Singles group, I avoided James' Sunday Mass. In early November, I cancelled our tentative plans to meet half way for lunch. I had a thirty page scene due to Dale the following week. I wrote about the New Year's Eve when I tried to break up with Dave and included a flashback to when I was eight and first felt the calling. Even if I had finished it, I didn't want to give up a Friday. I usually went to Mass and then settled in at the local bookstore with a café mocha and blueberry scone as I tried to wrestle with the truth. Dale told me I had summarized and needed to rewrite using scene and sensory details, so I got to work. She was a feminist scholar with biceps like concrete, four published books, and a husband who raised their two young daughters. She sat at the head of the conference table with no notes, just our text, *Tell It Slant,* and was thirty seven, only three years older than me. Although I was intimidated, I loved the class so much I sat up front and contributed all the time. One night while reading Gail Sher's *One Continuous Mistake: Four Noble Truths for Writers* as crickets chirped outside my window, I wrote in the margin, *I feel so at peace.*

My poetry professor M. was just as brazen and tireless. She had thirteen published books and students of all ages who adored her. For the first half of her life, she imitated the English Romantic poets. Then one day around forty, she woke up and began writing what she wanted to write: free verse about the tight-knit love she felt within her Sicilian-American working class home and the shame she felt outside it. She commanded us to go to "the cave," the dark part of ourselves that we hide from others. She got us to write deeply personal poems in twenty minutes, giving us five to ten autobiographical prompts to choose from. She expected us to read aloud what we'd written no matter how rough or raw, as she yelled at us to speak up because she was hard of hearing. At first I thought, *A poem in twenty minutes, is she kidding me?* but I felt so safe and at home that after several tries, I had something. I began writing poem after poem about Tom, including the one about the dream I had of him in a suit watering the lawn of my childhood home that he'd never seen. I wanted to hug him and yell, "Tom's alive! Tom's alive!" but as soon as I stepped toward him, he started to disappear. I couldn't let go of the fact that on the last day I saw him alive, I hadn't waited until the music therapist left before I said goodbye. I should have been around for him and my mother more. Why did I have to wait until he was dying to realize just how much he meant to me, to really show my love?

I made a friend, Lorraine, who I often went to Saturday night Mass and coffee with. She was chatty and pretty with shoulder length black hair and grey eyes. She hadn't wanted to get a PhD either, but here she was all the way from Houston excited about her dissertation on Christopher Marlowe. I admired her for relocating so far, but she said she had to get away; all her Mexican-American friends were getting married and having babies. I couldn't believe it. I met someone my age on the first day who shared my struggle. Squinting into the late August sun, I told her, "My dissertation is going to be a memoir about how I was going to become a nun but then I didn't and how much I struggle as a single Catholic." I added, "I can't believe I just told you that. I tell almost no one that."

"You sense something special about me."

"I suppose," I chuckled, caught off guard by her confidence.

"That's going to be a wonderful book."

I knew she was flattering me, but I didn't care. She was a sign from God that I was in the right place at the right time and that there would be readers for my book one day. I felt a little less alone, but also insecure. In our Dickens class, Lorraine came up with sixteen possible themes from the first ten chapters of *Oliver Twist*. I came up with one. It also took me over three hours to write a three and a half page response. I meticulously went back through the chapters, and then edited each of my sentences before I finished them. While Lorraine spoke nonstop, I half listened as I rehearsed how I'd word my comments when she was done, but then I let other classmates jump in, convinced that what I'd written was paltry and simplistic, and that as soon as I spoke, everyone would know I didn't belong in a PhD program. When we got our responses back, the professor said I needed to complicate my argument. I criticized myself: *I'm not really capable of deep intellectual work. I don't belong here. I'm not good or clever enough. What a mute.*

I was even harder on myself as a TA, teacher's assistant. The students' exceptionally high SATs convinced me I wasn't capable of teaching literature. I spent most of the time addressing their multiple writing errors. It took me an hour to grade two papers, twenty-five hours to grade fifty. With five papers of two to three drafts each required of every student, TAs had over five hundred drafts to comment on. Just when I was returning one set, I was collecting the next, but they kept making the same mistakes. I was pointing out too many of them. I didn't know how to focus on two or three of their most common ones. At the end of the semester, one of the student evaluations read, "I kept waiting for the TA to go into depth about the literature, but she rarely did."

I started praying a morning offering each day, "*Oh my Jesus, I offer you all my prayers, works, joys, and sufferings of this day in union with the Holy Sacrifice of the Mass throughout the world. I offer them for all the intentions of your Sacred Heart—the salvation of souls, the reparation for sin, the reunion of all Christians...*" I still felt lonely and frustrated. God wasn't beaming Himself down and curing my perfectionism and scrupulosity. He wasn't sending me someone special to absorb my fears and anxieties, someone I could rest and unwind in. Except for Mass, I wasn't spending quality time in prayer, giving myself a chance to be more deeply filled by His Son and Spirit. I'd stop going to Eucharistic Adoration, because the closest chapel was over thirty miles away and only open a few hours a day.

By mid-November, I was dying for sex. One night I was talking to my mother, hoping she'd detect my loneliness. I didn't want to tell her and burden her more; she was going through enough grief. Besides, what was I going to say, "*Ma, I want sex?*" I also didn't want to hear her say that I should think about meeting someone, because it would only hurt more. After I hung up with her, I called back, desperate, but I got a busy signal, which I took as a sign I wasn't meant to tell her. There was no one else I could call. My sisters and friends with kids were too busy and tired. Barbara had been burnt in the past, so I was sure she wouldn't understand, and Kara would probably tell me, "Well *then* meet someone, girlie." Even Sister Erin probably wouldn't have been helpful.

She would've insisted, "You're *not* called to celibacy, Maria."

On the day before Thanksgiving, I showed up at the hospital to surprise James, something I'd never done before. With no papers to grade for four days, it was time for me to relax and get a little attention. I looked the secretary in the eye and asked in my best professional voice, "I'm here to see Father Infanzi." When she asked if I had a family member in the hospital and I said, "No," she wouldn't let me in, said Father was busy seeing patients. A minute later, she allowed a former patient, a man, through. "Of course, sure, go right up," she said, "Father will be thrilled to see you." The words felt like a punch from God. I wrote James a note that I left with the secretary—*Don't ever accuse me of not trying*—and then told him on the phone later that night what "that" secretary had done to me.

"Ugh," he said, "I can't believe she did that," which didn't make me feel any better.

Two days later, we were ice-skating in Central Park. My mother had left the house early for a retreat, and Nellie and her family who had been visiting were headed home, but I still had James pick me up on the service road, so he couldn't ask to come in at the end of the night. While he and I were waiting on line and got into a conversation about childhood neighbors, he remembered the girl who lived two doors away. "Her name was Lainie. Come to think of it, I'm going to get in touch with her again," he said with delight as if he was imagining what she'd look like now. "Why in the world would you bring up another woman when you're standing here with me?" He blushed, said, "It's nothing like that."

In the rink, I proceeded as if nothing had happened, tying his skates for him and putting his hands on my waist so we could skate one behind the other. The following week a student asked me, "Did I see you skating at Central Park over Thanksgiving?" I looked at him calmly and said, "Yes, yes you did," but I panicked. *Does he know the man I was with is a priest? Does he know James?*

At Christmas, I was filled with more self-pity than usual. If Tom had still been alive, he would've lit up the outdoor smoker for the spiral ham while my mother made the manicotti, and then he would've mixed Manhattans, and asked me what I was having. I would've said, "Seltzer," afraid to blend holidays and alcohol, and he would've poured it in a wine glass for me with a twist and a smile. While I'd spent most of the morning in my bedroom crying like a faucet, my mother was downstairs withdrawn. She wouldn't let me help her with dinner. She missed my grandmother and Tom terribly. Toward the end of the day, I insisted on giving out goody bags to my nieces and nephews even though they were already loaded up with gifts and sugar. I was trying to win everyone's approval, make up for everything in me that I was certain was lacking, but I hadn't filled the bags with identical treats and when one of the kids starting crying, I grabbed the bag and flung it across the room. All five children looked at me startled and afraid. Julie pulled Daniel who was three, the youngest, away from me.

"You're going to pull your kids away from me? You think I'd actually hurt them after everything I do for them? Your stresses are the visible kind. Mine are invisible. I deal with them all by myself, but they're just as real," I yelled. All it did was make everyone gather their things as quickly as possible and get out. My mother didn't talk to me for days. She was angry that I wasn't grateful for all the blessings in my life, that all I saw was what I didn't have. She was so right, but I couldn't see. Except for scaring the children, I wasn't even that sorry. Now I had to apologize to their mothers.

After Christmas, the next time I heard from James was the day of the Space Shuttle Columbia disaster. It was also the 6th anniversary of our first kiss. He sent me an email telling me he loved me. I was ecstatic. For the next week I agonized over whether to send him a Valentine. I had this feeling he might not reciprocate. After all, how much longer before he realized I didn't want him and moved on to a woman who did? The readings in my Religion and Lit class didn't help. There was Plato: "Love... ventures to make one out of two...Each of us then is the matching half of a man. And everybody carries on an eternal search for his other half." And John Donne: "When love with one another so / Interanimates two souls, / That abler soul, which thence doth flow, / Defects of loneliness controls." But it was the Song of Songs that made me cave: "Let him kiss me with the kisses of his mouth – for your love is more delightful than wine." I gushed in my card, *I love you too, James; I always have.* I also made us homemade bookmarks from a greeting card that I cut in half—one side for him, the other for me— so that if someone found them after we were dead, they'd know we belonged together. At the end I added: it's best if you don't call me.

He didn't. Neither did he email or send a card. Valentine's Day came and went, and then another week and another with no word. There was no way he wouldn't respond unless there was someone else, but I convinced myself that he was playing by my rules again. Home for spring break, I tried to avoid the Masses he typically said, but I ran into him anyway two Sundays in a row. The first week he asked me out for tea. He was subtly distant like he was hiding something, but he was also apologetic for not responding to my Valentine and excited to hear about my courses. I told myself that I still made his heart stop and that God had allowed me to run into him, because He knew I needed to be reassured of his love. By the following Sunday, I was disgusted again. He *gets to be up there on the altar, but I don't? I'm never going to be his equal in the Catholic Church. The only person he loves is himself.* I wrote, *Trying to hold onto him to minimize the chance he'll hurt me is not real love or trust.* I couldn't even commit to paper that I knew something was going on. Home again for Easter, I let him cajole me into a nighttime walk in a park where he tried to fondle my breasts. I finally drew the line. I didn't acknowledge his birthday or go to his 10th ordination anniversary that St. Stephen's celebrated with a cake in the rectory. I started attending Mass at another parish. When my mother asked why, I told her I was staying away from James Infanzi. Surprised and relieved, she said, "Finally, good. He's all wrong for you. Selfish, immature. You need a man who knows what he wants," and then, "He doesn't even know his theology the way he should."

EH, my first autobiography professor who was still

mentoring me, recommended that I spend the summer writing about my experience at the Motherhouse. "The truth can never hurt you. It's fantasy that'll kill you," he told me. I wrote it on a post-it, taped it to my desk, and then went home for the summer. How was I going to capture a place I'd only been to once and admit on paper everything I'd felt there, including how angry I was at James? Instead, I wrote about the summer I turned eight when Nellie was born, and I lured Arturo, a shy, quiet boy in my troop, into a kiss. In writing it, I realized that I'd used an innocent boy, but I couldn't acknowledge that I was doing it again, this time to an exceptionally kind, introverted, and prayerful man named Mark who I'd met at the Monastery. I went out with him a couple of times hoping I'd grow attracted to him and forget James, but it didn't work. I thought about him all the time, especially when I was around couples. I wanted to call him so badly, hear his cough-y voice. When I got a birthday card from him, I decided I was going to call him. What harm could there be in getting a little comfort however fleeting? But I didn't have to call him. Three days later I ran into him at a baseball game with my mother's Italian club. She had gone to the bathroom when I looked up, and there he was.

"Get out of here!"

"Hi," he said, surprised but guarded.

"Get out of here," I repeated, unaware of the double meaning.

"I'm sitting on the other side with some of the men from the parish. I looked in this direction and couldn't believe my eyes. What are you doing here?" he asked, taking the empty seat across the aisle and crossing his legs to the side. Only half of him faced me.

"The same thing you are."

"How's school?"

"Well, I finished my first year."

"That's great. I'm sure you're doing great," he said, inhaling deeply.

"It's been nice to be home."

"When do you go back?"

"Less than two weeks."

"Happy Birthday by the way."

"Thank you."

"How was it?"

"It was a birthday." My mother had treated my sisters, four of my girlfriends, and me to dinner at a lake-side restaurant with velvet chairs and a jazz singer in the loft. We laughed, toasted, and ate really good food, but a few minutes after we were seated, the tent outside filled with a bride and groom and all their guests. For the rest of the night I felt them pressed against my back. It didn't help that I felt outside the conversation, which centered on the mean things that school kids say to each other. Except for Kara and me, everyone was a mother. At the end of the night, I felt so lonely, I didn't want anyone to leave, but I knew they had to get back to their families and that Kara would be too tired to stay out longer. As soon as I climbed into bed, I called her crying, trying to explain how I felt and apologizing for my ungratefulness. I still don't think I told her the truth about James. She tried to cheer me by telling me something cute her niece had said, but I didn't want to hear it.

"James, I was going to call you *tonight.*"

"You were?"

"Yes, I can't believe this. What a coincidence," I said, holding his gaze. "I really was going to call you. I know you probably don't believe me."

"No, I believe you."

"This is way too far away to be from each other," I said, motioning to the aisle of steps between us. "Move over. I'll sit next to you." I waited for the man selling beer to pass us and then scooted next to him.

"I've been praying a lot lately to Tom."

"For Tom?"

"No, no *to* Tom and to my uncle who passed away this summer."

"Oh, I'm sorry."

"Thank you," he said pinching the sides of his knee to get the crick out.

"I've been praying to both of them a lot."

"That's good, I guess," I said, puzzled but letting it go.

"Do you want to come sit near me on the other side for a while?"

"I –uh," I said, worried what my mother would think as I saw her returning. "Mom look who's here, Father Infanzi," trying to sound casual.

"Hi J—," he said, calling her by her first name, which always annoyed me. She deserved much more respect from him than that.

"Hi, Father. How are you?" the strained surprise all over

her face.

"I'm okay, thank you. And you?"

"I'm well," she said, heading to her seat. A woman not too far from her began talking to her. I excused myself and went to sit with James for a few minutes. It was the top of the fourth, the bases still pristine, the night cooling like a preview of fall. I shook hands with his friends, mostly grandfathers from the parish who politely said, "It's nice to see you."

"Do you want a sip of my soda?" James asked.

"Okay." I took the oversized cup from him. As soon as I tasted it, I grimaced and gave it back.

"Oh, right," he said laughing nervously, "I put some rum in it, you know just from those little bottles. I thought, it's a nice summer night, a little drink, not a big deal. Stopped at a liquor store on the way over. You don't like rum?"

"That's not it. I wasn't expecting it," I said feeling uncomfortable.

"Ahhh, what a great summer night," he repeated, stretching his legs out into the aisle. "The weather's perfect, I'm relaxed, I'm out with friends." I looked over to my mother who was no longer talking to anyone.

"James, I have to get back," I said, getting up to go but holding his gaze as if I were saying, *Call me.* When I returned, my mother was shivering, so I went to get her a cup of coffee on the other side of the stadium, and walking back, I saw James standing in a corner on his cell phone with his head bowed down, a sly smile on his face. The concession stand suddenly became dots in my peripheral vision as the coffee steamed circles into my dazed face. God was giving me another chance to face the truth. He was on the phone with a woman, the woman who was the reason why I hadn't heard from him since February. I still tried to deny it. *He always calls his father or one of his brothers when he's at a game, nostalgic for the past. Being a suspicious, insecure, nagging woman can turn a man who's not unfaithful into one who is.*

After the game, he called me twice, the following night and a couple of weeks later when he was driving back from a vocation night at the seminary for high school boys. He wanted to apologize if he had made me think he wanted to start things up with me again. He also wanted to know why, when we'd had sex, I wasn't willing to do certain things. He was trying to figure out if he could get me to do in bed the things the other woman must've been doing in bed—the one I pretended didn't exist—and whether I was worth considering when he left the priesthood. I was flattered and disgusted that he still thought about it all these years later, but once we hung up, I went back to my denial. *He's just trying to be a better priest.*

For the next four months we had no contact. I thought about emailing him a few times, but I always talked myself out of it. I wrote forty more pages of memoir for Dale, this time about James: how mesmerized I was when I spotted him greeting the little boy with Downs, how floored I was when he showed up in Admissions, how enamored I was at the Advent concert. I wrote nothing about my relationship with God or about my ambivalent feelings for James. I had completely forgotten that he'd forgotten me after bumping into me in Admissions. I wrote him so idyllically that the day it got workshopped, I wanted to tell my classmates, *Please don't judge or pity me.* They didn't do either, but Dale said, "I don't get the whole God-thing. Why don't you and this priest Infanzi get together already?"

Three days after Christmas he left me a message. He sounded like he had something to tell me. I waited two days before calling him back, but he wasn't there and I didn't try again. The next time I heard from him was the middle of January, a few days before I returned to school. At first we were both cautious and cool, but then one of us said something sweet, and we started finishing each other's sentences and chuckling. He didn't say there was anything new, so I was relieved until the following night when he called again. It was about five o'clock, that time in winter that Grandma Giulia always used to say is when *mi scura u cori*, the heart goes dark. He asked me twice if we could get together, there was something he wanted to tell me. I said no, tell me over the phone.

"In June, I'm taking a leave of absence from the priesthood."

I dropped my head in my hand, felt my stomach bottom out. Even though I'd always known, it felt tragic. "What? How long will it last?" I played dumb.

"I'm saying a leave of absence, because that's the first step, but I don't," he cleared his throat again, "think I'll be returning. I struggled mightily in deciding whether to tell you, Maria. *Mightily*, but I didn't want you to find out from someone in the parish."

"That would have been horrible."

"I could get a gut ache just thinking of it. And you know

how people talk."

"This is a lot to take in," I said, still standing, afraid if I sat, it'd sink in more.

"I've been very unhappy for a long time. I haven't slept well since I first set foot in this place. The lack of sleep has been ruthless. The sleeping pills, going to bed anticipating not being able to sleep, the anxiety over the anxiety of not being able to sleep. Just staring wide-awake and then having a full roster of sick calls the next day. It's been brutal."

"I know," I said, softening my voice, understanding a little better. "You've talked about it a lot."

"It just hasn't gone away. And the men here? Not one who's a real man. They make fun of people, of women. No one here is a priest for the right reasons. Either they love the power, or they became a priest because they had no other options."

"It's like you couldn't find one friend at that rectory. Maybe if you could have, maybe if you found even one man who was around your age and your sensibilities, you'd st—"

"What?"

"No, nothing."

"I went on a retreat in the fall with Father Benedict Groeschel, he's...."

"*I* know who he is," I said getting smug. I read his *Courage to Be Chaste*. People shouldn't choose marriage or celibacy, because they're afraid of or look down on the other vocation. They should understand and value both in order to make a good decision between the two.

"He assured me there's more than one way to serve God,

233

to build up the Kingdom."

"Yep, there is," I said getting angry. Every time I heard a lay person use the phrase, they were usually referring to how marriage helps build the Kingdom. Heaven forbid I ever heard anyone say that the single life can too.

"I don't want to be one of these priests who's duplicitous."

"No, of course not," I said, partly sarcastically.

"I'm convinced it was the loneliness that made me an insomniac."

Was. I bowed my head again, gripped the rim of the bureau, heard myself ask, "Is there another woman?"

"Not another woman. Just someone," he paused, "I've gotten to know this year."

Over the years, he'd always told me that he could never find anyone like me. He looked around all the time, compared me to lots of women, even those who'd show up to the rectory with their fiancés. Now he'd found her; he was leaving the priesthood for her, a woman he might have known for less than a year when he supposedly loved me ever since "he was a little boy." Maybe if I had immediately responded to his email in February instead of waiting to send him something in the mail. Maybe if I had ignored my conscience and invited him to come see me at school or indulged his need for attention all along this wouldn't have happened. He was going to wind up married to her, and I was going to wind up single forever. He didn't say anything else about her, and I didn't ask. All I could say was, "I see."

"If you change your mind and want to see me to talk, call me."

"No. Give me a day, and you call *me*."

The next day I walked around the Monastery in a robotic haze. I was doing a mailing for the Singles group, which was painfully ironic enough. Two volunteers started talking about whether priests would ever be allowed to marry. It was all I needed to hear. What if James left for this woman, and then one day priests could marry and he'd be able to return to the priesthood married to her? He'd get both, and I'd get nothing. There was no way the Pope was going to allow married priests unless there was a priest-convert from another denomination who was already married. Even if a Pope down the road did allow it, I don't think a man could leave the priesthood and just come back whenever he pleased. Besides, it sounded like he wanted out altogether. I called RF to ask her if she thought I should see him. Because I still hadn't told her the full truth about our relationship, she said, "Yes." When James called that night, I should have set him free, wished him a good life. I should have asked for and accepted God's grace and strength. Instead I fell into Satan's trap again.

The next night we met at a chain restaurant much closer to home than we would've dared in the early days. I made sure I was late. I walked alongside the restaurant toward the entrance and saw him through the glass, the butterflies speeding up in my stomach. There he was with his tall man's body and face like a *puer aeternus*, eternal boy. I rapped on the glass three times to get his attention, but he didn't notice, which frustrated me especially when a couple our age looked directly at me before realizing I wasn't for them. Once I was inside, we leaned in sparingly and kissed each other on the cheek. He looked as handsome as ever.

"You were trying to get my attention weren't you?"

"Didn't you hear me?"

"I thought I did, but by the time I turned around it was too late. You were gone," he said, as if he detected the irony.

A young waiter grabbed menus and led us under a canopy of Tiffany-style lamps passed two tables packed with teenagers to a booth in the back. He left the menus on the table and told us he'd be back to take our orders.

"I can't stay long," I said.

"That's okay. I don't have a lot of time either. I'm saying the 5:30 Mass. I said my Rosary on the way over here."

"*You did?*"

"Yes, I was very nervous about seeing you, said, 'C'mon God, help me out here.'" We took off our coats, fighting to keep our eyes off each other's bodies.

"Tell me again why you're still single?" he asked.

"I guess I'm very specific about what I want. We're going to talk seriously, right?"

"Yes."

James ordered the veal capriccioso, changed his mind to the penne puttanesca, and then changed his mind a third time. "You know what? he told the waiter, "I'll have both. I'm really hungry. You can bring them out together, because we don't have a lot of time." I ordered a lemonade. I hadn't been able to eat or sleep since his phone call.

"I don't mean to sound like I'm in control here, but after I leave it's either going to be you or her."

"Really? Wow. As if you're the only one who gets to

make that decision," I said hiding the extent of my hostility. I should've walked out.

"If you ceased to exist this very moment, I would still be leaving the priesthood," he said, lowering his voice, looking around.

"That's a lovely way to put it."

"You know what I mean, Maria. One of my friends just became a pastor. I've spoken about him to you before. He lives in a rectory by himself. I'm looking at my life. I don't want that," he said, wrinkling his face. "When I was visiting my parents this summer, they told me they want to leave their new house to me. I don't want that. What's a man going to do with a house by himself? And there's another priest I know who was recently admitted to the hospital, because of his drinking, but no one's owning up to it. I'm convinced it's the loneliness of celibacy that made him drink."

"You're going to talk to me as if you have the patent on loneliness, James?" I wanted to throw my water in his face.

"No, of course not. It's just that I didn't have the same sense you had not to enter the convent when it didn't feel right. I'm convinced I went into the priesthood, because I was in med school and didn't want to be there but didn't know what else to do. Because my family is so religious, when I passed the Catholic Church every day I was certain She was calling to me. It seemed the right way out," he said and then paused. "Being celibate your whole life is so unnatural."

"You don't have to tell me, but so is being married to the same person for life. Marriage has its things, too, you know. Someone could get married and then the spouse gets incapacitated somehow," I said, desperately. "Or maybe not even something so extreme. There are no guarantees." It was okay for me to have to stay in the struggle with celibacy, but he got to walk away from it, from the Church, from me for good? Where was the man who once told me that the crucifix in St. Stephen's bothered him because it made it look as if Christ was hanging neatly? "His body should be dragging miserably," he said. He seemed so genuinely disturbed that it made me look closer. Was even that a lie?

"Does the priest scandal have anything to do with this—like it's hard being a priest at this time?" I asked even though I was pretty sure it didn't.

"No, I've been feeling this way for a long time. My family thinks my soul's in danger. Steven is even threatening to call the bishop."

"You can't stay because it's what they want," taking a sip of water before I changed my mind.

"I appreciate you saying that, Maria."

"Even if he did call, the bishop can't stop you, can he?"

"No, it's not that. I don't want anyone to know. I'm like you. I like my privacy. I want to wait until my last day and then tell the head chaplain, because the nurses," he paused. "They love the rumors."

It's one of the nurses.

"Penne puttanesca and veal capriccioso for you," the waiter interrupted, placing both dishes down in front of James. "And I'll bring your lemonade right over," he said looking at me. James salivated as he moved the pasta to the center of his setting.

"What ever happened to 'You're the only woman I'd ever leave the priesthood for?'" He looked around to see if anyone heard me. "I'm not lowering my voice one bit."

"There are not too many girls, women, like the two of you. You're both very lady-like except she's very… *strong-willed*. It's an interesting combination," he said, arousal sweeping over his face as if he just pictured her naked. "I wasn't looking for it. We knew each other. I had no idea she was so interested. I can be really naïve sometimes." He took a forkful of penne and chewed happily with his mouth closed like a perfect gentleman as I seethed silently. The fact that I didn't force him to leave the priesthood for me and didn't continue sleeping with him made me *weak* willed? "I would say more, but at the moment I want to protect her."

"Protec—protect *her*? Are you kidding me? What about *me*? You've know her for *a year*," I said, though looking back, it was probably longer; I didn't want to know. "You and me, it's been seven years," I added raising my voice, shaking my pointer finger wildly in his face. "Do you have any interest in protecting me? Yeah, you know what, I'm going to walk out now, and when I do, I bet you won't run after me, because you have never once fought for me," I said melodramatically, reaching for my jacket, bluffing.

"I won't, because I'm not going to make a scene," he said as if he was enjoying finally having the upper hand. "I didn't mean for any of this to happen. After I saw you at the base-ball game I tried to break it off with her, but she called me an impossible number of times a day, and the other nurses noticed how depressed she was becoming, not eating, that I felt bad not to go back to her. It was part chivalry, part weakness on my part. I called you that night when you were back in school, because she put me up to it. She could tell something had happened to me at the baseball game, so I told her about you, that I'd seen you at the game. I wasn't the same for a while, Maria. That call was about me trying to forget about you, but can't you see that it didn't work, hasn't worked?"

I put my jacket down. "That night I was naively thinking that you were trying to be a good priest, but really you've been getting some this whole time."

"You don't have to say it like that," he said blushing, creeping closer to the table and looking around.

"I'll say it anyway I like. And besides that's exactly what it is. Getting some. You think sanitizing your language changes the truth? You don't think *I* couldn't convince you that you don't have a vocation?" I said leaning into the table, pressing my fingers tighter into the fake wood. "You don't think I couldn't use my body, this body?"

"Of cour—," he laughed nervously.

I touched the base of my water glass, my lemonade never having arrived. "But that wasn't my place. You had to want to leave," I said, pretending it's what I wanted. "Do you love her?"

"Let me not answer that now."

"Oh, really?"

"What about you? Let's talk about you. What do you want?"

There it was: the most important question, the one I was dodging, so I could continue playing the victim and incriminating him. Even though I still felt keenly alone at times, I was slowly beginning to appreciate my solitude. Being single allowed me to pick up and move, to take a giant step closer to what I'd wanted to do ever since I was in third grade—write. Most times I liked coming home to my apartment, unlike all those years earlier when the silence paralyzed me. I had a long way to go, but I was starting to trust God's will a little more and mine a little less; I was reaping the gifts. Imagine when I gave myself to Him completely? It was like the inscription near the little-boy-Jesus statue in St. Agatha's: *The more you honor Me, the more I will bless you.* But if I said this, I'd be admitting that God is enough, that I didn't need James or a sexual relationship to be happy. I'd be letting him go to her, which I wasn't going to allow—at least not without a fight.

"I don't know what I want yet."

"You once said having kids is hard."

"I think it is hard." I had finally started waking up.

"Do you want kids?"

"I've never stopped wanting to be a wife and mother." It wasn't untrue. St. John Paul II called it the "spousal order" – giving ourselves for the other in a total and undivided manner, whether to one's spouse and children or, if celibate, to those who come into one's life, loving someone for who they are and not what they can give us. I wanted to be that kind of woman. Anytime I cared for one of my nephews or nieces or listened to someone who needed my time, I was a spiritual mother. Anytime I sat in Adoration or worked on the Singles group or taught or wrote from my heart, I was a spiritual wife co-creating with the Holy Spirit. As much as I would've cherished my own kids, I knew I didn't need them to feel fulfilled.

"There's something else I want to discuss. It's important to me."

"What?"

"How do you feel," he looked around and then leaned in so no one would hear, "Would you have sex any way other than the traditional? You seemed uncomfortable in the past."

"You haven't seen me in *five* months." *We haven't had sex in over five years.* "You're bringing it up this way? Couples grow into these conversations, James, if they even have to have them at all. "

"I'm not *not* going to discuss it. We're both adults. It's very important to me. All these husbands who say my wife won't do this, she won't do that," he added with a look of disgust.

"If I were secure in the love, there'd be no issue. If it's okay with the Church," I added, which was somewhat of a cop-out. The Church doesn't forbid any marital sexual act as long as it's open to conception.

"What about money? What do you think you'll be making when you graduate?"

"I use the figure I was making when I left career development four years ago and add on cost of living increases. I don't need more than that." I wanted to spit in his face. "*You?*" I said brightly.

"I want to do something with hospital administration, that much I know. But sometimes I think it might be fun to open my own pizzeria."

Fool.

"As long as I live I will never forget what it was like to look at you at that baseball game, Maria, especially before you had seen me, because you were disarmed. You looked so beautiful. I couldn't get you out of my mind."

"Thank you."

"What are you doing tonight?"

"My sisters and I are going to see *Cold Mountain.* It takes place during the Civil War."

"I heard about it."

"I like movies like these, because they fill in gaps in my knowledge," I said, slipping, but then catching myself, "I have to get going. What do we do now? Live our lives?"

"Yes. And maybe you can start browsing houses upstate."

"I will." I wasn't.

When I got home, he called to tell me that he felt an abiding sense of peace, that I was going to hear from him, and that he loved me. I told him I loved him too. He also said I should call him sometimes, that he needed to know that I wanted him. A week later at school, I called him at midnight on a Friday, testing to see if he'd be home. He wasn't. I tried the next morning but got his voicemail again. He returned my call that night, but I didn't know until the next day, because I'd been on the phone with a school friend Gloria crying over him. I knew that he had to have been with the other woman whose name I still didn't want to know. Gloria had recently told me that a man who she'd been involved with over twenty years ago had resurfaced. He had since been married twice. Every time he came around for her she felt as if she was being tested by the devil. The same thing was happening with me. I had allowed Satan to lure me into this triangle. When James and I finally spoke, he told me he couldn't get me *or her* off his mind and that he couldn't proceed with either of us until June when he left, which I knew was a lie. I told him, "You should really come see me."

The next morning after celebrating the seven o'clock Mass, he drove the nearly two hundred miles to my place. Dressed in jeans and a white, cap-sleeve shirt even though it was freezing out, I was vacuuming the apartment when he called to check if he had taken the right exit. A couple of minutes later the phone rang a second time. "I love *you*," he said. "*What?* I just told you that I love *you* but only after I had hung up the phone," I said, stunned, still clinging to the idea of a fateful synchronicity between us. I had no idea that he thought he had just dialed *her*, that he had told her that he was driving up to break things off with me. Greeting each other at the door, we kissed, but I stopped before he could put his hands on me. I'd closed my bedroom door before he arrived, because I didn't want him to see it, let alone go in. After lunch in another dim chain restaurant where I told him I was afraid about him leaving the priesthood, he said, "*So am I.*" Once we returned to my complex, I saw it—a pink, crumpled up tissue in the compartment of his car door—proof that this woman was real and that she was probably suffering. I acted like I didn't see it. He nudged me and winked, "Let's go upstairs for a quickie." "No, James," I said careful not to sound too exasperated, but I let him up for a few minutes. After locking eyes and kissing, I told him I'd let him go until the end of June, but God help him if he continued to see her. I pretended it wasn't a useless demand as he looked away from me. At the very least, I'd make him feel as guilty as possible.

On the phone with him a few times over the next few months, I allowed myself to think I was winning. Then on the Friday before Palm Sunday, I drove in the middle of the night to surprise him at his morning Mass. He was shocked and distracted the whole time, which should have made me feel guilty but didn't. Afterward he cautiously greeted me with eyes that were as blood shot as my own and a kiss on the check. At the diner, I got stared down by the waitress while he got "Good morning Father," and "How are you Father," and "Can I get you more coffee Father?" which nauseated me. Neither one of us said a word about her. I knew if I brought her up, he'd get that horny look on his face confirming that he was still sleeping with her. Two days later on Palm Sunday, my phone rang at four in the morning.

"Hello?" I asked startled.

"You don't know me."

"*Who is this?*"

"Marcia, the person James is having a relationship with," she whispered.

"What?"

"I have to know now if he does this to every woman. I have to know if he is evil. I was with him last night. He made love to me."

"Is he there with you *now?*" I cringed.

"No, of course not."

"Why are *you* calling me, telling me this?"

"Because then he got strange right afterwards and I knew, I just knew. I asked him, 'She's in town isn't she?' The two of you had breakfast Friday morning."

"How did you get *my* number?"

"I'd rather not say."

"Well I think you better say. Did you steal it from him?"

"No. You and I have a mutual friend. The two of you went to school together."

"Who is it?"

"I don't want to put her in a bad position. She gave me your number. It was very innocent," she pleaded, lying, though I had no way of knowing. She'd called the Monastery posing as someone interested in the Singles group and convinced the elderly monk at the desk to give her my number. "Does he do this to everyone?—If I hear my husband's footsteps I'll have to go," she added sounding scared.

"You're *married?*"

"Yes. But I found out recently that my husband has had indiscretions, several. So now he leaves me alone when he knows I'm going to see James. And I have to whisper because I'm in my son's room. I don't want to frighten him."

"You have a son, too?"

"Yes, he's nine. I have to put the nail in the coffin. How does he do this, a man of God? A man of God, how?"

"This isn't God, Marcia, this is James. There's a difference," I said, my edge melting a bit. She sounded fragile like a small bird or a tea cup. I imagined her with light hair and eyes and fine features. For the next half hour, I let her tell me her side, which I knew I needed to hear: James had initiated their relationship, not her. She had gone to him for counseling, told him how dead she felt inside, and that she and her husband had nothing left. Then one day he reached out and touched her, and looking in her eyes, he said she could feel alive again; that's when she knew he had intentions. After he saw me at the baseball game, though, he was different toward her. She knew something was up so he told her about me: we had fallen in love six years earlier but didn't pursue each other because I was becoming a nun. We'd only slept together a couple of times, and he always felt like he had to walk on eggshells around me. He told her that she looked as young as I did even though she was six years older. The morning he drove up to see me at school in February, he was driving to break things off with me and calling her to tell her he loved her. He had only dialed my number by accident. She would've never become intimate with him if she didn't think she and her son had a future with him. She even had her fertility tested, because she knew he wanted to have kids; she had the eggs of an eighteen year old, she added. She had already met his family. He told his father and brother he was going to marry her.

I dropped down on the bed as the streetlight forced its way in around my blinds. It was more deceitful and hurtful than I could've imagined. She was married with a child. He had ridiculed me to her. Yet, I didn't cry, not a tear. "Marcia, he didn't break anything off with me that day. He told me that he loved me. When he dropped me off at home after we had had lunch out, he nudged me in the car, said, 'C'mon let's go upstairs for a quickie.'" I didn't admit to her though that the visit was my idea, that I was trying to keep him from her.

"He loves the chase," she said.

"I would agree."

"I told him that he hates women."

An overgrown pine brushed against the siding, and the chimes sounded from the back patio. Maybe that's why he was so turned off by the priests he lived with—because they reflected him? I still couldn't accept it. Hadn't he loved me at all, ever?

"You know there have been others?" she asked.

"Not others plural, just the single mom."

"There's been more than her." Then she added with, what sounded like spite, "And people in the parish know about you."

I bowed my shaking head in my hands, imagining what people must have thought of me who had seen me on the altar lectoring and receiving Holy Communion. I felt ashamed but also defensive. Who would they be to judge me especially if they were happily married?

"How does he do this, a man of God? A man of God, how? I look at the cross and I get sick."

"Are you spiritual, Marcia?"

"I used to be."

"Jesus isn't doing this to you," I said looking at my favorite picture of Christ that I had hanging on the wall. He's wearing a white robe bunched loosely around his collar, has a neat beard and shoulder length brown hair, and his face looks sun-burned as if he'd spent a great day fishing with his friends. At first glance he looks casual, but his eyes are searching me with a tender and intense love, the very same love he has for Marcia and for James. He hung on the cross for each of us, loves each of us as, St. Augustine said, as if we're the only one. But I thought I was better than them. No matter what James thought, she and I were not similar. She was married with a child, having an affair with him, and pathetically calling me, whom she had never met, to cry over him. As for James, he was the worst excuse for a human being; I was *nothing* like him.

"Are you still in love with him?"

"I, uh. Yes, I am."

"After six years?"

"I know."

"And in that six years, there hasn't been anyone else who you…You run a singl-, a singles group, Christian singles and there's never been anyone?"

"Not anyone *I've* wanted to be with, Marcia," I said, my pride back.

"No, no of course, that's what I mean. I'm sure there have been men but no one you want?"

"No." There was no way I was telling her I still felt called to celibacy, that she could have James.

"How could there be such a thing as true love if someone like you is alone?" she asked sounding afraid.

I stared at the pile of mail on my bureau that went from being the neat, symmetrical pile my mother had left with the catalogs on the bottom and the bills on the top, to the way it was now that I'd gotten my hands on it, an inverted tower about to topple. The red-lit digits of the clock read almost five. I wasn't alone. I was loved for all eternity, but I still believed that God was giving me little choice about my life the way He had Jesus, that He didn't really love His only Son. I still couldn't see that I had set myself up for exactly this. Who was this woman to pity me? I wanted to tell her off. Instead, I said gently, "I wouldn't base your life on me, Marcia. I'm unusual. Either you and your husband will find a way to reconcile, or you'll divorce and meet someone new." Before we hung up I also told her that she and I had to let James go, a united front. I challenged her to have the same strength and resignation she heard in my voice. It would be the perfect ironic punishment if we both walked away from him. I asked if she could do it. She repeated, "I uh, I have to. I have to put the nail in the coffin," but then she said, "I have to go. My son is starting to stir."

II.

I told myself that once James knew that I knew everything, he'd feel so remorseful and angry at Marcia for hurting me that he'd write her off for good. He slept with her again. I finally yelled, "DON'T *EVER* CALL ME AGAIN!" Racked with contempt, I wrote "The Fact that Someone Like Me Isn't the Clear Choice," a rant of all the ways I thought myself superior to him and her. I was angry at myself but wanted revenge on him. I considered contacting one of his high school buddies who lived nearby and had recently broken up with his girlfriend. What poetic justice it would be if I started dating him. A month later on James' fortieth birthday, I was in so much pain thinking of him and Marcia having sex that I called RF for an emergency session. I told her everything that had happened over the last six weeks. I might've also finally admitted that I'd slept with him. After apologizing for telling me in January that I should see him, she ordered, "Go online right now and search narcissism." The list of characteristics included: exaggerated need for attention and validation; envious; a lack of responsibility, boundaries, and empathy; and persistent feelings of fear, anxiety, and shame. Some of it sounded like me. When I got to the end of the list, though, a light went on: *closely associates themselves with people and institutions they perceive as superior and authoritative.*

I closed my laptop, feeling a little better, when I heard my neighbor moaning through the walls. At first I thought someone was hurting her, but then I knew better. Horrified, I covered my ears and ran into the bathroom, but I could still hear her, so I fled to my bedroom, and shut the door, but her deepening pleasure chased me down until the sound of her climax shattered throughout the apartment. I screamed "*Aaaaaaaaaaaah*" with tears streaming down my face, certain that the devil had found a way to make Marcia's orgasm reach me from a hundred eighty miles away. I wanted to hunt the devil and James down, grab them by their skeevy throats, throw them against a wall, watch them choke in my hands.

I finished the semester with heightened intensity. I resumed writing—a chapter titled "Fort Lee" about my initial meetings with the nuns and the angst I felt visiting the convent the first time. I was more determined than ever to get the memoir done and finish my doctorate. There was no way I was allowing him to get in the way of what I was supposed to do with my life. I wasn't going to be thirty-seven with no manuscript. I was going to start being really honest about everything and tell the whole truth of how horrible James Infanzi had been *to* me. I picked up *Love Hangover* by Shewanda Riley and Germaine Hawkins, unready for what she had to say: "Ask God, 'Show me *me*' not, *'Why did he do this to me?'*"

The weekend before Memorial Day I went on a Singles retreat led by Father Ryan, a brisk, forty-something Jesuit priest who was so kind and down to earth, I told him about James and how I'd lied to my family all these years. He listened without judgment, and told me that when someone begins to discern a religious calling, it's not uncommon to fall in love. Maybe he was speaking from experience. Either way, it made me feel less odd and ashamed. I also told him that I felt called to the single life, but that I wasn't happy. Crossing his legs, he leaned in and asked, "Does your family have anything to gain by you remaining single?" which made me pause. All these years, I'd been angry at them for my calling, but no one expected or wanted me to remain unmarried. In fact, if I continued to be troubled about it, they'd have nothing to gain. I was of course free to make my own choice. My mother especially wanted me to be happy. I looked at the crowded bookshelf, and then at him and said, "No, Father, there's nothing for them to gain." It was as if a lie had left my body. Then he gave me absolution and encouraged me to come clean. The next day, before I poured cereal into the bowl, I said, "Mom, I need to talk to you."

"What is it?" she asked, perking up like the morning

glories on the porch.

"Father Infanzi is leaving the priesthood at the end of June."

"What!"

"He's probably leaving to marry a woman he's having an affair with. And there have been others. He's had affairs during his priesthood," I repeated as if I needed her to ask.

"What about you, Maria? Did *you* ever have an affair with him?" she asked looking in my eyes.

The images of James and me especially from that first year flooded me: he and I on my couch sometimes until four in the morning, then a few hours later him handling Christ on the altar with me sitting just a few feet away, me knocking on rectory doors on Monday morning to get rid of the choke on my soul, acting in front of my family as if I was doing nothing wrong. I no longer wanted to bear the weight. "Y—yes, I did Mom."

It was the moment when she could have gotten indignant and angry. Instead, her face softened easily, quickly. Then she said the words I needed to hear ever since I was eight, "It's okay, Maria. You're only human."

"Oh, Ma, I'm so *sorry* for what it caused you and the family," I said breaking down, my eyes swelling with tears.

She got off the stool and took me in her arms as if I were a little girl again and had hurt myself. At sixty-three with her hair almost all white, she looked like the female face of God. All these years I'd behaved as if her love for me was conditional. Now I knew how wrong I was. I was so grateful, so relieved, that I felt as if I could finally breathe. God had forgiven me a long time ago, but it was my mother's mercy I'd also desperately needed.

"I want to call him," she said, the gentleness in her face replaced with vindictiveness, as if she were trying out for a part in a movie.

"Mom, no."

"Why not?"

"Because knowing him, he'll actually feel flattered by the attention. He'll love getting it from you, even this kind. What you'll try to do by reprimanding him will be lost on someone like him."

"I still want to call."

"Mom, don't please."

"Tom knew all along."

"Knew about him and me?"

"He couldn't stand him. Thought he was doing a number on you. But I didn't believe it. Turns out Tom knew more about things than I ever wanted to give him credit for," her eyes filling with regret. "He wanted to talk to you about it. But I begged him not to say anything, because I didn't want him to accuse you of something I didn't think you were doing. Besides, I was afraid to confront you, Maria. You were not at all easy to talk to," she said, straightening her back. I winced at the truth. "Are you going to tell your sisters?"

"Yes. I just wanted to tell you first."

"I think it'll be a good step in taking responsibility for all of this."

"I know."

"Janine was angry with you. She felt she was the one

who had found Fath—" she said, catching herself, "Infanzi, and how she thought she found a friend. She felt you stole him."

I nodded but thought, *Why was she the only one allowed to need him?*

"But all this aside, this is reason to rejoice. It's finally an ending," she said relieved. I knew she was right, but I was still afraid. Now that I was telling my family, I could no longer fool myself. If he showed up one day and begged me to give him a chance, I couldn't, at least not without alienating them all over again. Janine and Julie pointed this out very clearly two weeks later around my mother's kitchen table as the sound of an ice cream truck came through the screen door. I told them everything from beginning to end except, instead of saying I had sex with him, I implied it. I was afraid of angering and disappointing Janine, whose face tightened as soon as I said his name. "I'm so sorry for not telling the truth sooner. I'm sorry for everything I've just told you and anything I haven't." Julie said, "It's as if the convent didn't stand a chance because of him." I reassured them that he was ultimately not the reason why I didn't become a nun.

"You're going to have to stay away from him; you know that, right? He's toxic," Janine said, her nostrils flaring. My mother was quiet. Julie winced. I was saddened. This was the man whom Janine once said would've made a wonderful husband, who teared up when a handicapped boy who had been blessed by the Cardinal broke out into a glorious smile, who always spoke to the one person in a room who nobody else bothered with, or at least that's what he told me he did.

Where had that part of him gone?

"Are you still in love with him?" I think it was Janine who asked.

"At this exact moment, yes. But I believe that's changing. I know that's a strange way to put it, but it's what I feel is happening. I know I can let go of him. I just haven't chosen to do so until now. "

"It's good you've told us, because now you know that if you change your mind about him you won't have our support," Julie added. Then as we said our goodbyes around the counter, she added, "It makes me sad that you went to that restaurant in January knowing what he had done to you." She was right of course, but I wanted to tell her, *Easy for you to say.* I still felt sorry for myself. I was also still trying to deny my calling. In fact, I had a date later that week with a college instructor named Leo who I'd recently met at a Catholic mixer. We were going to Domenga's on the ocean to eat paella and drink sangria. I fantasized running into James there in his Roman collar and introducing him to Leo—"Oh hi, *Father;* this is *Leo*"—as I tossed my hair over my bare shoulder; then when he was seated at a table with a parishioner-family and couldn't keep his eyes off me, I imagined Leo kissing me on the mouth. I prayed, "Lord, if there's something blocking Leo from calling me, please remove it. It's already June 4, Lord. *Please.* I want to have a *good* summer." He called the next day and asked me out for the following weekend. Three days later, when I was in Manhattan interning, God found another way to remind me of my calling.

I'd planned on going to noon Mass at St. Paul the Apostle, but I was running late, so I walked around Lincoln Center instead. The relief and gratitude I felt for my family's forgiveness—Nellie, too, had been understanding—bubbled up in me like the fountain outside the Metropolitan Opera, which I walked close to so I could enjoy the spray. Continuing past the American Ballet, I heard the beginning of "New York, New York." I followed it north where Juilliard, the NY Public Library for the Performing Arts, and the Metropolitan Opera converge, and sat down at a table where people didn't look like they belonged to each other. The orchestra was a high school troupe from the Midwest dressed head to toe in black and white except for their cummerbunds that stood out like bright purple dashes across the stage. Their conductor was also all in black, his back to us, his fingers dancing methodically in the summer air. When they were several chords into their next song, I listened harder to confirm I wasn't mistaking it, but sure enough, they were singing the "Prayer of Saint Francis": *Oh, Master, grant that I may never seek / so much to be consoled as to console / to be understood as to understand, / to be loved as to love with all my soul. / It figures,* I thought lovingly, *I didn't make it to Mass, but Mass has made it to me.* Then, when they were done and the throng of us applauded, the conductor turned around, and there, wearing a white clerical collar was a Roman Catholic priest.

Chapter Eleven

Dream

It was no surprise that Leo or the two other men I dated over the summer didn't work out. I used them to avoid my vocation and then got angry when they stopped calling, the same thing I let happen with James *again*. He'd said his last Mass, got a job at another hospital, and bought a house, though he hadn't started the process of official dispensation from the priesthood. He told me that he was taking the next year to fix his life, begged me to please give him a chance, that things with Marcia were "dead." I knew he couldn't mean it, that even if could, there was my vocation, but I didn't tell him yes or no. I still couldn't bear the idea of him married to someone else. A few St. Stephen's parishioners who knew nothing about my involvement with him said to me, "You know he's leaving the priesthood for someone? The rumor is he's getting *married*." Maybe, just maybe, I thought, if he never brought Marcia or any other woman to his new house, he and I could have a clean, fresh start.

Over the next six months, I heard from him twice more:

at Christmas, when he sent me the same boxed card and generic letter he sent to all his friends, defending his decision to leave the priesthood, and a week before Valentine's Day to tell me that I hadn't heard from him, because he was still trying to get his life in order. I knew he was sleeping with her again. I wrote back, "It's over for good."

Five weeks later on Holy Thursday at the Triduum retreat, I was sitting on the floor of the chapel, as close to the empty tabernacle as I could get, feeling incredible peace. I was reading Debra Farrington's *One Like Jesus: Reflections on the Single Life,* a small, beautiful book about all the brave single people in the Bible beginning with Jesus and how single Christians are *not* alone. I looked up toward Christ on the cross, and there was James.

"I thought you said you were going to leave me alone, that I wasn't going to hear from you ever again," I said, feeling the same attraction and anger as always.

"I meant it at the time."

"The reason I can't be with you, James, has more to do with my own calling than it has to do with you," I finally said. "I don't think becoming a nun or a priest is the only way for an unmarried person to give their life to God. I think a single person can do the same." I still couldn't say, *It's what I want.* Then he started telling me how beautiful I looked and how I never change. I talked with him for close to an hour, alternating between being sarcastic and sweet, telling him about my school year, how I had passed the first of three field exams and was ready to take the second, to which he gave me the same flirtatiously proud grin he always did. "When was the last time you were with her?" I quickly changed my mind, "You don't have to answer that."

The next day during spiritual direction with Sister Erin, she said that my remaining there with James the previous night was a form of aggression, a way of getting back at him. Of course it was, but I still wasn't fully aware of it. "You don't think that's what I was doing, do you?" I asked RF during my next session. "It's not only aggression," she said, "You're a woman and want to feel desired."

I hated myself for regressing, for letting him believe that the door was still open, for hurting myself again. I knew that letting go meant making it impossible for him to contact me, but I still didn't do it. I even asked him for copies of some of his homilies to help me fill in details for the memoir. He sent them all, and I went through them all: reliving his handwriting, his words, and the tone and gestures that had accompanied his delivery. I mailed them back to him at the hospital. There was no way I wanted his home address—to picture the street, the house itself, the woman he had over.

Nellie giving birth in June to her second child, a delicately beautiful baby girl Eliza, triggered my jealousy again. When my mother pried it out of me, she said, "*You're mean,*" which stung almost as much as it had twenty-nine years earlier when Nellie was born. I told her I was seriously considering going ABD, all but dissertation. As I got closer to finishing, I was afraid to have PhD after my name and to be moving even further away from having my own Eliza.

"*Yeah, and if you don't finish, you'll find a way to blame me for it,*" my mother retaliated, the truth shocking me back to my desk.

In August, the two of us took the trip to Sicily that I'd wanted to for years. It turned the summer around. We sipped champagne and espresso and ate mouthwatering food with women friends we met from California and Australia. At the Doric Temple, on a miraculously crisp day, we took long strides up ancient steps and walked among the ruins close to the edge of the hill overlooking Segesta; I put my hands on the columns that had been built five centuries before Christ and felt *new*. Then in the small town outside Messina where my mother lived her first eight years, her cousin Filomena took us up the two-and-a-half-mile hill to *campagna*, where my grandmother, grandfather, and Aunt Anna used to make the trip by foot with sacks of grass on their heads to feed the animals, no matter the weather. My mother and I rode standing up in the back of her wobbly, wooden pick-up, dressed in Sunday clothes because we'd just come from Mass, clutching the sides of the truck, laughing. At the top, we stopped in the courtyard of a church that had a charming view of the village below with its maze of old, curving, cobble-stoned roads. Filomena, who had just met me, said, "*Statti vergine pu Signuri coma mia, ma su fai fallu volontario,*" Be a virgin for the Lord like me, but if you do, *choose it freely.* I smiled less uneasily than I would've a few months earlier.

Back at school that fall and looking up the call number for *The Lonely Crowd*, a study that I thought would help refine my last field exam, I saw James' name appear in my email. I ignored it and wrote the next section of the memoir, fifty pages about the eight months from the night I ran into James at the baseball game through Palm Sunday when Marcia called. I titled the pages "Exit Interviews," painting myself as the innocent victim and the two of them as over-sexed culprits. The following month when he showed up at my apartment, I finally let him go, though not without one last battle.

It was a Sunday night, and I had just gotten back from a weekend home and was pulling out laundry and books from my trunk when I felt someone behind me. I turned around, and there he was in long shorts and hooded sweatshirt, look-ing more like a shadow than a man. He had left the city while I was still there and had spent the previous three and a half hours roaming my apartment complex, going back and forth to my floor to make sure I hadn't come in from a differ-ent entrance. The night before, driving home from a cousin's wedding and seeing the Verrazano Bridge come into view, he decided his coworker was right—why was he waiting until I graduated in May to ask one last time?

"*James?*"

"I don't want to scare you," he said, putting out his hand as if trying to protect himself.

"I'm not scared."

"Can I take a couple of steps closer to you?"

"I didn't say you couldn't." I was trying to act cool, but I was shocked and gratified that he'd made the long drive. As he stepped under the lamppost, I could see he was due for a cut and shave, that his eyes were red.

"If you think you see greys here on the sides of my head, you're wrong, it's just the way the light's hitting it."

"Funny how that works."

"I'm losing my voice, so I'm not operating from a place of strength."

"Good."

"While I was waiting for you, I saw a couple walk by, and my heart sank because I thought the girl was you. Then I thought to myself, *Who are you not to want this for her?* Please just give me a second. How was your summer?"

"Good." *Should I say I was in Sicily?* "I was in Sicily."

"Really? Were you there for your birthday? How was it?"

"Yes. Very good."

"I just have to tell you even if it makes you mad. You look so *beautiful* tonight."

"Thank you." *Even after having sex with her every weekend, he still wants me.*

"Maria, you don't know how difficult she's made it for me. Today alone she called me fifteen times. *Fifteen* times. It was something I should've never gotten myself involved in. I know that now, but I was feeling lonely knowing you were over three hours away. You're the only girl I've ever loved. Even if you let me walk away, it won't change the fact that you're the only girl I've *ever* loved."

"When you barged in on me Holy Thursday while I was on retreat, I had every right to lash out at you, demand that you tell me when the last time was that you slept with her, but when you said 'I'd rather not say,' I let it go. This time I'm asking until I get an answer. When was the last time you were with her?"

"A month ago," his face reddened. "You don't know how

difficult she's made it for me. My friend Tony—you know Tony? He says it's like the movie *Fatal Attraction*. I hadn't seen or talked to her in three weeks and then something good happened to me, and I wanted to share it with someone."

A small, low flying plane whirred above us, its lights blinking in the direction of the local airport. A month ago could have meant either thirty days ago, or, because it was the beginning of a new month, two days ago. 'Something good' probably meant that he won big at Atlantic City or golfed another seventy. Neither scenario dawned on me until he was gone.

"I only came here to tell you what I'm hoping for. I'm going to leave. Now it's completely up to you. Thank you for hearing me out," he said turning to go, hanging his head. If I had asked the Holy Spirit for courage and meant it, I would have let him go. Instead, pulling out my overstuffed duffel bag and struggling to get it over my shoulder, I said, playing my old role, "I'm supposed to keep letting you walk away from me James? How many times are you going to keep making this so hard for me?" which got the response I knew it would, "Maria, let me help you with that." At first I overdramatically refused, "I've been unloading my car by myself my whole life. You think I can't do another night of it?" But then he asked again, and I gave him the bag, and grabbing my laundry by the neck, I led him up to my apartment where he asked to come in for ten minutes. We sat on opposite ends of my couch, the same pink leather one on which I'd lain with him all those years ago. He told me a story about a day when he and his brothers were young, and their father had hired someone to take them fishing, but the man's motorboat broke a quarter of the way out. The man begged James' father to let him make it up to them the next day. His father didn't trust the man or his boat, but when he said, "Please, everyone deserves a second chance," his father felt bad. The boat worked perfectly the next day, and they had a great time. "Can't you give me that same second chance?"

"Second chance, James? *Second* chance? Try, the twentieth chance. Besides, this is not a boat ride. This is my life."

"You're going to stay single, Maria, and I'm going to wind up with someone who's not for me?"

"You're starting to sound like those people who over the years when you were a priest said to you, 'What a waste.' You believe I'm a waste if I don't get married?"

"*No, no,*" he said nervously. "About a half dozen people have given me the phone numbers of women they think I'd like. One of the people who wants to set me up was on the phone giving me this woman's number, and the husband shouted out in the background, 'She's gorgeous.'"

"Wow, these people didn't skip a beat when you left the priesthood, huh? You're telling me this why?"

"I'm telling you, because I haven't been able to call any of these women because of you. Tony tells me that when it comes to business I should follow my head, but when it comes to these matters, I should follow my heart. James believes this too," he said pointing to himself. "But I need to be held," he said crossing his arms snug across his chest, "like a baby, and I'm not going to apologize for that. If it's not going to be you, it has to be someone. Just so I don't eat dinner alone on Friday nights, just to have someone to talk to."

I looked out my sliding glass doors to the row of apartments facing my unit. *This is your last chance,* a silent whisper nagged. *He will not be back after this. He will wind up with one of those new women or back with Marcia. You will be gone, out of the picture. People from St. Stephen's will talk about him and the woman he marries as if you never existed. If you choose him, you'll finally vindicate yourself. You'll have a tall, handsome husband, a gold ring on your left hand, a place in the world. You'll no longer have to walk into every occasion by yourself, deal with people's silent pity or curiosity. You'll no longer be the only one on both sides of your family who never married. You'll be explained. There's no sense or use being celibate if you're not a nun or a priest. You'll have the chance to live the picture you've always wanted to be in. Once you're married and having sex regularly, you'll be able to heal him.*

No, you won't, the other side fought. *You won't be enough for him, just like your mother said, and he won't be enough for you. You marry someone because you love and trust him and want to spend your life with him; you don't get married to give you a place in the world. God has already done that for you— Jesus has. You're a daughter of the Most High God. This is the title that matters the most. You may want to believe you can heal James; he may want to believe you can heal him, but you can't. Only Christ can heal each of you.*

"I've been faithful to her."

"To who? To Marcia? I'm supposed to feel good that you've been faithful to her."

"I just want you to know that I didn't sleep with anyone else since I've been with her. You've made me so happy just sitting here talking to you," he jumped. "*This* is what a man needs. I asked Matt several months ago if his cousin could prescribe sleep aids for me again, so I could be faithful to you."

"Meaning that you can't fall asleep at night without sex?"

"It's not the sex. It's being next to someone."

"James," I said trying to be patient. "I run a singles group, and while I don't know everything about everyone who comes through the doors, I'm pretty sure no one needs drugs or sex to fall asleep at night."

"An anxiety set in for my mother, too."

"What?"

"When my brother Christopher was little, he almost swallowed a chipped tooth while he was in the dentist's chair. The dentist was able to get a hold of it before it went down, but in that moment when my mother thought my brother might choke or worse, something was set off in her. From that point on she became anxious, unable to sleep like me."

"Anxious about things that had nothing to do with your brother having been in danger but were just triggered by it?" I asked, trying to understand.

"Yes. She was the same age as me."

"James, I'm so sorry, but I can't do this anymore. If you came here tonight and told me that the last time you were with her was March or April when you saw me last, if you had never brought her to your house, if I was the only woman you'd bring there, then maybe I could think about this, but I can't."

"Then what if I show up again in April and am able to tell you I wasn't with her or with anyone in six months?" he pleaded.

"But it's not just that. It's also what I tried to tell you on Holy Thursday. I'll say it again. Maybe being a priest or a nun is not the only way to give one's life to God. The single life can be a vocation too." I still couldn't say, *It's mine*, even though I was enjoying more peace and freedom. Just that day, driving Route 80 belting the lyrics to Mercy Me's "Imagine," about seeing Jesus face to face one day, with the enormous Delaware River on one side and a rugged rock wall on the other, I was overwhelmed with awe and gratitude. I felt God's largesse. He was, is, *my* rock, bigger and stronger than any of my fears or sin. As I continued driving, I looked forward to the solitude of my apartment after a busy weekend. One of my poems about my father had won an award, and I'd been invited to read it along with the journal's other contributors. My mother was in the audience smiling uncomfortably, because she was in the poem too, but she clapped proudly. Afterward we went to five o'clock Mass and then for Chinese, where we ordered the Happy Family that she insisted on paying for. The following morning, this morning, after a breakfast meeting with the Singles group planning committee, the five of us lingered, drank lukewarm coffee, and pulled our chairs closer to the table, taking turns talking and listening like a family.

"Maria, please don't tell me no. Not tonight. If you have to say no, just wait to tell me another day," he said, shaking his head. I'd never heard him sound so desperate and afraid. I felt as sorry as I had that night when I was nine, and my father showed up at my and Julie's bedroom window begging us to let him back in. My mother had locked him out of the house plenty of times, but this time she changed all the locks. He called out, "*Belle, Belle, Figlie Miei*," beautiful daughters of mine, tapping his thick, calloused fingers on the window between the bars that he had installed a few months earlier after a robber had broken in. I woke up, but Julie didn't, not even when I repeatedly called her name for help. I felt horrible pretending I was asleep especially when Papa finally walked away, and I heard the crunch of leaves beneath his rubbery work shoes. I worried where he'd go, where he'd be without us, his family. Maybe some of it was my fault. Maybe if I hadn't needed my mother so much, they wouldn't have fought so often. I felt so much guiltier about James. I had lured him and used him and kept him dangling. I was a liar too. I had to stop. If I really believed what I say I believe, that Christ rose on the third day, that his horrific death was not in vain, if my religious faith meant anything and I wasn't simply talking the talk, then it was time for me to set him and me free. But I didn't want him to get into an accident on the way home, so I saw him to the door and promised I'd call him with an answer soon.

I put on Joel Osteen, the TV evangelist, who talked about having to let go of yesterday in order for today to be a true beginning. I decided that the following day I would skip classes to scrub my apartment, including the outside of the windows, which I hadn't cleaned in the three years I'd been living there. Then I went to bed where, in a fitful sleep, I had a multi part dream. In the first part, a pair of supervisors from my apartment complex, whom I'd never seen before, sighted James on the grounds and had come to my door like some strange combination of investigators and EMTs. They placed me on a gurney and asked me how long I went out with the man who had been spotted. "That's just it, we never got to go out with each other, not in a normal way like a real couple," I said. "That figures," they responded. Next, they sealed my body in plastic bubble wrap and wheeled me outside where they removed me from the gurney, attached me to the top of a high tree, and told me to jump. I was terrified, but I jumped anyway, and once I hit the ground, I was safe and free. I walked over to James who was talking on his cell phone with his back to me the way he had at the baseball game. Then the supervisors held up a picture of James' license plate in front of me as if they were giving me a number in a line-up, holding me accountable.

I woke up suddenly, startled by the image of myself trapped in thick plastic, thinking about what James had said, that he hadn't spoken to Marcia in three weeks but then something good happened and he didn't want to be alone, and she wound up going over. I fumed, the room stifling hot even though summer was long gone. I begged, "Jesus, Mary, Joseph, please help me get back to sleep," and then again a half hour later until I was eventually calm enough to drift into the next two parts of the dream. I went with James to a hearing in a courtroom that looked like a funeral parlor. There was a woman there to facilitate his dispensation;

James said she was his aunt, but she was too young to be. At the end, the court reporter handed me—not her—the transcript, and then suddenly a group of First Holy Communion children in white shining garments burst into the room and circled me with joy. In the final part of the dream, I was in a room sweeping what looked like black beads but felt like bugs pouring down on me from the ceiling. Squirming, I thought they'd never end, but after a couple of minutes, as a new and final batch was about half way to the floor, they shed their cocoons, and big, beautiful butterflies fluttered all around me.

In the morning with the dream mostly a memory and my feet not yet on the floor, I decided I'd call James at four, so I wouldn't upset him at work. But first I cleaned everything: drawers and cabinets and baseboards and floors. I threw the shower curtain, liner, and bathmat into the washing machine. I used bleach on all the fixtures. I took all the silverware out of its tray, cleaned it, and put it back. I used glass cleaner and paper towels on the inside of the windows and vinegar and newspaper on the outside. When I finished, I called James, but he wasn't there, so I left a voicemail explaining that I was letting him go for good, and then I had to add, "I hope when you're married someday you won't be like the rest of society who looks at chaste single adults like they're tragic figures." I went to the fitness center hoping the endorphin kick would relieve my grief, but Oprah was interviewing Faith Hill about her fairy-tale marriage to Tim McGraw. Afterward, I collapsed on my couch where I probably would've remained the rest of the night had I not gotten a feeling like there was an invisible lover pushing me out the door, saying, *Go, go* but who was also on the other side, waiting. I remembered that St. John's had an evening Mass, so I pried myself off the couch and showered off the grime. After Mass when everybody had left, I sat silently in front of the tabernacle and asked the Blessed Mother to please one day allow James to feel everything he'd put me through multiplied, so that he'd finally understand and return to Jesus. Then, as I got up to leave, the First Holy Communion children from my dream came back to me, their faces like flowers risen through frozen snow.

Epilogue

It was another six years before James gave up for good, and I was whole enough to embrace my vocation. At first, he sent white roses and letters, and I tried to fool myself again: why can't I write a memoir about how much I struggled to be single and yet wind up married? Dale asked a similar question one day when we were in her office going over the last part of the memoir. I had told her about James' recent letter and how hard it was to be writing a story I was still entrenched in. Ever since I'd written the first drafts of "After Mass" and "Fort Lee," she looked at me differently. Before, she thought I was a coward tiptoeing around the story, but afterward, she told me, "*This* is your story. You're finally writing it. I'm proud of you." Now she was encouraging me again, "You have to finish this memoir. Single women need it. The exile they feel is not just personal. It's *systemic.*" Then she softened her voice, looked at me kindly, "Maybe there's still a chance for you and James. If anybody knew *my* romantic past, they'd never believe I could sustain a commitment either."

Five months later, I defended the memoir and received my doctorate. After making my opening comments and fielding questions from my committee members, the room was abuzz with discussion. The memoir had taken on a life of its own, but it wasn't yet the book it was supposed to be, the fullest and best version of itself. The truth. Dale took me out to celebrate and told me she understood that *I* believed I had a celibate calling, but that my readers were going to believe that I remained single because I was afraid to get close to anyone. She also said I should take a year off before I started revising, and that I shouldn't rely on publishing to give me the validation she could tell I was still looking for. She added that she and I had gone to two opposite extremes: she went with a lot of men to try and heal her childhood, and I avoided them to try and heal mine. Her husband thanked her all the time—he would've never wanted to wind up just him and the cats. She told me I needed to date.

I wanted to tell her, "No, you don't understand, I'm not afraid. I just know I'm not meant to marry," but I still couldn't get it out. I told her about Patrick, a screenwriter I'd gone out with a few times a year and half earlier who didn't want a long distance relationship and had recently emailed me because he knew I was finishing school and moving back to the city. I was certain God was rewarding my four years of hard, lonely work with a tall, sexy man for the summer. Before three months had passed, both of us were disappointed and frustrated. As Patrick put it, religion was as important to me as sex was to him, something I still couldn't own up to. One day when we were fooling around at his house in Breezy Point, he said pulling away, "If you told me, 'Patrick, I love you, I want you, I want to tear your clothes off,' maybe I could wait until marriage, but I'm not getting that from you." He was right. I didn't even invite him to my graduation party. I wanted *to want* to invite him, but the thought of him there felt unnatural to me, even suffocating. For weeks after we broke up, I was crushed. One day driving to the university where I'd gotten a teaching position, I called Barbara crying, "I'm so sorry to bother you, but I feel such dread. I don't want to go to work. I don't mean today; I mean ever. *I miss Patrick.*"

Each time I dated—three times over the next five years— it ended the same, even with Ben, who was mature and kind and seriously Catholic. I was playing house all over again, still searching for attention and pleasure at the expense of men. I tried to explain this to Sister Erin, but she said I wouldn't feel that way if the man and I owned the house together. She missed the point entirely, but it didn't matter. I was the one setting my hand to the plow and then looking back. I was like the character Much-Afraid in the allegorical tale *Hinds' Feet On High Places* by Hannah Hurnard, who The Good Shepherd leads to High Place but only once she is able to drink the cup he has asked her to drink, when she tears herself away from her "cousins": pride, resentment, self-pity, bitterness, and fear. Throughout the journey, she faces new obstacles that make her want to cling more to her "cousins," but with the help of sorrow and suffering, her two guides, she's able to let go. The Shepherd has to keep strengthening her, because she makes progress and then regresses. Sometimes it seems that she has not moved forward at all.

Except for these episodes of regression, though, I was, with God's grace, moving forward. I began practicing a Christian form of meditation called Centering Prayer, which helps open one to contemplation, to resting in God. First practiced by the Desert Fathers in the third century and inspired by the writings of several Christian mystics, it was updated for lay people in the 1970s by three Trappist monks, including Father Thomas Keating who founded the Centering Prayer movement. The source of the prayer is the Holy Trinity dwelling in us. Sitting with eyes closed for twenty minutes twice a day, you let your thoughts float by the way you would passing sailboats if you were sitting on a lakeshore. When you get overly tangled in them, you say silently and gently a one or two syllable sacred word like joy or peace or faith, or you gently notice your breath. Each time you do this, you're consenting to God's action and presence in your life. You're letting go. Practiced faithfully, it helps free us from our attachments, chips away at our selfishness. Without us knowing when or how, the Divine Physician heals our wounds, the ones we know and the ones that are hidden. During my first session when I was asked to silently choose my sacred word, *Abba*, Dad, sprung up in me. I was so startled, I teared up. The Holy Spirit knew exactly what I needed. I wasn't afraid of silence anymore. I craved it. In addition to the daily practice, I found a group at a nearby parish whom I prayed with a couple of times a month. It often wasn't until the last minute of the twenty minute "sit" that I finally let go. Sometimes I even missed the second sit, but I showed up every day.

I went to a Divine Mercy Sunday Mass, first established by Pope John Paul II in 2000, the same day he canonized Sister Faustina Kowalska, a deeply devout nineteen-year-old nun who Jesus appeared to in 1931 in the image of Divine Mercy. He wore a white garment and held his right hand raised in blessing while pointing his left hand to his heart as two rays of merciful light poured from it, one red and the other pale, representing the blood and water he shed on the cross. He asked Sister Faustina to paint this image of him with the inscription, "Jesus, I trust in You," to have it blessed on the first Sunday after Easter—to be called the Feast of Mercy—and to have it publically honored. Once her confessor, Father Michael Sopocko, was convinced she wasn't crazy, he introduced her to Kazimierowski, the artist of the first Divine Mercy painting. He also encouraged her to record all of Jesus' conversations with her in a diary—*Divine Mercy in my Soul*—published forty-three years after her death. The message was and is that God's mercy is far greater than our greatest sin. Ask for it. Love and forgive others the way He does us. Trust your heart to His Son. The more we do this, the more grace we'll receive. At the age of thirty eight, gazing into Christ's healing heart on the Sunday after Easter, I felt the purity of genuine remorse rise into mine, and then, after confession and Eucharist, my sin wiped away like dew in a summer sun.

The Shack, a book by WM. Paul Young, also played a pivotal role, especially the scene when God—Papa—who's depicted as a compassionate, playful African-American mother, cries as she shows the main character Mack the nail marks in her wrists, the same nail marks in *Jesus'* wrists. She had been crucified with him, felt every whip, thorn, and nail. She also felt every blow that Mack had received as a boy from his abusive, alcoholic father. As tears fell from Papa's face, tears slid down mine, cleansing my wounded view of God as a distant and cruel taskmaster and reestablishing my belief in the Holy Trinity as three loving persons in one. Finally willing to understand that God was crucified with Jesus and with each of us whenever we suffer, I started to grow up.

One evening my mother told me that Nellie and the kids were coming for a visit and flying into Kennedy, not the more convenient Newark Airport. My mother didn't drive on highways anymore and didn't like inconveniencing my sisters, so I knew I'd be the one battling the traffic on the Belt. It was the least I could do. I was rooming in *her* house, so I could live on a half-time salary while I worked on revising the memoir, but resentment rose to my face. When she asked, "*What* are you so angry about?" I was afraid to answer, but I couldn't hold onto it anymore. With heart hammering in my chest, I told her how her and Nellie's relationship had always made me feel shut out and that I was always afraid if I said so, I'd anger her. She seemed surprised as if she never realized or thought of it before, and then she told me she was sorry. I felt freer than I ever had. Later, pulling up to the terminal and seeing Nellie and the kids and their enormous luggage, I couldn't wait to get them in the car and home with us.

James found out which university I was teaching for and emailed me every few months to ask if we could see each other or talk on the phone. I always declined. I probably shouldn't have responded at all, but I was afraid he'd get angry and back at me somehow, though I honestly couldn't imagine him doing so. On vacation at the Grand Canyon for my fortieth birthday, I was about to start fantasizing him and the family we didn't have when the image of him threatening to drop a girl over the canyon shot through my mind. I gasped. At first I thought she could've been our daughter, but then I realized I was that girl. If I had married him, he would've continued to hold my heart over a precipice. Or maybe I just told myself that. Either way, it no longer mattered. At one of his very favorite places in the country where he'd told me he *felt* God, I let go of him to God. I flung all my resentments and fantasies over Mather Point. I prayed a sincere blessing over him and his life. When he emailed me a few months later to let me know his dispensation from the priesthood came through, I wrote back that I wished him all good things, but that it no longer paid to be in touch with me, that I was spoken for. I didn't say by God, but he knew. Three years later, Janine bumped into him at a doctor's office where she thought she overheard him telling the receptionist that he now had a family of his own. When she eventually told me, it was strange to hear but, finally, not painful.

Christ tells us in the Gospel of John, "*It was not you who chose me, but I who chose you and appointed you to go and bear fruit that will remain...This I command you: love one another.*" I believe something similar about our vocations, that God has chosen *how* He'd like each of us to bear that fruit and love one another. We can say no; it's our choice, and I think He'll bless any path we choose if we live it with integrity, but I think the path He has in mind for us is the best. One day in the midst of watching my sister and brother-in-law during a long, painful stretch of their marriage, one of my nieces asked in her precious, nasal voice, "But still, Aunt Maria, isn't it better to get married than to stay single?" I don't think she was asking me as much as she was trying to figure out the truth for herself: none of us should choose a path to try and avoid pain. Any life worth waking up to will eventually involve some form of suffering. Trying to fight or avoid it when it comes is not only futile but deepens the crisis. There is no "better" path than the one that's ours. If we listen carefully enough, God lets us know, and He will not disappoint, will not be outdone in generosity, though it could seem that way for an awfully long time. As the years have gone by, He has not only taken away my desire for natural marriage and softened my sexual urges but has filled me with more interior freedom than I could have imagined. He has covered me in His peace. I have wound up with the better part, sitting at Jesus' feet listening to him, my Prince in Disguise, my door to eternal life, but also to the one here that I finally walk through on my own, though never alone.

Acknowledgments

To say this book wouldn't have been possible without my mentor Professor Ed Hack is a grand understatement. From a graduate course in autobiographical writing over two decades ago right up until many of the last rewrites here, you have taught me, Ed, how to write, how to access the emotional truth of my life, and how to stand in that truth as uncomfortable and hard as it has been. You have taught me to "dream my way" back into memories in order to make them vivid and new. You have been a shoulder to cry on and a listening ear; you have witnessed my growing pains—writing and otherwise—with great patience and love. You have been a writing-father extraordinaire. Thank you eternally, Professor, for helping to *pull* this book *out* of me.

To my writing-mother extraordinaire, Maria Mazziotti Gillan, for your selfless and tireless instruction and for teaching me to take risks. You never ask for anything in return except for your students to go to the "cave" and give their very best. Yours and Laura Boss' inspiring workshops have introduced me to exceptional poets whose talent has always challenged me to go deeper and reach higher. Thank you for putting me in contact with so many of the right people and places over the years, Maria, and for generously answering my many questions. Like all your other fans, from the moment I had the privilege of meeting you and your prolific body of work, I was hooked. Thank you and love from my heart.

To the esteemed authors who unselfishly read this manuscript and provided advance-praise, I can't thank each of you enough for your time, expertise, and incredible generosity. To Leslie Heywood, thank you for your critique of the first and final versions of this book, and for your effective graduate memoir workshop where I received feedback that was essential for the development of this book.

To everyone at Apprentice House Press, based at Loyola University Maryland: Christina Damon, Carmen Machalek, Meghan DeGeorge, Molly Werts, Shelby Ehret, and professor-director Dr. Kevin Atticks—thank you. Thank you, especially Kevin, for your guidance and understanding and Christina for your long hours and personal investment. It's been such a blessing to work with *all* of you. Because of you, this book is going out beautifully to the "world." Thank you for helping to make the many years I spent writing and revising it worth it in the end. I'm so happy it wound up in your talented, eager, and patient hands.

To my many luminaries and colleague-friends in the Italian American academic and artistic community, including the Italian American Studies Association and the Italian American Writers Association, for the much needed and appreciated guidance, inspiration, and fellowship. A special thank you to Dr. Anthony Tamburri for your continued mentorship and belief in my work. And to my author-friend K. Curto with whom it's both a joy and a tremendous help to share this journey.

To the library staff at the City University of New York who provided such a hospitable and friendly place for me to write this book and to take my breaks. And to JJ for your enormous smile and personality and for helping to keep the silent floor silent.

To M. Bisbee-Beek, thank you for taking on this book with enthusiasm, appreciation, and understanding. From the first time we spoke, I sensed you were the right person to shepherd it where it needs to go.

To the Sisters of Charity, especially Sisters Teresa and Erin, and to Father Dennis—as they are all named here—for always having my best interest at heart and for gently helping me to discern God's *loving* will.

To my three soul friends—TP, CHM, and LP—thank you so much for being constants in my life over the last twenty plus years. Thank you, LP, for your prayers and for your thought-filled feedback on the manuscript.

To my extended family, the ones here and the ones who have passed on, thank you for your love, legacy, and friendship. A special thank you to my beautiful aunts whose unceasing prayers for me have been answered and to Aunt Rose for being so open in sharing with me what the early years were like, which helped me to better understand the past and filled in gaps in my memory and knowledge.

To my nieces and nephews, when you were little and asked what this book was about, I told you it was for adults. Now you know what I mean. I pray that you will have the strength and courage to avoid the snares that life can present, and I hope you'll always know how profoundly God loves you. I love you so much.

To my sisters, thank you for the laughter we share, the lessons we've learned, and for your unceasing support. Thank you for holding my heart in your hands and for allowing me to hold yours in mine. A lot of who I am is a result of us having shared our youth. I wouldn't want my life as inextricably wound with anyone else's, including yours CG. To DT for being like a brother—someone I can call in need—and for letting me use the beautiful Shore house where some of the early versions of this book were written.

To my father AG, thank you Papa for all the sacrifices you made, along with Mom, to ensure that we always had more than enough, and for teaching me, by example, what discipline and work ethic look like. Thank you for being the creative, generous, and hardworking man you are. I couldn't have asked for a father who was a better provider or a more colorful storyteller than you. *Ti voglio bene.*

To my canonized friends who have always been so good to me, interceding for me with regards to this book and to anything else I needed for myself and those I love: St. Anthony of Padua, St. Elizabeth Ann Seton, St. Bernadette Soubirous, Sts. Francis and Clare of Assisi, St Teresa of Avila, and St. Therese of Lisiuex.

To the Holy Trinity—Father, Son, and Spirit—and to the Holy Family—Jesus Lord, Blessed Mother Mary, and St. Joseph—my truest and most important luminaries with whom I wrote this book and without whom no good thing is possible. Three is *the* best number. Thank you for Love that never lets go.

To my mother, JM, my best friend and hero of this story, thank you for always accepting me even when you were rightly worried and unsure about my choices, including my writing of this book. Your unfailing love, forgiveness, support, and prayers have been the backbone of my life, Mom, and the *joy* of it. Thank you for all the ways you've given me life and continue to, for teaching me every good thing I know, and for always wanting me "Close to You." I love you to infinity.

About the Author

Maria Giura PhD is also the author of *What My Father Taught Me*, a collection of memory poems, which was a finalist for the Paterson Book Prize. Her writing has appeared in several journals including *Prime Number*, *Presence*, *VIA*, *Italian Americana*, *Ovunque Siamo*, and *Lips*. She has won awards from the Academy of American Poets and the Center for Women Writers and is a judge for the Lauria/Frasca Poetry Prize. Giura has taught Literature and Writing at St. John's University, Montclair State University, and Binghamton University where she earned her doctorate in English. She lives in NYC.

Apprentice
House Press
Loyola University Maryland

Apprentice House is the country's only campus-based, student-staffed book publishing company. Directed by professors and industry professionals, it is a nonprofit activity of the Communication Department at Loyola University Maryland.

Using state-of-the-art technology and an experiential learning model of education, Apprentice House publishes books in untraditional ways. This dual responsibility as publishers and educators creates an unprecedented collaborative environment among faculty and students, while teaching tomorrow's editors, designers, and marketers.

Outside of class, progress on book projects is carried forth by the AH Book Publishing Club, a co-curricular campus organization supported by Loyola University Maryland's Office of Student Activities.

Eclectic and provocative, Apprentice House titles intend to entertain as well as spark dialogue on a variety of topics. Financial contributions to sustain the press's work are welcomed. Contributions are tax deductible to the fullest extent allowed by the IRS.

To learn more about Apprentice House books or to obtain submission guidelines, please visit www.apprenticehouse.com.

Apprentice House
Communication Department
Loyola University Maryland
4501 N. Charles Street
Baltimore, MD 21210
Ph: 410-617-5265 • Fax: 410-617-2198
info@apprenticehouse.com • www.apprenticehouse.com

CPSIA information can be obtained
at www.ICGtesting.com
Printed in the USA
FFHW012012201119
56086300-62120FF